State of Mind

NUMBER TEN:
Tarleton State University
Southwestern Studies in the Humanities

State of Mind

Texas Literature and Culture

TOM PILKINGTON

Texas A&M University Press
College Station

The paper used in this book meets the minimum requirements
of the American National Standard for Permanence
of Paper for Printed Library Materials, z39.48-1984.
Binding materials have been chosen for durability.

♾

Library of Congress Cataloging-in-Publication Data

Pilkington, Tom.
   State of mind : Texas literature and culture / Tom Pilkington. — 1st ed.
      p.   cm. — (Tarleton State University southwestern studies in the humanities ;
no. 10)
   Includes bibliographical references and index.
   ISBN 0-89096-839-X (alk. paper)
   1. American literature — Texas — History and criticism.   2. Texas — In literature.
3. Texas — Civilization.   I. Title.   II. Series.
PS266.T4P55   1998
810.9'976409 — dc21   98-22261
                                                                                CIP

For Betsy & Michael,
with love

Texas is a state of mind,
but I think it is more than that.
It is a mystique closely approximating
a religion. . . . The word Texas becomes
a symbol to everyone in the world.
There's no question that this
Texas-of-the-mind fable is often
synthetic, sometimes untruthful, and
frequently romantic, but that in no
way diminishes its strength
as a symbol.

JOHN STEINBECK
Travels with Charley

CONTENTS

PREFACE

*The puzzle of Texas is that it is simultaneously diverse and
unified. Climatically, topographically, economically, the east
has no connection with the west; yet the Texans' sense of
themselves, their cultural identity . . . links the rancher from
San Angelo with the timber merchant from Nacogdoches like
mountaineers at different heights yet on the same rope.*

— STEPHEN BROOK, *Honkytonk Gelato*

An article in the *Dallas Morning News* a few years back addressed, at least
indirectly, a subject I find fascinating. The piece concerned the twentieth
anniversary of *Texas Monthly,* a magazine that has become "as much a part
of the Texas cultural landscape as the April bluebonnets that color Hill
Country fields." Much of the popularity of *Texas Monthly,* as the article
implicitly acknowledged, derives from its ability to provide slick new pack-
aging for the hoary "Texas myth." A magazine-industry executive was
quoted as saying, "I do not believe there is another state where anything
like *Texas Monthly* would work." Indeed, Michael R. Levy, the financial
wizard behind the success of *Texas Monthly,* in the early 1980s attempted to
launch a West Coast periodical called *California* that would be to that state
what *Texas Monthly* is to Texas. It was a dismal failure. Too late Levy discovered that "Californians apparently have individual lifestyles, not a single
mind-set."[1]

The essays that follow were written for different occasions and purposes. What they have in common is that all are reflections, usually rooted
in personal experience and observation, on the literature and culture of
Texas. Though I focus mainly on literature, I often find myself dealing with
subject matter that is somewhat broader — in a word, with culture. One of
the definitions my dictionary gives for the noun *culture* is "the customary
beliefs, social forms, and material traits of a racial, religious, or social
group." It is in this sense, with emphasis on the term *social group,* that I use

the word. To put it another way, I agree with Clifford Geertz, who says in *The Interpretation of Cultures*, "man is an animal suspended in webs of significance he himself has spun, I take culture to be those webs."[2] Culture is, by its very nature, a product of the human mind and imagination, and it is what makes a group of people distinctive from all other groups.

Myth, it seems to me, is the handmaiden of culture. Myth ordinarily is the means by which a group's customary beliefs, social forms, and material traits are continuously reinforced and, just as important, are inculcated in newcomers, whether they are outsiders requesting admittance or children and young people seeking full membership in the group. Myth, writes Richard Slotkin in *The Fatal Environment*, is a "deeply encoded set of metaphors that contain all the 'lessons' we have learned from our history and all of the essential elements of our world view."[3] In sum, according to the great anthropologist Bronislaw Malinowski, "myth is above all a cultural force."[4]

It is hardly news that the aforementioned "Texas myth" is precisely what supplies Texans their sense of identity, their sense of "differentness," of uniqueness. No other state of the Union has such a full-blown and extravagant mythology. The reasons for this fact are many, but one seems preeminent. A myth traditionally has its origin in the sacred beginnings of a people. Texas was once an independent nation. Thus it had its own "founding," generated its own colorful history, its own pantheon of legendary heroes. The "sacred" dimension of the myth that emerged from the state's dramatic birth is poignantly suggested by Larry McMurtry in his 1968 collection *In a Narrow Grave: Essays on Texas.* The first chapter bears the metaphoric title "The God Abandons Texas"—the "god" being "old Texas," a phrase guaranteed to evoke in most native Texans feelings at least quasi-religious.

Given the state's history and mythology, therefore, given its size and diversity, given its cohesive, self-conscious culture, Texas is, as historian T. R. Fehrenbach has dubbed it, a "nation within a nation"[5]; or, to adopt a term from the cultural geographer D. W. Meinig, it is an "empire"[6]; or, to echo the gushings of *Ultra,* a now-defunct Houston magazine, it is a "principality." (*Ultra,* incidentally, in its first issue in 1981, declared itself "the national magazine" of Texas and crowed, "We *know* that the United States couldn't exist without Texas, but that Texas could exist perfectly comfortably without the rest of the U. S."[7])

Culture and myth are closely related to art. Art—whether literature or painting or music or forms of the popular arts such as film and television and magazine journalism — inevitably reflects a people's beliefs, values, mythology. Geertz asserts that "Societies, like lives, contain their own interpretations. One has only to learn to gain access to them." A work of literature, while an intensely personal experience for both writer and reader, is also part of those collective "webs of significance" of which Geertz speaks. It is a cultural artifact. Thus literature mirrors — and interprets — the culture from which it springs. If this statement is true as a general proposition, it is doubly or triply true of Texas literature. In talking about Texas writing, I cannot avoid referring time and again to Texas culture and myth. I have no intention of engaging in the kind of "thick description" that Geertz employs in his work as an anthropologist, but I proceed from the assumption that literature sheds light on culture — and vice versa.

The pieces I have gathered here were all written (in their original versions) within, roughly, the last decade and a half. The landmark event of that time period, with regard to Texas literature and culture, was the 1986 Sesquicentennial celebration. For all the blather and folderol that issued from the Sesquicentennial, it proved a stimulus to the recognition and appreciation of Texas writing. Subsequent developments have been encouraging: for example, gubernatorial proclamations, beginning in 1994, establishing an annual Texas Writers Month (originally held in March, now held in May); the organization of a large and lively annual book festival in Austin that is presided over by the state's first lady; the hugely successful Texas Bound series of readings of stories by Texas writers at the Dallas Museum of Art. These and other events give evidence that there is actually a sizable audience out there eager to know more about Texas literature. It is my intent that the following reflections and ruminations speak to such an audience.

Most writers incur scores of debts they can never repay. My first and largest debt is to my parents, Tom, Sr., and Alice Pilkington, both deceased. My parents were not well educated in a formal sense, but they understood the value of education, and they instilled in me, if only directly, a love of books and learning. Every Saturday morning, when I was a child, they dropped me off at the old public library in downtown Fort Worth, where I happily browsed row upon row of inviting books, selecting the upcoming week's reading matter, while they did the week's grocery shopping.

A lifetime of reading, begun in the Fort Worth public library, has left, as Edith Sitwell once put it, "other writers' birds flitting around" in my head. Many people have advanced, in large ways and small, my education in Texas literature. I especially acknowledge a considerable debt to Don

Graham and James Ward Lee, friends and colleagues of thirty years and more. Together Don, Jim, and I have gnawed on and worried over the bones of Texas writing for so long I sometimes lose track of which bits of gristle are theirs and which mine. My colleagues at Tarleton State University, Craig Clifford (godfather of the Stephenville Literary Mafia) and Mike Pierce (a historian who, astonishingly, is also well-versed in literature), have frequently been sounding boards—though hardly passive ones—for my ideas about Texas books and writers. These—and others—have contributed much to my thinking on the subject. I hasten to add, however, that they should not be saddled with responsibility for any errors of fact or outrageous judgments that may have found their way into the ensuing pages.

Finally, I offer thanks to Tarleton State University for an appointment as University Scholar. I am particularly grateful to Dr. B. J. Alexander, Provost and Vice President for Academic Affairs, and to Dr. Barry B. Thompson and Dr. Dennis McCabe, former and current presidents of Tarleton State University, for the original appointment and for its continuation. The release time from teaching duties that accrues to the position has assisted greatly in the completion of this project.

State of Mind

CHAPTER I

Prologue

The Myth of the Texas Empire

*Texas does not properly belong to the South, the West,
or even the Southwest; it is an empire, an entity, totally its
own. . . . if we were writing about Europe instead of the
United States, one might easily be tempted to a
paragraph about Texas "imperialism."*

—JOHN GUNTHER, *Inside U.S.A.*

When one speaks of Texas, superlatives, usually having to do with size and expansiveness, seem to leap unbidden to the tongue. It is scarcely surprising that Edna Ferber (or one of her editors) affixed the title *Giant* to her popular and controversial 1952 novel about the state. Ferber's book was intended as a searing indictment of the crudity, racism, and general excess that, in her view, characterize the behavior of Anglo Texans. Yet the net result of her book and, even more, the 1956 film version of the story has been to enhance the idea of that mythical Texas readily recognized by most citizens of the United States—indeed by most citizens of the world.

Giant—an appropriate, perhaps inevitable term to designate the largest of the forty-eight contiguous states. *Empire*—another word that has been used to describe Texas many times by many people. There is no denying that from the beginning Texans have entertained dreams of empire. In the mid-nineteenth century, during the decade of the Republic, the young nation staked a claim to large portions of present-day New Mexico, Oklahoma, Colorado, and Kansas, plus a chunk of Wyoming. Many Texans at the time, even as their country struggled to survive economically and militarily, schemed to expand its borders all the way to the Pacific. Several times—at least twice during the days of the Republic and again during the

Civil War—the government of Texas dispatched ill-fated expeditions to invade and conquer New Mexico.

When Texas gave up its status as a sovereign nation and joined the Union, its imperialism of necessity became largely economic and cultural rather than territorial. The American ranching industry, for example, had its origins in South Texas following the Civil War, as Anglo stockmen adapted Mexican ranching techniques to the handling of longhorn cattle that ran wild in the brush country of that part of the state. In the last decades of the nineteenth century hundreds of thousands of head of Texas cattle were herded to railheads in Kansas and beyond, and those trail drives transported not just beef for hungry northern consumers, but also a culture and a way of life. They brought with them, in addition, the cowboy, who was to become one of the central figures of American mythology.

In fact, Texas cattle culture spread northward and northwestward until it encompassed virtually the whole of the Great Plains and the mountain West. According to John Gunther,

> The cow country of the United States . . . stretches up from Texas like a broadening funnel. Texas is its root and heart. . . . In this whole immense region, from Brownsville to the Canadian border, any cattleman is at home anywhere. The mores are the same; the vernacular and manner of speech are the same; the habit of mind is the same.[1]

Starting in 1901 with Spindletop, oil provided another powerful stimulus to the exportation of Texas culture. For decades the preponderance of the oil produced and consumed in the United States came from Texas—as did most of the workers, technicians, geologists, and other assorted types needed to keep black gold flowing. When oil was discovered in other states—and in other parts of the world—the denizens of the Texas oil patch often moved in to lend their skills and expertise. In recent times Texas accents have dominated the oil fields of New Mexico and Wyoming and Alaska and Saudi Arabia—and even, as a television documentary some years ago demonstrated, the streets of Glasgow, Scotland.

In addition to the vast economic and cultural influences exerted by Texas cattle and oil, the state has seemed to be the object of perennial fascination for people living outside its borders. In the realm of fashions and lifestyles, the brief but astonishing phenomenon known as "Texas chic"— which flourished from the late 1970s to the mid-1980s—might well be cited as an example of Texas cultural imperialism. During that time it was not uncommon to spot Wall Street bankers wearing cowboy boots and Stetson (or, if they were really hip, Resistol) hats and learning to dance the two-step.

More recently the Dallas Cowboys football squad — which has long billed itself as "America's Team" — may have become, thanks to a return to winning ways, Mexico's team. Years ago the Cowboys began sponsoring telecasts and Spanish-language radio broadcasts of their games into Mexico. With the growth of interest in American football in Mexico, the overwhelming majority of fans in that country, according to a wire-service news account in January 1993, favor the Cowboys. However, as the account went on to explain, a vocal minority of Mexicans root against the Cowboys because they claim the Texas team, in its marketing practices, is guilty of — and I quote — "cultural imperialism."[2]

Nearly three decades ago, D. W. Meinig, an outlander who taught geography at Syracuse University in New York, visited Texas a couple of times, applied his analytic talents to a stack of maps and historical and demographic data, and wrote an illuminating study entitled *Imperial Texas: An Interpretive Essay in Cultural Geography* (1969). Meinig points out in the book that Texas's imperial ambitions have always been felt most acutely, sometimes oppressively, by people in neighboring states, such as New Mexico and Oklahoma. There is the matter, for instance, of those military campaigns against New Mexico, events that to this day many New Mexicans — especially Hispanic New Mexicans — have not forgotten.

Moreover, roughly the eastern one-third of New Mexico is widely known, even to New Mexicans, as Little Texas, since most of the people who settled the area were Texans, and its culture is virtually indistinguishable from that of West Texas. The entire state of New Mexico, in fact, has long felt the hot breath of migrating Texans and the infusions of Texas capital into its economy. Meinig concludes that "the imperial dreams of Texas Republic days have at least to some extent been accomplished by the mundane movements of Texan ranchers, farmers, merchants, bankers, and oilmen."[3]

I could continue in this vein indefinitely, but the point, I hope, has been made: Texas is, in some sense, an empire. But to be an empire, whether territorial or cultural, is not an unmixed blessing. Empires have received a great deal of bad publicity in modern times. In the second half of the present century, the great European empires crumbled under the political and moral pressure exerted by disgruntled natives and world opinion. And in a somewhat less serious but no less fervent context, there have been over the years many vocal critics of Texas imperialism. Coloradans, as well as New Mexicans, for example, often complain bitterly that at almost any time of the year too many Texas tourists clog the highways and byways of their state — skiing in winter, basking in cool mountain breezes in summer. To add to their discomfort, much of the money that has financed the "development" of Colorado and New Mexico has come from Texas. Many residents of those states are more than a little contemptuous of Texas money, though, like E. A. Robinson's Miniver Cheevy, "sore annoyed" are they without it.

Such criticism is the downside of empire. The good side, one that has not been seriously considered in our time, is that empires — whatever evils they may engender in practice — are built on energy, expansiveness, and, most important of all, vision and faith. These are things, intangible though they may be, that Texans have traditionally possessed in abundance. Thus the Texas empire, such as it is, has been propelled by nothing more substantial than a people's conception of themselves — by myth.

As frequently happens, there is a considerable disparity between the myth and the reality. Texans like the sound of the word *empire;* they like to think of themselves as citizens of their very own country. T. R. Fehrenbach asserts that Texas has always been a "nation within a nation." If that is the case, Texas was, during the period between the Civil War and World War II, the equivalent of a Third World country, a banana republic. It was ruled (after Reconstruction) by a feudal oligarchy of plantation owners, cattle barons, oil tycoons, and, not least, corporation lawyers from outside the state. The majority of its people — black, brown, *and* white — lived in near-desperate poverty. According to historian Norman D. Brown, fully two-thirds of the farmers of East Texas at the turn of the twentieth century were sharecroppers,[4] a form of servitude memorably depicted in George Sessions Perry's 1941 novel, *Hold Autumn in Your Hand.*

At about the same time, the enormous ranching operations of West Texas depended on cheap labor supplied by cowboys; the cowboy, a mythological figure of gigantic proportions, was, in actuality, as Eugene Manlove Rhodes called him, "a hired man on horseback" who rarely accumulated land or cattle for himself.[5] In the early decades of this century, the Texas oil fields were truly filthy, dangerous, appalling places. William A. Owens, in *Fever in the Earth* (1958), vividly chronicles the cycle of the boomtown, where every budding tycoon who brought in a gusher built his financial stake atop a pile of bodies — the dead and maimed who paid the price for others' success.

The late Bernard DeVoto once called the American West a "plundered province."[6] The reasons DeVoto's assessment was demonstrably valid at least into the 1950s are detailed in a little-known book by the celebrated historian Walter Prescott Webb — himself a Texan — entitled *Divided We Stand* (1937). Writing in the depths of the Great Depression, Webb showed how the North kept the West and South in economic vassalage by means of patent monopolies and discriminatory freight rates. As late as the 1940s, journalist Gunther succinctly summed up the problem as regarded Texas in his popular travelogue *Inside U.S.A.*:

> [D]espite its fantastically great economic power, Texas represents the kind of "exploitative" or "colonial" economy typical of all western states; it lives basically by the multifarious production of raw materials — cattle, cotton, sulphur, petroleum, a hundred others — but most of the reservoir of production is owned outside the state. . . . It has been badly fleeced by outsiders in its time.[7]

Only after World War II, which stimulated the growth of urbanization and the diversification of the economy, did most Anglo Texans begin to enjoy the security of safe and healthy work and a reasonable level of prosperity. The golden age of the Texas economic boom lasted about fifty years. And now, as we near the start of a new century, the health of the economic empire seems uncertain. For decades family farming and ranching have become increasingly less feasible as ways of making a living; in the 1980s the collapse of oil prices literally devastated the Texas economy, and now the American oil industry is almost nonexistent; and in the early 1990s the closing of defense plants and installations exacted a heavy toll of jobs in the state's larger cities. On the bright side, there are those who believe that trade with Mexico will be the salvation of the Texas economy. And Austin, at least, has become a high-tech boomtown. What lies down the road, of course, is anybody's guess, but as I write, the immediate economic future seems problematical.

But most Texans — natives and longtime residents, at any rate — remain proud of their state. In 1969 Meinig, in *Imperial Texas,* peered into the cultural future and predicted that, despite substantial immigration into Texas from other parts of the country, the Texans' mind-set would change only with glacial slowness. The typical Texan of the future, he said, would be much like that of the present (that is, the late 1960s). Though its validity for the twenty-first century may be questioned, Meinig's forecast to this point has proved largely accurate. Many Texans still think of themselves as a breed apart from, and probably superior to, the common run of Americans. The tendency to employ the word *Texas* as an adjective — as in Texas food, Texas music, Texas art, and so forth ad infinitum — rather than diminishing over the last few years, has if anything gathered momentum. A domain in which the tendency is clearly apparent is literature.

Many Texas writers and scholars — myself included — have begun to think in terms of Texas having generated its own literary tradition, separate from the national and regional traditions of which it is a part. The assumption seems to be that any self-respecting empire ought to be able to produce a body of decently accomplished literature. As is true of other facets of the myth, the grandiose assumption may have little connection with reality.

Texas literature, in fact, is a cultural development of fairly recent vintage. I realize I leave out of consideration here the ancient oral literature of American Indians who lived in what is now Texas, as well as the folk literature of various ethnic and racial groups within the state, not to mention the occasional exception to the rule such as Cabeza de Vaca's sixteenth-century *La Relación*. Having said this, I contend nevertheless that literary enterprise in Texas has been a going concern only since the 1920s. The reasons for this late development of interest in belles lettres should be obvious. Refinements such as art and literature are luxuries generally enjoyed by settled, mature societies whose citizens have attained a certain level of leisure and formal education. A populace engaged in the rugged business of making homes for themselves in a hostile environment has little time to read or write even the most rudimentary things, much less poetry, fiction, and philosophy. Only in the last few decades has it been practicable, or possible, for a Texas Institute of Letters to sponsor annual prizes for the best Texas books in a variety of categories.

The state's "literary record" prior to 1920, then, does not really comprise very much literature. It is a collection of historical documents and narratives that possess, in varying degrees, literary value — grist for the historian's mill, but hardly sustained achievements of the creative imagination. Since the 1920s, however, dozens — nay, hundreds — of Texas writers have added slowly, layer by layer, to the Texas literary tradition. Unfortunately, during that time, the East Coast and California have transformed Texas into a "plundered province" in the cultural realm; these regions have strip-mined the state of much of its most valuable writing talent. The names of Texas writers in the twentieth century who at one time or another joined the ranks of the exiles and expatriates to other parts of the country and the world are far too many to enumerate here. Too many of our best writers have not found the intellectual atmosphere in Texas congenial to the artistic temperament and have moved on, at least temporarily, to more salubrious climes. Texas writers, for the most part, continue to write about Texas, but they often live somewhere else.

Furthermore, Texas writers who have managed to penetrate the consciousness of most Texans—to say nothing of most Americans—can be counted on the fingers of one hand. In politics and football, Texans love winners, and the same is true of literature. They honor the memory of J. Frank Dobie for the acclaim he attracted in the 1930s and 1940s. Those in the know respect Katherine Anne Porter (herself an expatriate) for the huge international reputation she garnered during her lengthy career. And most recently Larry McMurtry has become the state's favorite literary offspring, mainly because his novel *Lonesome Dove* (1985) was awarded a Pulitzer Prize that won him worldwide notoriety. That pretty much exhausts the list.

If the star system is invoked as the standard of judgment, therefore, the Texas literary tradition seems rather shallow. Undeniably we have turned out more famous politicians, business leaders, military men, and football players than famous writers. This fact no doubt says much about the values that govern Texas culture and society. Every empire must have its priorities. Will Texas's priorities ever change? Perhaps. I believe I have seen, in my nearly three-score years, a growing respect, or at least tolerance, among Texans for the life of the mind, for intellectual activity that does not produce immediate practical gains. But myths have a strength and intractability all their own. The myth of empire—rooted, as it is, in the ideals of action, determination, and common sense—still dominates the Texan mentality. As long as it does, can we ever expect another Katherine Anne Porter or Larry McMurtry to blossom in some Kyle or Archer City in the hinterlands? Again, I answer "perhaps." This response, I grant, is weak and tentative—but it is also hopeful.

CHAPTER 2

Ancestors

The Roots of Texas Writing

*How shall a man endure the will of God
and the days and the silence?*

— ARCHIBALD MACLEISH, *Conquistador*

Where did it all begin? Where do the origins of Texas literature — written literature, anyway — lie? Some say the beginnings stretch all the way back to the sixteenth century. Others (myself included) believe that Texas literature, for practical purposes, dates from the 1920s. I want to start by talking about Alvar Nuñez Cabeza de Vaca and J. Frank Dobie, a duo of pioneer Texans — one native, the other "naturalized" — whose substantial shadows still fall athwart the cultural map of the state. Though both are important for reasons that go beyond literature, these two men laid the foundation for literary accomplishment in Texas.

ALVAR NUÑEZ CABEZA DE VACA

The riddle that the narrator of Archibald MacLeish's long poem *Conquistador* poses is very like one that Cabeza de Vaca may have asked himself during the eight incredible years that he roamed the coastal marshes and the mountains and deserts of what is now Texas and the American Southwest. Like the great conquerors, he marched "by a king's name," discovered a "famous country," and suffered "unknown hardships."[1] But the only enemies he fought and subdued were his own body and will. His exploits, though they stimulated further exploration of the regions north of central Mexico, contributed nothing in the way of treasure to his king or country. But his remarkable journey will be recalled as a triumph of the human spirit when the plundering and bungling of his more celebrated contemporaries have been long forgotten.

Most students of American history know, in bare outline, the facts of Alvar Nuñez Cabeza de Vaca's amazing adventure, but interpreters of our national culture have, I think, overlooked the Spaniard's role as a literary prototype. His wanderings, which covered six thousand miles and eight years, have been hailed as one of the most remarkable achievements in recorded history. At the end of his sojourn in the wilderness, he returned to Spain, where he wrote an account of his stay in the New World and presented it to his king, Charles V. In 1542 the report was published in Zamora under the title *La Relación,* and it has fascinated and puzzled readers ever since.[2]

Cabeza de Vaca came to the New World in 1527 as a royal appointee with the Narváez expedition. His commander, Pámfilo de Narváez, had been granted the right to explore and conquer "Florida," which at the time included all of the land around the northern perimeter of the Gulf of Mexico, from the tip of present-day Florida to the Rio de las Palmas (the Rio Grande). In the spring of 1528, after a stormy winter in Cuba, the Spanish "governor" led ashore a party of some three hundred men, including Cabeza de Vaca. Prodded on by greed and foolhardiness, the Spaniards soon lost contact with their ships, which they never again sighted. They struck out northward on foot, and upon reaching the area that is now the Florida panhandle, the leaders of the decimated troop — the number of which had been greatly diminished by disease and sniping Indians — devised a plan to build boats to carry them along the coast to the west until they reached Pánuco, an outpost near the present site of Tampico, Mexico. Somehow five barge-like vessels were constructed, and in early fall the remnants of the expedition put out to sea. Some pressed onward to the coast of Texas, but none was able to go farther.

Cabeza de Vaca's barge, the occupants of which were near death from hunger and exposure to the elements, was washed to land probably on Galveston Island. The exhausted Spaniards named it Malhado (Misfortune) Island, for obvious reasons. When the shipwrecked men had somewhat regained their strength, they decided to resume their sea journey to Pánuco. Removing their clothes to keep them dry, they set about the task of relaunching their barge. No sooner had they pushed it out from shore, however, than it was capsized by a gigantic wave. Several of the men were drowned, and those remaining alive were left completely naked. From that time, in fact, until Cabeza de Vaca and his companions reached the Spanish settlements of southern Mexico, they possessed not a stitch of clothing: "we went naked through all this country," he writes in his narrative, and he notes, "not being accustomed to going so, we shed our skins twice a year like snakes."[3]

For a while Cabeza de Vaca lived among the Indians of the Texas coast, who treated him as a slave, often beating him and threatening him with death. But after a year or so the Spaniard discovered that he could attain a degree of freedom by serving as a go-between for warring tribes. He eventually became a roving trader among the Indians of East Texas. His trading territory seems to have reached as far north as what is now the Dallas–Fort Worth area.

Cabeza de Vaca often accompanied the Indians with whom he traded on their migrations in search of food. At various seasons of the year they fished the bays and inlets of the coast, harvested the pecan crop along the Colorado River near Austin, and gathered the fruit of the prickly pear cactus. It was near present-day San Antonio, during the prickly pear season of 1533, that Cabeza de Vaca was reunited with three other surviving members of the Narváez expedition who were also living among the Indians: Alonso del Castillo Maldonado, Andrés Dorantes, and a "Moor" named Estevánico. Together the four began to make plans to flee, but it was a year later, in September, 1534, before they were able to make good their escape. The Spaniards chose to move inland, rather than south toward Pánuco, because of their desire to be rid of the cruelty of the coastal Indians; also, as Cabeza de Vaca later writes, they felt sure that they would find the interior "more amply provisioned" than the coast.[4]

As was their expectation, the tribes to the west greeted them much more hospitably than had the coastal Indians — though they did not find an abundance of food until they reached the rich agricultural valleys of central Mexico. The first Indians they met after their flight were called Avavares, and it was among them that the Spaniards made their reputations as healers. These Indians suffered from terrible headaches, and apparently thinking they had nothing to lose, they asked the Europeans to relieve their suffering. The Spaniards developed a ritual they were to employ many times in the future: over each supplicant they made the sign of the cross, prayed, and blew on the seat of his pain. Afterward all said that they had been made well. In each village the sick were brought to the Spaniards to be healed, and rarely was a "patient" dissatisfied. Thus the wanderers found a means of continuing their journey. As their fame spread to the villages ahead, they were warmly, even reverently welcomed. Their hosts along the way were more than willing to provide food and guides to the next town. In fact, the "guides" soon became an escort that numbered in the hundreds.

After leaving the coast, the Spaniards most likely journeyed westward through the Hill Country of Central Texas and across the Edwards Plateau to the Pecos River. It was somewhere in the area west of the Hill Country that they came upon a village in which the inhabitants were so wretchedly poor they had to subsist for several months of the year on powdered straw. However scanty their food supply, the Indians were usually eager to share it with their famous visitors. They were not so eager, however, to welcome the wanderers' train of native followers. These "guides," it seems, were given to looting and plundering, and Cabeza de Vaca, who could do nothing to control them, tells of the fear they inspired in many of the Indian settlements through which they passed. Villagers were invariably excited by the appearance of the Spaniards, whose fame as healers had preceded them, but the natives' initial joy was soon replaced by severe anxiety.

When they came to the Pecos, Cabeza de Vaca and his companions followed the course of the river north into New Mexico. After crossing the Sacramento Mountains, they reversed directions again, striking out across the desert toward the present site of El Paso. Cabeza de Vaca describes their journey through a great wasteland, then their being guided by a woman to "a river which ran between mountains where her father's house lay." Almost certainly this is a description of *el paso del norte* (the pass of the north), which is formed by the Franklin Mountains on one side of the Rio Grande and the Sierra Madre of Mexico on the other side.

After their long journey across Texas, the Spaniards forded the Rio Grande in southern New Mexico and continued on to the Gila River country of Arizona, where they finally turned southward toward Mexico. In three months, still aided by friendly Indians, they crossed Sonora and part of Sinaloa. Near the town of Culiacán, in March, 1536, they met a startled Diego de Alcarez, who was in the area as commander of a slave-hunting expedition. After some unpleasantries between Alcarez and Cabeza de Vaca — precipitated by Alcarez's mistreatment of Indians — the four wanderers were given an escort to Mexico City, which they reached a few months later.

In Mexico City, they were provided with living quarters and outfitted with new clothing. But, writes Cabeza de Vaca, "I could not stand to wear clothes for some time, or sleep anywhere but on the bare floor." The Spaniards' adventures in the uncharted lands to the north and their dramatic appearance in Mexico City caused a small sensation. The tales the travelers brought back with them—tales in which they insisted they had seen evidence along their route of "gold, antimony, iron, copper and other metals"—were listened to with respectful attention. These stories, no doubt greatly exaggerated as they passed from person to person, soon revived rumors of the fabled Seven Cities of Cíbola and eventually led to the Coronado expedition. In effect, they set off the chain of events that resulted in the colonization of the American Southwest.

But Cabeza de Vaca's more lasting significance has been literary and cultural, not historical. *La Relación* makes Cabeza de Vaca more than just a physical trailblazer; he was also a literary pioneer, and he deserves the distinction of being called Texas's first writer. His narrative is, without question, the most remarkable byproduct of his eight-year odyssey in the wilderness. *La Relación* possesses many of the attributes of a good novel—especially its subtle presentation of character and its dramatic tension, which is a natural outgrowth of its true story line.

Its scope, as befits its function as a "report," is broad enough to include much information about the country through which the wanderers passed—the variety of its climate, its flora and fauna, the customs of its natives. Cabeza de Vaca was apparently an interested observer, even under the most extreme conditions, and his descriptions of man and nature in pre-European Texas and the Southwest are helpful to historians, anthropologists, and other present-day scholars. The facet of the narrative that has intrigued readers through the centuries, however, is less easily defined. The laconic style of *La Relación* often conceals more than it reveals, but it is the recurring understatements that prove most suggestive in their implications. I want to discuss a few of those implications.

Though Cabeza de Vaca was by birth a European, his narrative was shaped by the exigencies of a new and strange environment, and it seems to me a peculiarly American document. One of its underlying themes, for example, is the physical and emotional struggle for an accommodation between races—a conflict that has never been very far removed from the American consciousness and one that has always been a factor in the works of our best and most vital writers. Further, the narrative leans decidedly toward the metaphysical. And finally it is couched in an allegorical framework (for Cabeza de Vaca it was also a structure of reality) that has often been employed by American writers, great and obscure. In these ways, *La Relación* points to forms and thematic concerns of much American literature that followed.

Cabeza de Vaca's attitude toward Indians — his increasing sympathy and admiration for the native Americans he met along his route — is the crux of the racial theme. The history of the Spanish in the New World shows that they, like other colonizing groups, were arrogant and often brutal in their relations with the Indian population. Cabeza de Vaca, when he began his great adventure, must have had in him something of the conquistador's haughty view of the Indian. He was, after all, an aristocrat, and his grandfather, Pedro de Vera, had cruelly suppressed the Canary Islanders and, in so doing, incurred the denunciation of the Church. But after eight years among the Native Americans, Cabeza de Vaca's attitude toward them had changed to one of kindness and (within the limits of his time and place) understanding.

Though the modern reader may find a touch of condescension in Cabeza de Vaca's advice to his king concerning Native Americans, it is nonetheless worth quoting: "to bring all these people to Christianity and subjection to Your Imperial Majesty, they must be won by kindness, the only certain way." As he progressed in his journey, the Spaniard became more and more aware that Native Americans, despite their (to him) bizarre customs, were indeed human beings who, like himself, responded to friendliness and charity. Part of this recognition was perhaps the result of his natural compassion for human misery and suffering, which he had an opportunity to observe firsthand as the sick of village after village were brought to him for treatment. But apart from pity, he approved of the Indians of the interior for their admirable physical and mental traits.

It is revealing that the Indians, in reciprocation, came almost to worship the four Spaniards. Cabeza de Vaca comments that, at the end of their journey, Alcarez, the slave-hunter, had told the assembled Indians that the wanderers were Christians like himself and his men. The Indians refused to believe him, for "we had come from the sunrise, they from the sunset; we healed the sick, they killed the sound; we came naked and barefoot, they clothed, horsed, and lanced; we coveted nothing but gave whatever we were given, while they robbed whomever they found and bestowed nothing on anyone." This, in succinct contrast, was the difference between men who had learned a great lesson during their eight years of hardship and privation — the lesson of brotherhood and human kinship — and officials fettered by the colonial mentality.

La Relación, then, in its account of racial difference and of the misunderstandings and conflicts engendered by that difference, anticipates much later American writing. It is a forerunner in another sense because of the unmistakable spiritual quality it radiates. It is perhaps a commonplace of literary criticism, but an essential one, to insist on a fundamental distinction between European and American letters. In general, European literature — fiction in particular — excels in the recounting of the minutiae of life, in depicting manners, social and political, whereas American books are more often concerned with ultimates: with the individual's relationships to God, to the universe, and to his own soul. Most works of American literature, says W. H. Auden, "are parables; their settings, even when they pretend to be realistic, symbolic settings for a timeless and unlocated (because internal) psychomachia."[5] Cabeza de Vaca's narrative was ostensibly composed as a chronicle of physical ordeal, but many readers who have searched for its deeper meanings have detected a corresponding odyssey of the spirit, have seen in it a kind of true-life parable.

The element of spirituality in the work that immediately snares the reader's attention is the Spaniards' activities as faith healers. Cabeza de Vaca included in *La Relación* a catalogue of miracles of healing that he and his companions supposedly performed on the Indians they met along their way. Some commentators have claimed the miracles were not genuine; the Indians were lying, the argument runs, when they said they were cured, or perhaps their ailments were psychological in origin and the Spaniards managed to relieve them by means of what we would now call the self-fulfilling prophecy. Others have been more charitable in their interpretations.

One of the most interesting interpretations is in a curious little book by the poet Haniel Long, called *Interlinear to Cabeza de Vaca*. Long's Whitmanesque theory goes something like this: Cabeza de Vaca found in the wilderness the secret of tapping that reservoir of power that is in each of us, a power few of us are ever able to exert. By being stripped naked, spiritually as well as physically, the Spaniard was thrust "into a world where nothing, if done for another, seems impossible." He had learned by the end of his journey that "the power of maintaining life in others lives within each of us, and from each of us does it recede when unused."[6]

Whether or not the reader accepts Long's latter-day transcendentalism, he must admit the difficulty of explaining the "miracles" in purely rationalistic terms. They seem in any case to have had a profound effect on the one who performed them. Cabeza de Vaca's experiences elevated his spirit to a domain above the physical landscape around him and contributed to the near mysticism — or perhaps it was only a kind of fevered asceticism brought on by hunger and pain — into which he apparently lapsed. The knowledge of human suffering and its psychological, if not physical, alleviation seemed to expand and alter his vision of life; it chastened him, taught him humility, and encouraged his spiritual growth — growth which paralleled with almost calculated artistry his geographic progress.

One of the recurring motifs of American literature is the voyage of exploration, of physical and spiritual discovery, the journey to the interior, in which the dominant figure is man isolated — alone in the wilderness, alone with himself. This thematic and structural device appears with great frequency in our writing. Voyages and journeys of discovery, Harry Levin suggests, "have served as real and imaginary vehicles for our literature from John Smith to Ernest Hemingway."[7] Levin's claim is demonstrably true, but we must look earlier than the English Captain Smith to find the first account of the American journey inward: Cabeza de Vaca's *La Relación* is, in fact, the prototype of such accounts.

La Relación's anticipation of the direction of much American writing that followed suggests that our literature is what it is because, given the nature of our national experience, it could be nothing else. The exploration and settlement of vast tracts of "empty" land are crucial components of the American's (and the Texan's) heritage, and these historical facts have had to be examined and interpreted in works of a truly national character. A convenient medium for their dramatization has been the journey of discovery. As a literary convention it allows the writer to juxtapose the objective dangers of physical isolation with the subtle and sometimes more demanding trial of spiritual isolation.

The American journey of discovery ends in one of two ways, in hope or in bleak despair. Often it has concluded with the latter, with its course leading nowhere. De Tocqueville warns that the American environment tends to throw the individual "back forever upon himself alone and threatens in the end to confine him entirely within the solitude of his own heart."[8] Thus the American wanderer frequently discovers only a blank, the spiritual equivalent of the nihilistic landscape through which he has trekked. In the case of Cabeza de Vaca, however, rescue seems to have found him a wiser and nobler person than he was when he began. The Spaniard did not rage and storm at fate for casting him ashore among savages and the elements. He accepted the suffering forced upon him, and as a result he grew and learned. The land fascinated him, and more importantly he came to acknowledge his kinship with the Native Americans. It is fitting that he became the first Texan, the first American — his citizenship having been forged in the crucible of pain and privation — to experience and report a sequence of events that, with variations, runs in a continuous stream through our literature.

J. FRANK DOBIE

J. Frank Dobie's role as founder and, later, arbiter of Texas literary culture began in the 1920s. His fresh renderings of Texas and southwestern folklore earned him a large local and national reading audience; they also helped to initiate a literary tradition in a region where no such tradition had previously existed. As decades passed, however, Dobie's writings gradually became secondary in importance to his acts and pronouncements as a citizen, and those acts and pronouncements generated his considerable reputation as an indomitable, if rather cranky, individualist. Dobie's significance as a public figure and controversialist was immense, and just about everybody who ever met him or heard him talk was charmed by him. Indeed it has been suggested that Dobie's *only* real importance lay in his dominating personality and that this fact accounts for his current plummeting reputation as a writer. For it is unquestionably true that, as impressions of Dobie the man — the mischievous grin, the unmistakable shock of white hair, the resonant cow country voice — fade from memory with the passage of time, his fellow Texans have tended more and more to forget about him. Impressions of Dobie the writer have not, apparently, been sufficiently favorable to offset dimming memories of Dobie the man.

I want to argue that Dobie's artistry as a writer was more subtle and accomplished than some recent commentators have recognized. When he was alive, Dobie's many books, as they appeared with inexorable regularity, were usually greeted with high praise from reviewers, and they usually sold well — even to people who never read them. Since his death three decades ago, however, those works have been examined in a much more detached and tough-minded fashion than they normally were when the author was alive. In fact, they have drawn sharp criticism from a number of observers and for a variety of reasons.

The books have been attacked, for instance, by the so-called scientific folklorists, who deplore the writer's lack of devotion to folklore as a systematic and rigorously precise discipline. (Dobie's professed, and only half-joking, attitude toward the collection and publishing of folk materials was that he never let the truth stand in the way of his telling a good story.) Richard Dorson, a former president of the American Folklore Society and a noted professional folklorist, was especially harsh in his condemnation of Dobie's approach to folklore. Dorson accused Dobie of being a purveyor of "fakelore," a "prolific romancer of Southwestern lore whose only purpose is entertainment and nostalgia." Dorson contended further that "Dobie's formula based on color, nostalgia, and sentiment had, in general, set back the discipline of folklore."[9]

From another flank, Dobie was assaulted by a younger generation of Texas writers and intellectuals who, following Dobie's death in 1964, made it fashionable to sneer at the author — along with his friends Walter Prescott Webb and Roy Bedichek — as the cornerstone of an outmoded literary establishment. Larry McMurtry, of course, has leveled a series of withering volleys at Dobie. McMurtry has claimed that Dobie was too much a sentimentalist, was often an indifferent stylist, lacked the ability to structure his books coherently, was something of an anti-intellectual (in that he distrusted his own imagination and intellect and was "plagued by a persistent sense that his books were a reduction of life rather than an amplification of it"); overall, according to McMurtry, Dobie was "a hasty and impatient writer."[10] To go McMurtry one better, Gregory Curtis, editor of *Texas Monthly* magazine, dismissed Dobie a few years back by dubbing him a creator of "bedtime stories for boys in junior high."[11]

In all these criticisms there is probably a measure of truth, but there is also a good deal of exaggeration. In my opinion, the least justified of the criticisms (at least as it applies to his four or five best books) is that Dobie was a sloppy craftsman. Actually, if we may judge by available evidence, including the testimony of people who knew him well, just the reverse is true. The author labored long and hard at every stage of composition; any flaws that mar his works are not flaws of haste or impatience. His research, both in books and in the field, was extensive. He wrote and rewrote in an effort to chasten an unruly language. He often published the same story in a number of different places, always considerably revising and usually improving the tale with each republication.

Admittedly there was always in Dobie an impulse toward the sentimental and romantic, toward a style that was too flowery and poetic. He was aware of that impulse, and though he was not always able to suppress it, he fought it and in most cases managed to tone it down in his published writings. The older he got, the more he strove for clarity and economy, for the appropriate rhythm, pace, and tempo. Here is a sentence picked pretty much at random from a Dobie essay: "The flowers of a rainy spring and the grasses of a showery summer are good and beautiful and sufficient even though they vanish." The cadence here is clearly that of the King James Bible, the first and most basic influence on Dobie's style. The content, I suppose, is vaguely romantic, though it does not oppress my sense of reality to consider the writer's thought. On the whole, it seems to me a rhetorically effective statement. In most of his writings, particularly those he put between hard covers, Dobie's is a very conscious and sophisticated prose style, and I suggest that would-be writers might well profit from a study of that style.

I want to focus briefly on a single book, *Coronado's Children* (1930), as a kind of microcosm of Dobie's methods and techniques as a writer. In many ways *Coronado's Children* is Dobie's best and most characteristic work, and it is historically important because it was the book that brought the writer his initial fame and a fair amount of fortune (it was a Literary Guild book club selection). The volume takes its title from the fact that the Spaniard Coronado in his sixteenth-century quest for the elusive Seven Cities of Cíbola was the first prospector to search for legendary riches in what is now the American Southwest. The myriad of dreamers who have since scoured the region driven by tales of lost mines and buried treasure are the spiritual progeny of the credulous Spaniard. *Coronado's Children,* then, is a collection of legends and stories concerning the innumerable treasure hoards supposedly concealed by the rugged southwestern landscape. The tales included in the book were drawn from what an academic folklorist would call field research, from oral interviews, and from a long list of printed sources. (Dobie expanded the same materials, incidentally, in a later work, *Apache Gold and Yaqui Silver,* published in 1939.)

Coronado's Children is pure, quintessential Dobie, and those who dislike Dobie's seemingly casual approach to stitching a book together will not like this one. The tales seem to be arranged randomly, with scarcely any attempt at a linear, logical narrative progression, certainly no build-up to a grand climax. I think the reason Dobie favored this kind of loose structure was not because he was incapable of imposing order on his work, but because he saw himself in the great tradition of oral storytellers and felt that, in some ways, he was handicapped by having to use a pen rather than his voice. He modeled his works after the style and organization of the great tale-tellers he had known. His books thus seem choppy and disorganized because they are composed of many short tales clustered around a common subject or theme. With good reason he called his works "mosaics," for these books are meant to approximate the narrative breaks and disconnections, the associative flow of thought of a storyteller's monologue. The books are successful, however—*Coronado's Children,* in particular—because their hidden and underlying threads are never broken, and each tale develops and enlarges an overall pattern.

As Dorson and McMurtry remind us, there is God's plenty of romance and sentiment in Dobie's writings, and *Coronado's Children* undoubtedly contains its share of overtly romantic passages. Here, for instance, is Dobie's description of one of his informants, an old cowhand named Andy Mather. "The mountains of the West and the canyons of the plains are mapped in his grizzled features. I see him now, a great hat on his head, wearing a vest but no coat, all booted and spurred and ready to ride, but sitting with monarchial repose in an ample rawhide-bottom chair on his shady gallery." That description may not be objective—or dull—enough to please a "scientific folklorist," but it is effectively charming nonetheless.

Besides, it's really a stylistic extreme and not at all representative of the prose employed in most of the tales in *Coronado's Children.* The majority of the stories are told in a straightforward, matter-of-fact style that, in its cumulative effect, creates an ironic tone that would do credit to a Jonathan Swift. After relating a particularly tentative and circumstantial series of events concerning the search for a lost mine, the narrative voice concludes the tale as follows: "Thus, with little chance for error or exaggeration, has been preserved a record of probably the first American to be lured to a search for the Los Almegres mine." There is irony in this statement. Dobie knows, and the reader *should* know, that there has been plenty of room for exaggeration and error. But the writer, like Swift in many of his satirical works, is consciously playing the role of gullible narrator.

Time after time in the book Dobie says that he is merely conveying facts as to the size and location of some lost treasure. But the facts, of course, aren't really facts at all; they are the dreams and projections and delusions of those half-mad searchers who never lose hope, who know that treasure is just a few feet of digging deeper or can be found just over the next hill or at the foot of the next rainbow. Facts to a true believer are not necessarily facts to a detached observer, and it is this inherently ironic truth that Dobie uses fully and effectively in *Coronado's Children.*

To underscore the point, Dobie's irony was so subtle that, after the book was published, hundreds of readers contacted the writer proposing partnerships to uncover the lost gold and silver he had supplied accounts of. But Dobie, even if he had believed the tales he recounted, was not interested in treasure as such. He was much more fascinated by those people who dedicate their lives to looking for it.

The essence of Dobie's method, as writer and artist, it seems to me, is what may be called a form of symbolism. He used this symbolic method effectively, for example, in his books about southwestern animals. He admired the longhorns of the Texas brush country for their qualities of endurance and adaptability; by implication, these are also qualities he felt human beings should possess. In another book, he rhapsodized about the wild mustangs and their fierce love of freedom; when it is recalled that his book *The Mustangs* appeared in 1952, in the midst of a witch-hunt usually referred to as "the McCarthy era," the allegory of his tales of the free-roaming horses of the prairies should be obvious.

In *Coronado's Children* lost mines and treasure seem to be symbols of the unattainable that humans continually strive for, the illusions by which we all live. It is the search that is important, not its successful completion. As Henry Nash Smith once wrote, "the obsession with buried treasure that is the unifying thread of *Coronado's Children* is curiously noncommercial. Dobie's desert dreamers wear out their lives in bondage to visions of gold and silver, but the treasure they lust for could never be converted into digits entered on books of a national bank in a forty-story skyscraper."[12] In many ways Dobie approved of the treasure-hunters because they had hope and purpose and vision, and these are motivations necessary to fulfilling any goal. But to balance the equation, he also recognized their moral and spiritual blindness.

Perhaps the best chapter in *Coronado's Children* — certainly the most oft-reprinted one — is the episode titled "Midas on a Goatskin." This brief narrative recounts the author's interview with Dee Davis, "The second sorriest white man in Sabinal." Dee knows the exact locations of a half-dozen fabulous treasure hoards, and he will get around to recovering them, he says, as soon as conditions are right. Dee Davis, sitting on a goatskin in the door of his shack spinning treasure tales as his wife waters zinnias and morning-glories in the yard, is Dobie's unforgettable emblem of human desire and human shiftlessness held in uneasy suspension.

Coronado's Children, I think, succeeds as a work of art because, like all Dobie's best books, it uses local and regional materials to illuminate the timeless aspects of human nature. And the book *is* a work of art. Indeed, it is at this point that the criticisms of the scientific folklorists miss the mark. For, despite his enthusiasm for collecting and studying southwestern lore, Dobie was not essentially a folklorist. He had a great respect for the power and truth of folklore. He once said that "of all forms of human expression, folklore is the most sensitive to environment; it is the autobiography, unconscious and unsigned, of a people." Dobie collected folk-tales with great zest, but he used those tales as raw material and inspiration, not as finished products safely preserved in an index and properly cross-referenced as to motif and tale-type number.

Stories filtered through a writer's intelligence and transmuted by an artist's imagination are naturally going to be changed from their original form. Dobie did not hesitate to make such changes, since he believed his efforts were humanistic and artistic, not scientific. He was not attempting, as would the academic folklorist, to transcribe faithfully the tales gathered from field research. He was trying instead to transform them into literature. More often than not—despite the fact that, like most writers who have long careers and produce many books, his performance was uneven—he succeeded in doing just that.

CHAPTER 3

Herding Words

The Emergence of Texas Literature

*I grew up in a herding tradition and that's determined
everything I've done. I was never good at herding cattle,
but writing is a way of herding words . . . and I suspect
by my constant driving around the country I'm
practicing a form of trail-driving.*

— LARRY MCMURTRY, *New York Times Book Review*

When it first began to enter my consciousness, roughly three and a half
decades ago, that my own, my native state had produced some writers who
were worth reading, those writers at the time were ordinarily thought of
as southwestern writers rather than as Texas writers. In fact, one critic,
Lawrence Clark Powell, a southern Californian with a keen interest in
southwestern literature, in the late 1950s conferred upon that arch-Texan J.
Frank Dobie the title "Mr. Southwest."[1] This act was no doubt performed
in public acknowledgement of Dobie's yeoman service in publicizing the
lore and legendry of Texas and the American Southwest — that vast and
somewhat amorphous region stretching from West Texas to California. At
any rate, in the 1950s, 1960s, and well into the 1970s, most bibliographies,
literary histories, anthologies, and other reference tools of the sort that
dealt with Texas writers at all considered them as part of a larger regional
culture — that is, the culture of the Southwest. Today, fewer people speak
of Texas writers as contributors to southwestern literature; most employ,
almost automatically, the phrase "Texas literature."

An example of this shift comes from the nonfiction of the state's best-
known living writer, Larry McMurtry. McMurtry's 1968 collection, *In a
Narrow Grave: Essays on Texas,* contains a chapter called "Southwestern Lit-

erature?" — with emphasis on the question mark. In that essay, McMurtry talks mostly about Texas writers, but don't overlook the word *southwestern* in the title of the piece. Thirteen years later — October 23, 1981, to be precise — McMurtry's iconoclastic article "Ever a Bridegroom: Reflections on the Failure of Texas Literature" appeared in the *Texas Observer.* It was a shot heard round Texas — maybe even round the world — and McMurtry's contention that Texas literature has been, to this point, a dismal "failure" detonated an explosive controversy, with charges and countercharges ricocheting through the state's literary circles. I will not comment on the controversy here, except to say that it has not died out completely to this day. To me one of the most interesting things about McMurtry's *Texas Observer* essay is that it assumes, unlike the 1968 piece, that there is a recognizable body of writing that we may call "Texas literature," failed though the author believes it to be.

Further evidence of the triumph, in the 1980s, of the concept of a separate and distinct Texas literature came in the form of a gaudy, three-day symposium on "The Texas Literary Tradition," held in Austin in March, 1983, and sponsored by the University of Texas as part of its Centennial celebration. Three years later, in September, 1986, in Denton, the University of North Texas put on a shindig that bore the imprimatur of the governor's office and was called "Texas Images and Realities: The Governor's Sesquicentennial Conference on the Literary Arts." Audiences totaling well over a thousand people attended each of these conferences, and both the Austin and Denton get-togethers were covered by all the state's major newspapers, as well as by out-of-state papers such as the *New York Times.*

A citizen of, say, North Dakota or Kansas might well find such symposia passing strange. North Dakotans do not claim for themselves a North Dakota literature, nor do Kansans normally think in terms of a Kansas "literary tradition." North Dakota and Kansas writing is considered — if it is considered at all — as Texas writing used to be, as part of a more encompassing regional literature. Furthermore, people from other states may think the idea of a Texas Institute of Letters rather pretentious. The TIL was founded in 1936, during the state's Centennial exhibition in Dallas, to be a select body charged with fostering in Texas the creative act of writing (a sponsorship that often started at the rudimentary level of opposing censorship in whatever form it appears) and the critical appreciation of that writing. But a state having its own "institute of letters" strikes some as absurd — European rather than American — and down through the years there have been those, including Larry McMurtry at one time, who have chided both the theory and practice of the organization. Again, what other state has its own institute of letters?

It is easy, then, to poke fun at the idea of a uniquely Texan literature, just as it is easy to ridicule the "Texas mystique" in its varied and sometimes ludicrous manifestations. But the concept of a Texas literary tradition, to me, does make a good deal of sense. Certainly I have written much over the years that begins with the assumption that such a tradition exists. In the world of book-publishing, as in other areas, Texas is a widely recognized brand name, thanks to the universal currency of the Texas myth. Americans in general and Texans in particular buy books about Texas — lots of them. Book people — who, if they are successful, are also hard-headed business people — are aware of this attitude. Is there a bookstore in the state that does not sport a lavishly stocked and prominently displayed "Texana" section? National publishers often court Texas authors, because of their sales potential, while largely ignoring those from Wisconsin or Idaho. Moreover, a lively publishing industry, comprising both commercial and university presses, now flourishes within Texas, much of it catering to the local market.

Most Texans, I believe, think of themselves as part of a separate and distinct entity. Of the states of the union Texas is uniquely, to adopt a phrase apparently coined in 1915 by Zane Grey in his popular novel *The Lone Star Ranger*, "a world in itself." (Many a writer since, including George Sessions Perry in his 1942 volume *Texas: A World in Itself*, has perpetuated the cliché.) Or, as historian T. R. Fehrenbach asserts, it is a "nation within a nation." One of the advantages of employing Texas as a means of categorizing works of literature is that it is a well-defined geographical entity. We can look on a map — as we cannot in the case of a nebulous region such as the Southwest — and see its boundaries clearly outlined. Within those borders, Texas possesses more topographical, ethnic, and cultural diversity than do most of the nations of the world. And yet it is held together by a powerful, chauvinistic mythology that generates fierce loyalty from almost all who think of themselves as Texans. It seems to me, therefore, that the idea of a "Texas literature" is as justifiable — and, again, as subject to ridicule — as the idea of Texas music or Texas cooking or Texas apparel or, most grandiose of all, a Texas lifestyle.

Having said as much, let me proceed to assert — well, I guess A. C. Greene and Larry McMurtry said this quite a while ago — the importance of pausing occasionally to take stock, to consider Texas writing within the context of other literatures and other cultures. It is all too easy to forget that Texas literature is only a small and, many would say, relatively insignificant part of American literature, of Western European literature, and of world literature. John Graves is on target when he warns, as he did in a recent interview, that Texas literature "is just a segment of the whole and has to stand ultimately on how well it stacks up against writing from N.Y.C. or Minnesota or whatever."[2] What Graves is talking about here is the question of quality. Just how good is Texas writing? Is literary Texas an empire or a banana republic?

That there may be bad Texas books as well as good Texas books is a thought that probably never occurs to Texans who think about books at all. For Texans, Texas books — like Texas cattle, Texas oil (what's left of it), and Texas bidness — are, in and of themselves, good because they are Texan. I know several people, fellow Texans all, who own near-complete sets of the works of the aforementioned J. Frank Dobie. Dobie's books sit on shelves beside volumes by Stephen King and Anne Rice. These folks read Stephen King and Anne Rice; they do not, for the most part, read Dobie. Nonetheless Dobie is revered by many Texans. He taught Texans how to succeed at the culture game. He gave Texans a literary identity at a time when foreigners, that is, people living outside the state, refused to acknowledge there was such a thing as Texas writing — or even southwestern writing. Thus Dobie is seen as a natural resource, as important on the cultural level as cattle, cotton, and oil are — or were — on the economic level.

Obviously we need to be more critical in our approach to Texas literature than this naive, chauvinistic reaction allows. And without a doubt evaluations of Texas writing beginning in the early 1980s have been more penetrating and, one hopes, more sophisticated than they ever were in the past. A. C. Greene kicked off the decade by publishing several articles and essays that initiated a lively discussion of Texas writing throughout the 1980s. For example, Greene's "The Fifty Best Texas Books" appeared in the August, 1981, issue of *Texas Monthly*.[3] This list, later fleshed out and put between hard covers under the title *The Fifty Best Books on Texas,* seems in retrospect to have been offered with a kind of good-natured innocence. Greene did not make any extravagant claims for the books included in his catalogue. He simply said: Here are some good Texas books worthy of a serious reader's attention. As a matter of fact, in *The Fifty Best* (the book, not the article), Greene had the audacity — and the honesty? — to compare Texas writing with New Mexico writing and to find Lone Star letters clearly lacking: "Texas," he adjudged, "has not furnished indigenous materials for great novels" such as those by Oliver La Farge, Frank Waters, and

Adolph Bandelier. "It has drawn out no *Death Comes for the Archbishop,* and few products comparable to Richard Bradford's *Red Sky at Morning.*"[4]

Interestingly, the fact that Texas writing was about to take a bashing was signaled by the appearance of a piece by Gregory Curtis, a former student of Larry McMurtry's at Rice University and now editor of *Texas Monthly,* in the same issue of the magazine that carried Greene's "The Fifty Best Texas Books." Writing in his "Behind the Lines" column, Curtis proclaimed that "the curse of Texas letters is that for the most part our hallowed writers are themselves more interesting than their books."[5] This statement was followed by a thorough flaying of the hapless (and deceased) J. Frank Dobie and his disciples. Though he professed to admire the work of a bare handful of contemporary Texas writers, Curtis concluded that few of the state's authors have contributed literature that has "practical value" — that is to say, books that "tell us who we are now and who our ancestors were then."

Hard on the heels of the August, 1981, *Texas Monthly* came the *Texas Observer* that contained McMurtry's "Ever a Bridegroom." This soon-to-be notorious issue hit the streets with a bang in October, 1981.[6] As the subtitle of McMurtry's piece indicates, he believed that Texas literature had, to that point, been an irredeemable failure. The only Texas writer for whom he had unqualified praise was poet Vassar Miller, who can hardly be labeled a regional writer. (That, no doubt, was part of McMurtry's point.) At any rate, a sizable boatload of critics, commentators, writers, and reporters bobbed in the choppy wake of Greene and McMurtry, and ever since the subject of the quality of Texas writing has been debated in the pages of magazines and newspapers, from platforms and podiums across the state. A great deal of heat has been generated, and now and then a few glimmerings of light have been shed upon the topic. At least everybody now seems comfortable with the idea of applying serious and rigorous critical standards to Texas literature. There is little remaining validity to McMurtry's famous definition of literary criticism in Texas: two writers getting into a fistfight in a bar.

It seems to me that Texas literature is still a very young literature and that Texas, as a literary entity, has not really had an opportunity yet either to succeed *or* to fail. Texas' literary development appears to be following the larger pattern of American literary development. American literature, we must recall, has not always enjoyed its current lofty status as one of the world's great literatures. In the eighteenth and well into the nineteenth centuries, American writing was dismissed by Europeans as embarrassingly provincial and immature. American artists and intellectuals were very much aware of this attitude and were stung by the barbs of snooty critics such as the Englishman Sydney Smith, who wrote an infamous essay in 1819 for the *Edinburgh Review:* "In the four quarters of the globe," Smith asked, "who reads an American book? or goes to an American play? or looks at an American picture?"

In the early and middle decades of the nineteenth century, many American writers, including William Cullen Bryant, William Gilmore Simms, Herman Melville, and, most notable of all, Ralph Waldo Emerson — whose 1837 address "The American Scholar" came to be widely known as America's "intellectual Declaration of Independence"[7] — published strident, chauvinistic proclamations calling for American writers to break free of the chains of European cultural domination and to forge a uniquely American civilization and culture. These proclamations were no doubt prompted as much by anxiety and a nagging fear of inferiority as they were by confident expectation. But fortunately for American culture the talent that rescued these statements from the realm of windy rhetoric began to appear in the middle decades of the nineteenth century.

Even so it took a long time for American literature to be accorded its rightful status and respect. In the latter half of the nineteenth century Henry James, an American soon to become a European, could still lament that the American scene was not conducive to the artistic temperament because it contained "no castles . . . no ivied ruins" — in effect, no culture worthy of the name.[8] Throughout the twentieth century, writers and other artists have continued to complain about the crassness, the materialism, the violence of American society. What they have often overlooked is the vitality of that society — a vitality that has fueled a remarkable flowering of the arts in our time, just as it has fueled unprecedented economic growth. Though America may be, as some have claimed, currently in a state of literary decadence — its literary batteries having run down parallel to the entropic decline of its industrial machine — a glimpse back over the past century and a half of American writing reveals a grand and glorious record, an inventory of literary accomplishments that owe much of their power to the very crassness, materialism, and violence of the society from which they have issued.

Texas writers, therefore, can draw strength from the examples of earlier American writers and their sometimes painful struggle to be taken seriously. Most cogently, however, they can look for aesthetic inspiration to the recent literary history of a neighboring province. I refer to the so-called southern Renaissance. As late as 1917, H. L. Mencken contended that the American South was "as sterile, artistically, intellectually, culturally, as the Sahara Desert." Aside from James Branch Cabell, Mencken asserted, "you will not find a single Southern prose writer who can actually write. . . . [The South] has no art, no literature, no philosophy, no mind or aspiration of her own."[9] It was as if southern writers, Faulkner and the Agrarians among others, were lying in wait to ambush the reckless Mencken, for the blooming of southern writing that has been dubbed a renaissance began soon after the publication of Mencken's intemperate essay.

American literature — and for that matter southern literature — as formal endeavors, began more than two centuries ago; Texas literature, for practical purposes, is barely three-quarters of a century old, dating from Dobie's first published writings in the 1920s. Though the following is far from a precise analogy, Texas literature today stands at approximately the same juncture as did American literature when Sydney Smith asked his ill-timed question, or as did southern literature when Mencken launched his harangue. Perhaps Larry McMurtry is *our* Sydney Smith and H. L. Mencken rolled into one self-assured and beguilingly convincing critic. McMurtry has thrown down the gauntlet. "In the four quarters of the globe," he has asked in effect, "who reads a Texas book?" Who, that is, with even a shred of literary taste or self-respect? It remains to be seen whether circumstances will be as fortuitous for Texas literature in the near future as they were for American literature following the gibes of people like Sydney Smith, or as they were for southern literature after Mencken's venomous generalizations about southern culture.

Time is required for a literary tradition to develop. Even more time is needed for the just appreciation and critical understanding of the tradition to evolve. The latter — critical appreciation and understanding — is really a public relations problem that must be worked on slowly but relentlessly. Reviewers, critics, and commentators have to be sold on the idea of a literature's existence; that literature must be widely taught over a long period of time in public-school and college classrooms. (Recall that it was well into the twentieth century before college-level courses in American literature became commonplace.)

It seems to me that there are at least three stages in the study and appreciation of any literature that must be surmounted before the legitimacy of the literature is firmly established. The first stage is simply recognition: it must be recognized that here is a body of literature worthy of serious scrutiny and attention. The second stage is definition and description:

boundaries must be drawn, and catalogues of relevant texts must be compiled. The third stage is critical judgment and discrimination: evaluations of authors and works must be formulated, and the literature must be placed in a comparative context with other literatures.

Texas writing has more or less successfully weathered the first step; most readers, at least most Texas readers, are probably willing to grant the existence of a body of works that may justifiably be called "Texas literature." The status of Texas writing with regard to the second stage is more problematical. The parameters that encompass Texas literature have never been defined to everybody's satisfaction and may never be. A troublesome question, for example — and one that grows more troublesome with every passing year — is, Who are the Texas writers? (A similar question, incidentally, also vexes the study of American literature: were Aldous Huxley and W. H. Auden and Vladimir Nabokov *American* writers in any meaningful sense of the term? Were Henry James and T. S. Eliot?) With regard to Texas literature, there is no denying that J. Frank Dobie, Walter Prescott Webb, and Roy Bedichek — once worshipped as the "Holy Trinity of Texas Letters" — were Texas writers; they were born and bred in Texas, and they proudly boasted of their Texanness wherever two or three were gathered together to listen. Among today's authors no one would dispute the fact that John Graves, Elmer Kelton, and Benjamin Capps are Texas writers.

But what about someone like the late Donald Barthelme? Barthelme was reared in Houston but lived in the East during most of his very successful career. He returned to Texas a decade or so before his death in 1989 to teach creative writing at the University of Houston, his alma mater, but he had very little to say about his native state in his published writings. Interestingly, though, in the mid-1980s Barthelme was quoted as saying, "taking the thing state by state, there are more good writers in Texas than anywhere in the country save New York and California."[10] At any rate, despite McMurtry's published apology that he had ever questioned Barthelme's "credentials as a Texan"[11] (as he had in "Ever a Bridegroom"), it appears to me that doubts about those credentials, at least in the literary arena, have not yet been completely dissipated. On the other side of the coin, can authors such as Max Apple, Beverly Lowry, and Laura Furman, who grew up in other regions but who spent many of their productive years in Texas, be labeled, with any justice, Texas writers? Or for that matter can a certain well-known man of American letters, who shall remain nameless but who came to Texas (and maintained a home in Austin until his death in 1997) to write what he modestly called a "blockbuster novel" about the state — can he be called, or did he ever care to be called, a Texas writer?

McMurtry, in "Ever a Bridegroom," takes a hard line in defining the Texas writer: "only those born and raised in Texas," he asserts, "have the dubious honor of literary citizenship. Even writers who become absorbed in the state, and make good use of some part of it . . . shouldn't have to consider themselves Texas writers." The Texas Institute of Letters, on the other hand, takes a more liberal, not to say hopelessly diffusive, view of the question. The TIL seems intent on gathering into its fold any notable writer who crosses the Red River, whether by plane, train, or automobile.

A measured definition of the Texas writer no doubt lies somewhere between these extremes. Certainly migration, and the immigrant who is the human figure in the phenomenon of migration, is as much a part of the Texas myth as it is of the larger American myth. Migrant writers, like migrant executives of high-tech electronics industries, must be granted the right to become naturalized Texas citizens, following an appropriate period of acculturation and assimilation, of course. Dues of citizenship must be paid. The question is, How high should the dues be set? I do not know the answer to that question, nor do I intend to explore it further here. The point is, as interest in Texas books grows, the inexorable homogenization of American — and Texan — society makes it more and more difficult to say who is and who is not a Texas writer.

In the scheme I outlined above, the third stage in the study of a body of writing is sustained critical evaluation and appreciation, an activity that ultimately should yield a consensus as to the overall quality of the literature. The study of Texas literature has not yet reached this stage — or, if so, just barely. McMurtry's 1981 barrage from the pages of the *Texas Observer* ignited a firestorm of controversy as to the quality, or lack of quality, of Texas writing, in part, I think, because it violated the polite deference to each other's books that Texas writers and critics had tended over the years to maintain. Without question, McMurtry hit a nerve. There were outraged reactions and heated commentary from every corner of Texas culture. The ensuing turmoil even caught the attention of the *New York Times* and the *Washington Post;* indeed, it was considered important enough that in 1986 *Texas Monthly*'s Sesquicentennial "collector's issue," which bears the title "Texas, Our Texas: 150 Moments That Made Us The Way We Are," included an account of the verbal battle.[12] Now that the dust has settled a bit, we discern a growing accumulation of criticism — mostly drifts from the departed sandstorm — but it seems clear that extant criticism of Texas writing is still relatively slight. I am not foolish enough to suggest that what I am about to say represents an incipient consensus judgment on Texas writing, but I want to make a few comments — perhaps most are fairly obvious — on the quality of Texas literature considered within the context of American literature generally.

First, I think it should be noted that Texas literature suffers from the limited generic range that its writers, to this point, have exhibited. Novelists, short-story writers, folklorists, historians, journalists, and practitioners of various kinds of expository prose have flourished within the state's borders throughout most of the twentieth century. Poets and playwrights have not. As mentioned earlier, McMurtry, in "Ever a Bridegroom," could find only one Texas writer on whom he heaped unstinting praise: the poet Vassar Miller. Perhaps unfortunately, since Miller is undeniably an extremely talented poet, McMurtry's judgment has yet to be verified; Miller has so far failed to attract sustained regional, or national, critical acclaim or analysis. She suffers, it seems, not from being labeled a "Texas writer," but from being categorized as a "religious" or "mystical poet." But even if McMurtry's judgment that Miller is the cream of the contemporary crop of Texas writers is confirmed by future literary historians, she remains the exception that proves the rule. In Texas, prose-writers — particularly novelists — still ride tall in the saddle.

Second, let it be admitted, right off, that there have been no literary geniuses to emerge from Texas. (I cannot define the term "literary genius," but I know one when I read one.) A possible exception to this generalization is Katherine Anne Porter — if, that is, considering what I have said about the problem of definition, a case can be make for Porter's being branded a Texas writer, since she spent most of her literary life in voluntary and sometimes embittered exile from Texas. I, in any event, think of her as a Texas writer. So maybe Porter is an exception, or a partial one — a potential genius, anyway, who at her best wrote a handful of stunningly good stories, many of them set in Texas, that will be read as long as the English language and the printed word endure. Otherwise, I doubt that even the most optimistic Texan chauvinist would claim that the state has produced any truly great writers.

No, the brightest lights in the Texas literary galaxy rarely twinkle in the American literary heavens. Since his death in 1964, J. Frank Dobie — the founding father of Texas literature, for decades the state's cultural arbiter — has been pilloried by critics and blindsided by detractors. His literary reputation, once untarnished and impregnable, is now but a heap of rusted, abandoned scrap metal. The consensus now seems to be that Dobie's significance is largely historical rather than aesthetic. He was a literary pioneer who blazed a trail for later Texas writers to follow. But it is now plain to see, as it was not during his lifetime, that he was not a great writer.

I venture to say that the most distinguished — as opposed to bestselling — living Texas writer is John Graves, who in a sense works within the ruralist tradition initiated by Dobie, Webb, and Bedichek. Graves is a professional, a writer who applies an exacting standard to his own performance. In my view, he is the most skillful manipulator of language on the Texas literary scene today, a creator, as Joe Holley has said, of "forceful and eloquent prose."[13] Future generations will find, I predict, Graves's wonderful meditation *Goodbye to a River* (1960) — despite, or perhaps because of, its ruralist bias — both pleasurable and profitable to read. But I think that Graves, who is modest about his literary accomplishments, would probably agree with my judgment that, alas, he is not a literary genius.

At the present time, of course, the Texas author who enjoys the greatest national popularity is the ubiquitous Larry McMurtry. (Attempting to prevent McMurtry's name from popping up too frequently in an essay such as this one is like trying to stamp out the toadstools after a week of heavy rains.) McMurtry is a very inventive and prolific writer, and his winning a Pulitzer Prize for fiction for *Lonesome Dove* (1985) was a well-deserved honor. Texans are justifiably proud that a native son has "made it" as a nationally, even internationally, acclaimed writer, but McMurtry's standing with posterity is an issue that is far from settled. He has published too much — the low quality of his book-a-year performance since *Lonesome Dove,* for example, is especially dismaying — and I fear that his aggregate fictional output may contain more dross than nuggets of precious metal.

In spite of the tendency of literate Texans, then, to overrate their Dobies and Graveses and McMurtrys, Texas is not, on the other hand, the vast cultural wasteland that some have portrayed it to be. We have dozens of good, interesting, competent, and even undervalued writers who have practiced their craft with integrity and diligence during the past half-century or so. From East Texas, we have the three Williams — William Humphrey, William Goyen, and William Owens — who have yet to receive the regional, much less national, recognition they deserve. From West Texas, Elmer Kelton, Benjamin Capps, and Robert Flynn are excellent novelists who are often ignored by reviewers and critics. (In his survey, for example, McMurtry directs one disparaging comment toward Flynn, mentions Capps in passing, and slights Kelton altogether; only one book by the three, Capps's *A Woman of the People,* shows up on Greene's "fifty best" list.) From South Texas, Rolando Hinojosa and the late Tomás Rivera have given impetus in recent years to a vital and vibrant Texas Mexican literature that grows in strength and stature year by year. We have even witnessed, as Texas becomes ever more citified, the appearance of a few works about urban life in the state that are worthy of critical attention. I am thinking of books such as Billy Lee Brammer's *The Gay Place* (1961), or of two Dallas novels, Edwin Shrake's *Strange Peaches* (1972) and Bryan Woolley's *November 22* (1981), or of Laura Furman's *The Shadow Line* (1982) and David Lindsey's *A Cold Mind* (1983) and *Heat from Another Sun* (1984), novels that owe much of their narrative force to their Houston settings.

I allude, one more time, to McMurtry's conclusion that Texas literature is a failure. I, in fact, concur with McMurtry's judgment that Texas literature, within the context of the American literary tradition, is on the whole insular, ingrown, and inferior. I do not agree that Texas literature is therefore a failed literature. I prefer to think of it as a developing literature. (If there is such a thing as a developing economy, then I suppose there can also be a developing literature.) To reiterate, Texas literature is still young, still growing. I will not predict that Texas writing is about to blossom, the way American writing blossomed in the middle decades of the previous century. Given the lessons of history, though, I would not be surprised if it did.

To end with what seems an appropriate comparison, since we are talking about *Texas* literature and a writer like McMurtry unabashedly speaks of his profession as "herding words," I invoke the analogy of a nineteenth-century trail drive, which proceeded a leg at a time, confronting and surmounting obstacles, until the promised land of the railhead at the end of the long trail was reached. Texas literature has overcome a number of obstacles already, but the question is, How close are we to Dodge? Are the bright lights in view, or are there still many rivers to cross, many stampedes and dust storms yet to be endured before trail's end — and the bars and casinos and the pleasures of the flesh — is attained? Is Texas writing on the margins of a breakthrough, a triumphant culmination? We shall see.

A positive sign that such a culmination may very well be in the offing is that Texas, as a cultural entity, possesses the sustaining mythology, the sense of group identity, the self-consciousness and determination that seem to form the necessary support system for the emergence of a significant "national" literature. If any state or region in America is able to withstand in years to come the growing pressures of standardization and homogenization, it ought to be Texas. All of the rapid and sweeping changes the state is undergoing, even economic ups and downs—these, as T. R. Fehrenbach has claimed, may ultimately prove illusory, at least as far as their effect on the Texas mythos is concerned. Even as Texas becomes overwhelmingly urban and its population is transformed by the influx of people from other states and regions, the Texas myth lives on. "Midnight cowboys" and "urban cowboys" replace real cowboys, but in one form or another—to this point, at any rate—the myth of the cowboy has survived.

And the myth provides a powerful stimulus to literary activity in the state—indeed to artistic activity of all kinds. It supplies, as McMurtry's *Lonesome Dove* memorably illustrates, a rich texture of tradition, a frame of reference, within which the artist may work. Given these hopeful conditions, we have now, I suppose, only to await the arrival of a Texas literary genius. But genius, of whatever stripe, seems to be an accident of birth, as unpredictable in its origin as it is difficult to recognize and to nurture. Maybe there is a literary genius—a Texas Dickinson or Faulkner—out there right now, growing up in Muleshoe or Decatur or Jasper, or beginning to struggle with his or her craft in Houston or Dallas or Austin. Then again, maybe there is not. (Some developing economies develop; others do not. Why should developing literatures be any different?) But Texans are nothing if not optimistic. Texas literature, like Texas history, still seems, to Texans, an unfinished saga. Texas literature, we confidently predict, has its best days ahead of it. The only thing that appears certain, therefore—and the only forecast I am bold enough to make—is that Texas's literary future will be interesting and pleasantly surprising.

CHAPTER 4

This Stubborn Soil

Texas Earth and Texas Culture

Drought and storm, falling prices, banks and lawyers,
poverty and foreclosure broke more Texan hearts and filled
more graves than all the Mexicans and Indians.
The survivors came to see the land, their *land, hallowed*
both by their buried dead and by their dreams. Even the
losers who sank into bankruptcy and tenantry, and their
children's children in the cities, would be haunted
by the remembrance of this struggle.

— T. R. FEHRENBACH, *Atlantic Monthly*

The intimate connection between literature and the land cannot be doubted. According to the poet Richard Hugo, "The place triggers the mind to create the place."[1] As long ago as the late eighteenth century, Crèvecoeur, in his *Letters from an American Farmer,* insisted, in attempting to answer the question "What Is an American?": "Men are like plants; the goodness and flavour of the fruit proceeds from the peculiar soil and exposition in which they grow. We are nothing but what we derive from the air we breathe."[2]

Literary critic James K. Folsom suggested a couple of decades ago that the concept of literary regionalism is rooted in a belief that "man reflects in moral terms the physical nature of his environment."[3] British novelist and world traveler D. H. Lawrence, of course, was enamored of what he called "the spirit of place":

Every continent has its own great spirit of place. Every people is polarized in some particular locality, which is home, the homeland.

Different places on the face of the earth have different vital effluence, different vibration, different chemical exhalation, different polarity with different stars: call it what you like. But the spirit of place is a great reality.[4]

That talented provocateur, the late Edward Abbey, waxes eloquent in his variation on the theme:

Every man, every woman, carries in heart and mind the image of the ideal place, the right place, the one true home, known or unknown, actual or visionary. A houseboat in Kashmir, a view down Atlantic Avenue in Brooklyn, a gray gothic farmhouse two stories high at the end of a red dog road in the Allegheny Mountains, a cabin on the shore of a blue lake in spruce and fir country . . . or even, possibly, for those of a less demanding sensibility, the world to be seen from a comfortable apartment high in the tender, velvety smog of Manhattan, Chicago, Paris, Tokyo, Rio or Rome — there's no limit to the human capacity for the homing sentiment.[5]

Both Lawrence and Abbey speak of places in the heart — of home. They speak of places that possess, for the individual, a sacred dimension — a sacred space that truly emanates "the spirit of place." But the idea of home contains an inevitable duality. Larry McMurtry has said, "a hometown and a home are different things. The former is an accident, usually unfortunate; the latter is a goal, frequently unattainable."[6] There is, for each of us, an ideal home and an actual home. The ideal home we carry in the mind and in the heart; we belong to the actual home and it belongs to us, whether we want it to or not. Lucky are those for whom the actual and the ideal fuse in one magical place.

I have been reading and teaching southwestern literature for close to three decades, and I have often been struck by the circumstance that writers from New Mexico and Arizona — what we might call, with typical Texan chauvinism, the far Southwest — tend to get religious in talking about the land. D. H. Lawrence, for example, who lived off and on near Taos from 1922 to 1925, once declared that, when he first saw the brilliant light of New Mexico, "something stood still in my soul, and I started to attend."[7]

Rudolfo Anaya, author of *Bless Me, Ultima* and other fiction and a native of Santa Rosa, New Mexico, has paid homage to "*la tierra*" and to "the relationship between man and his place." Anaya describes what he calls "the epiphany in landscape" that is ignited by the "majestic and awe inspiring landscape of the Southwest . . . I don't believe a person can be born in the Southwest and not be affected by the land. The landscape changes the man, and the man becomes his landscape."[8]

The aforementioned Edward Abbey, whose home was near Tucson, Arizona, seemed to believe that God — or as much of the concept of God as he was willing to admit — resides in the southwestern deserts. Abbey rarely used the word *God* in his writings, and when he did employ the term, he often did so with whimsical intent. There is nonetheless a measure of high seriousness in the author's claim, in his wonderful book *Desert Solitaire* (1968), that he repaired to the desert "to meet God . . . face to face." The necessary qualification being that, for Abbey, "God" is an ineffable divine energy inherent in the elemental bare-bones reality of nature. "I am not an atheist," he says, "but an earthiest."[9]

These examples are from a trio of writers from New Mexico and Arizona who, in their works, respond to the landscape with aesthetic awe, even spiritual wonder. The list of examples could be extended considerably. On the other hand, *Texas* writers, I find, rarely speak of the land in religious terms — unless they happen to be searching for metaphors for hellfire and brimstone. For Texas writers, Texas is home, in the sense that it is the place where most of them grew up and that willy-nilly shaped their perceptions of the world. It is not, for them, a place of supernal beauty, a place that sets their souls aquiver. (For that kind of emotion, they ordinarily head for New Mexico or Colorado.) I think that, at some level of consciousness, Texas writers' primary allegiance is not to the land as a source of religious feeling — however broadly and loosely that term is defined — but to a land-based mythology that is the foundation of the Texas experience. In *The Trembling of the Veil,* the great Anglo-Irish poet William Butler Yeats asks a fundamental question: "Have not all races had their first unity from a mythology, that marries them to rock and hill?"[10]

A mythology, indeed, that weds us to "rock and hill." Yeats had in mind the rock and hill of Ireland and the mystical mythology of its cozy green countryside. Texas, however, is something else again. Texas is *big* country, and it produces (we Texans have been assured from birth) big men with big ideas and big ambitions. "The country is most barbarously large and final," writes Billy Lee Brammer at the beginning of *The Gay Place,* a well-known novel of Texas politics. "It is too much country—boondock country—alternately drab and dazzling, spectral and remote. It is so wrongfully muddled and various that it is difficult to conceive of it as all of a piece." In fact, the only way we *can* view it as "all of a piece" is through the wide-angle lens of culture and mythology.

Myth is one of those slippery terms that provoke endless argument. Everyone seems to have a slightly different definition of myth. To me, myth is *perceived reality* rather than *objective reality;* myth is what people want to believe rather than what demonstrably *is;* a mythos is a people's belief system contained in a cycle of familiar legends and stories. Every self-conscious group of people has its own unique mythology. Before the American nation could become a cohesive political and cultural entity, for example, a body of sustaining myths had to evolve and be widely accepted and believed. Consider the myth of "the American dream," or the myth of the "melting pot." America, to use Garry Wills's term, had to be "invented."

The same may be said of Texas. "Texans," according to that arch-Texan J. Frank Dobie, "are the only 'race of people' known to anthropologists who do not depend upon breeding for propagation. Like princes and lords, they can be made by 'breath,' plus a big white hat."[11] Texans may not be a "race of people" in the biological sense, but they certainly are in the Yeatsian sense, for they are united by a common mythology. And at the heart of the Texan mythology is the land.[12]

If I may, I want to refer briefly to personal experience. I do so because my experience is typical, I believe, of that of many of the current (though now rapidly fading) generation of Anglo-Texas writers. My home—my corner of Texas—is in south Tarrant County, not far from Fort Worth. The southeastern part of Tarrant County lies in a geographical zone called the Eastern Cross Timbers; the southwestern part is in the Grand Prairie. Our house must have straddled a fault line separating these two geographical areas—not as dramatic as, say, the Balcones Escarpment in Central Texas, but a fault line nevertheless. To the east the land is wooded, and the soil is rich and waxy black; in the early decades of the twentieth century, cotton was widely cultivated, and the ambience of the towns in that part of the county was decidedly southern. But then I could look to the west and see treeless prairie; not too many miles in that direction there were, when I was growing up, relatively large ranches where cattle were raised in extensive herds. Fort Worth, after all, bills itself as the city "where the West begins," and some of the cattle barons who used to make their homes there operated these ranches.

My grandparents came to south Tarrant County in the late nineteenth century. Three of the four came from the Deep South — from Georgia and Alabama. My maternal grandfather came from Illinois or Indiana; his precise origin is not clear from family records or memories. He came with his parents, who were German Jews who had migrated to the United States in the 1840s. All my grandparents — and all their children, at least in the beginning — tried, with only moderate success, to make a living by farming the land. Our property was, for the most part, in the scrubby, sandy land part of the county. My parents managed to scratch out a precarious livelihood during the Great Depression of the 1930s by growing vegetables and selling them to small grocery stores in Fort Worth. When I came along in 1939, they were just barely hanging on. They knew something had to be done to alleviate their marginal economic status. They thought of pulling up stakes and moving to California — as many others of that time and place were doing — but for whatever reason they were unable to leave the family homestead. Their solution, instead, was for my father to acquire a job in the city, in Fort Worth.

We were close enough to the city that we did not have to move there. In a series of old and unreliable automobiles my father commuted for nearly thirty years from our house in the country to his work in Fort Worth. For a long time we attempted to supplement the family income by raising produce to sell. Once I was old enough, much of the burden of planting, cultivating, and harvesting the produce fell on me. I had other chores to perform — in fact, an unending succession of chores. Until the mid-1950s, firewood was our only source of fuel for heating and cooking; I cut (with hand-saw and axe), carried, and stacked most of the wood we used. Cows and chickens needed tending. In season I worked for other farmers in the area, hoeing and picking their vegetables for meager pay. My least favorite activity, since it was hellishly hard on hands and kneecaps, was picking cotton.

It was all hard work, and I can't say I enjoyed it very much. It was often uncomfortable work, since there was no central heating or air-conditioning to retreat to. Indeed my most vivid recollections of that period of my life have to do with weather. We worried and fretted about the weather constantly: it always seemed to be too hot or too cold, too wet or too dry. I remember the dread with which we watched the "blue northers" descend upon us in winter. When a bruise-colored smudge appeared in the northern sky, we knew we were in for it; there would be days of huddling round the old wood-burning stove that was never able to keep warm more than a few square feet of our drafty living room.

John Graves is dead on target in one of his comments on weather in *Goodbye to a River:*

> There is less talk of "northers" these days. People sit softly at ten fifteen in the evening and watch while a bacon vender points to highs and lows and fronts on a chart, and then go to the wall and twirl their thermostats, and perhaps their windows rattle a little in the night, but that's about all. . . . In the country, though, a front is a fact still. There it's a blue line along the horizon, and a waiting, sweaty hush, and a hit like a moving wall, and all of life scurrying for the southern lee of things. There it's a battening down, an opening of hydrant valves, a checking of young and valuable stock, a walking across the swept lots with a flash-light, a leaning against the hard-shoving cold, a shuddering and creaking of old, tall frame houses. There it's a norther. . . .

To this day I compulsively watch weather reports on television, and now and then I still feel that old involuntary chill climbing my spine.

A lesson I learned early, and one reinforced by my parents from time to time, is that living with nature is a continual struggle to survive. I know we often felt a kind of unarticulated love for the land and weather, but respect and even fear were emotions that nature evoked from us more readily than love. I came to think of nature (once I discovered football in high school) as a triple-threat halfback that can score touchdowns suddenly and with a variety of weapons — flood, famine, and fire chief among them. Too much rain often left low-lying areas under water for days or weeks, mildewing crops, animals, even people. Too much sun and heat seared tender blossoms, killing plants and preventing fruition while the sand soaked up your sweat in the absence of life-giving moisture from the skies. Fire was a constant threat. Range and brush fires broke out often. I recall fighting them on several occasions. A couple of neighbors had their houses and possessions consumed by fire; once a fire began, there was the devil to pay stopping it, since the nearest fire-fighting equipment was twenty miles away in Fort Worth. It was not easy living on the land when I was growing up.

The story I have just related is true. It is as true, at any rate, as honest recollection allows. But already in my mind, increasingly as years pass and I tell the tale in bits and pieces to others, there has accrued to it a thick layering of myth. Besides, the story fits rather neatly into the larger "Texas myth." From the beginning, Texans have recognized — and have even taken pride in — the fact that Texas is hard country. Stories of hard times and hard country have filtered through our history leaving an unmistakable sediment of myth. "It's a hard land," wrote an anonymous immigrant in the 1840s in a letter sent back east to his old home. But he added as an afterthought, "it's a great place for a man with a family and a little money to settle down and buy himself a piece of land."[13] Overcoming great obstacles — surviving an appalling climate, loneliness, poverty — only added to the glory of the eventual conquest.

Texans have, in fact, turned the harshness of our land and climate to advantage, creating and propagating that most peculiar form of the Texas myth: the brag story. If our climate is almost unendurable, we boast of it: we have the hottest weather, the coldest weather, the most destructive tornadoes, the most vicious cyclones, and so forth. We assume, further, that hard times and a hard land have the hidden virtue of producing tough, strong people, independent people with strength of character and unbending wills. Most of the stereotypes of Texas history — cowboys and cattlemen, outlaws and lawmen — are weatherbeaten men who were molded by the exigencies of a harsh environment. When I tell my son, for instance, the story of my North Texas boyhood, my purpose — implicitly understood and often explicitly stated — is to show how I actually benefitted from the hardships I experienced. That may or may not be objectively true, but that is my personal myth. The Texas myth, then, is simply the intersection and collectivization of myriad personal myths.

Many of these personal myths, like mine, are land-based. T. R. Fehrenbach speaks of the "brooding presence of the land, with all its symbolism and association" in the Anglo-Texan soul. In Fehrenbach's view, many commonly held traits of the Texan character, both good and bad, emerged from a relentless struggle with the land and from the resultant feeling for the land that the experience engendered: "hard-driving pragmatism, a desperate belief in growth and material progress, an impatience with ideologies of any kind that did not serve to enhance man's mastery of the land."

The Anglo Texan's emotional attachment to his hard-won soil evolved into what Fehrenbach calls a "landowner ethos," in which "land, either its produce or what lay beneath it, was the source of all . . . wealth," and the landholder, whether rich or poor, became the "social ideal."[14] I would go further and suggest that, in the Texas myth, certain kinds of landowners are higher on the social scale than others and certain kinds of land-derived wealth seem more legitimate than others. Farmers, for example, are admirable because of their proximity to the soil, but ranchers are considered the myth's most noble product. At the other end of the scale there is a taint that has never quite been removed from the slightly suspect holdings of the oil tycoon.

This contrast is drawn in bold lines in what is perhaps the most mythic of all Texas tales, *Giant,* in both its literary and movie versions. For Bick Benedict money made from oil seems ill-gotten gain, while money made from cattle is made the old-fashioned way — it's *earned.* The point is raised just as strongly by the old rancher Homer Bannon in Larry McMurtry's 1961 novel, *Horseman, Pass By.* Even though he has lost his cattle to hoof-and-mouth disease, Homer rejects his stepson Hud's proposal that they recover their ruined finances by drilling oil wells on the ranch. Homer vows,

> there'll be no holes punched in this land while I'm here. They ain't gonna come in and grade no roads, so the wind can blow it away. . . . What good's oil to me? . . . What can I do with it? With a bunch of fuckin' oil wells. I can't ride out ever day an' prowl amongst 'em, like I can my cattle. I can't breed 'em or tend 'em or rope 'em or chase 'em or nothin'. I can't feel a smidgen of pride in 'em, cause they ain't none of my doin'. Money, yes. Piss on that kinda money. . . .

Much Texas literature, as the foregoing examples perhaps suggest, conveys a passion, ambivalent but nonetheless intense, for a harsh and demanding environment, for a soil consecrated by work and sacrifice. As an English teacher, I am committed to a belief in the power and truth of literature, and the Texas land myth is the underlying subject of a sizable chunk of Texas writing. I want to offer a few comments on a handful of books and writers that illustrate some of the ways that Texas authors have attempted to come to grips with the subject. The first is George Sessions Perry's *Hold Autumn in Your Hand* (1941), the only work of Texas fiction (that is, until Cormac McCarthy's *All the Pretty Horses* in 1992) to win a National Book Award. Perry was a town man; he grew up in a fairly comfortable middle-class setting in Rockdale, about sixty-five miles northeast of Austin. As Perry himself would later admit, he had an overly romanticized view of the farmer's life when he wrote *Hold Autumn in Your Hand.*

Still, Perry left us the best literary portrait of an East Texas tenant farmer during the Great Depression of the 1930s that Texas literature can put on display.

Perry's hero, Sam Tucker, is a simple man of the soil who has a dream. Sam wants to farm some land, the richest blackland soil he can find. In Sam's world, an important distinction among people—a distinction I can appreciate from my own growing-up years—is between sandy land farmers and blackland farmers. Sandy land is easy to cultivate, but its harvest is usually scanty; blackland is difficult to till, but its yield is much more abundant. Different kinds of farmers naturally gravitate to one type of soil or the other. Sam thinks of the rich black soil as being "a wild stallion to be tamed, where the sand had been a spavined old mare that would eat your courage and drink your own vitality and lay back down."

When the novel begins, Sam has expended several years and much energy in a futile struggle with the sand. He longs to farm sixty-eight acres of black earth in the San Gabriel River bottoms. The land, of course, does not belong to him, but Sam finally strikes a deal with the owner, whereby at the end of the harvest cycle he will have accumulated no money for himself; the profit, if there is any, will go to the landowner. Sam, however, looks upon the upcoming experience as his "play-pretty year." Though he cannot possibly better himself financially, he will have the satisfaction of proving to himself and his family just how good a farmer he is.

Sam's play-pretty year turns out to be a round-the-clock battle to survive. He uses the river to feed his family with its fish. He hunts the woods for pelts to sell in town for much-needed cash. Most of all he employs all his skills as a farmer to fight the land and the elements to bring in a crop. But at the close of the year Sam's situation is as marginal as ever. There is a suggestion at the end of the book that Sam's likely fate will be his removal to Houston to work in an automobile assembly factory. Perhaps he will join that flood of refugees from Oklahoma, Texas, and the Great Plains that migrated to California in the late 1930s and early 1940s—the ones that came to be known as "Okies."

But whatever Sam's future, his one play-pretty year, chronicled between the covers of Perry's memorable novel, is an unforgettable account of a Texas man of the soil. Sam loves nature and the land, the wellspring of all his values, all his vocational abilities. The implied pathos of the novel's conclusion lies in the fact that the economic and political system will not allow Sam further access to this life-giving source. A striking aspect of the book is the relevance of Sam Tucker's story, though it took place over half a century ago, to our own time; the staggering failure rate of America's family farms over the last couple of decades is still a newsworthy topic.

The second book I want to discuss is Elmer Kelton's *The Time It Never Rained* (1973). With this book we move from East Texas to West Texas. Elmer Kelton is a son of the West Texas ranch country that he brings so vividly to life in his fiction. Born on a ranch in Andrews County, Kelton grew up among stockmen and dryland farmers. The author's extensive firsthand knowledge of such people has been put to extraordinarily good use in the two dozen and more novels he has published since 1955. Many of these books are formula westerns, potboilers that still have a solid grounding in Texas history.

Kelton has also written several "serious" novels (a term he himself has employed). One of them is *The Time It Never Rained,* which is set during the disastrous seven-year drought of the 1950s. Damaging to all of Texas, the drought was particularly devastating to the western part of the state, already parched by scarce rainfall. The novel's central character, Charlie Flagg, owns a medium-size ranch west of San Angelo. As the story unfolds and the drought becomes more and more acute, Charlie is driven to ever-more-desperate measures to survive. He goes deeper in debt. He downgrades cattle-raising and upgrades goat-raising, even though he feels deep misgivings about the wisdom of this move. He cuts corners every way he knows how, but he steadfastly refuses to accept any form of government assistance. He never gives up on his beloved land. "It was a comforting sight, this country," Charlie muses as he stands atop a hill overlooking his ranch. "It was an ageless land where the past was still a living thing and old voices still whispered, where the freshness of the pioneer time had not yet all faded, where a few old dreams were not yet dark with tarnish."

Charlie stubbornly hangs on, fighting and suffering with the land, because "he felt a deep and binding obligation to the land itself. It mattered little who held the title; the land was a sacred thing. To see it bleed now brought him grief; it was like watching a friend waste away with a terminal cancer." In the book's last scene Charlie is pelted, flooded with the huge droplets of a drought-breaking downpour. But even the rain, when it finally comes, is devastating. It arrives just after Charlie's goats have been shorn and left vulnerable to the elements.

Kelton once said that, of all his books, *The Time It Never Rained* is his favorite, because "it was the most personal one I've ever done."[15] It is my favorite, too. And the reason it is my favorite is the character of Charlie Flagg. Charlie is one of the most memorable and remarkable characters I have encountered in recent American fiction. Charlie is, to use J. Frank Dobie's phrase, "out of the old rock." He embodies what we believe were the best qualities of the legendary Texan rancher: strength of will, independence, self-sufficiency. His primary commitment is to the land, harsh and unyielding as it is. His sense of right does not waver. He opposes equally the inert, clotted force of bureaucratic regulation and the evil of untrammeled power that too often crushes the powerless. Part of the appeal of Charlie is that he is an anachronism, one of the last survivors of a dying breed. He springs from an older, better time—a time when, it is widely thought, our forefathers acted from a deep conviction that seems increasingly implausible in the gray, ambiguous morality of the modern world. As we turn the novel's pages, we can only affirm the cliché: they don't make men like Charlie Flagg anymore.

The most important facet of Charlie's characterization is that he is a man of principles—principles rooted deep in the West Texas land and culture. His unbending resistance to federal drought relief issues from the rancher's fierce self-reliance and from a suspicion of outlanders bred of generations of proud isolation. But it would be a mistake, I think, to read into the novel a specific political message—that all government aid should be sternly and righteously rejected. The real lesson of Charlie's story—a lesson of tenacity that he learns, *absorbs* from the land and its creatures—is that, no matter the circumstances of our lives, we should never give up. "'Minute a man quits tryin', he's blowed up,'" says Charlie. "A man had to make his try, and when that didn't work he had to try something else. Try and keep trying. Endure, and try again." At novel's end there appears little hope for a new beginning—at least not for Charlie Flagg. He is too old and too debilitated. But he has triumphed nonetheless; he has endured.

Deservedly, *The Time It Never Rained* has been widely acclaimed for its high merits as a work of literary art. It has won at least two awards for excellence and was adjudged by critic Jon Tuska to be "one of the dozen or so best novels written by an American in this century."[16] That is a claim some may dispute, but at the very least the novel seems one of the major achievements of contemporary Texas writing. And much of the book's power derives from Kelton's sympathetic understanding and portrayal of Charlie Flagg's intense feelings for his plot of West Texas earth.

The third work I want to comment on is a small classic in Texas writing—indeed, in American writing—John Graves's *Goodbye to a River* (1960), a book I have already quoted from. At one point Graves states the general theme of his work as follows: "We will be nearly finished, I think, when we stop understanding the old pull toward green things and living things, toward dirt and rain and heat and what they spawn." The impetus for Graves's book, however, was supplied by the writer's love for a particular piece of earth — the stream and valley of the upper-middle Brazos River west of Fort Worth.

In the late 1950s Graves heard rumors that a chain of dams to be built along the Brazos would destroy forever the special character of the river. In order to recapture the stretch of water he had known as a boy, the author resolved to take one last canoe trip down it, keeping a journal as he went. *Goodbye to a River* is the literary result of that journey into time and space, a masterful blend of local history, philosophical musings, nostalgic reminiscences, and descriptions of river and surrounding landscapes, of animals and people encountered. The tone of the narrative is mellow but honest, and Graves carefully balances flashbacks to the past with acute and unromantic analyses of the present.

The message that Graves states over and over, in many different ways, is finally this: nature does matter, the character of a country is the destiny of its people. The upper-middle Brazos country is harsh; it is mostly hill country, infertile, not much good for agriculture, though from the start of human habitation there it has been farmed and the soil systematically depleted of its sparse nutrients. In recent decades it has been used for raising a few cattle and goats and for chopping cedar posts and for brewing bootleg whiskey in its hidden coves and valleys. But these are marginal occupations at best. The people who thrive there are those who match the land in its harshness — the loners, those types given to extremes, who give no quarter and ask none: the Comanches in the beginning, the cattlemen, the scruffy hill Southerners (who began to move into the area late in the nineteenth century) and their descendants.

Graves tells stories of all these people. He unfolds, layer by layer, the history of the upper-middle Brazos valley. And continually, a motif is reasserted: the land shapes the people who live on it, and vice versa. The writer quotes Old Man Willett of Parker County on what he has learned from the land: "A man needs it hard," says Old Man Willett. "He'd ought to have it hard a-growin' up, and hard a-learnin' his work, and hard a-gettin' a wife and feedin' his kids and gittin' rich, if he's gonna git rich. All of it. . . . [Then he not only appreciates it, but also] *does* it better." As I said, the upper-middle Brazos is hard country, and its lessons must be extracted from a painful struggle with its unyielding bedrock.

"Neither a land nor a people ever starts over clean," Graves tells us near the close of *Goodbye to a River:*

> Country is compact of all its past disasters and strokes of luck—of flood and drouth, of the caprices of glaciers and sea winds, of misuse and disuse and greed and ignorance and wisdom—and though you may doze away the cedar and coax back bluestem and mesquite and side-oats grama, you're not going to manhandle it into anything entirely new. It's limited by what it has been, by what's happened to it.

And a people, Graves continues, share in the fortune or misfortune of their land.

Goodbye to a River, though it recounts the story of a relatively small slice of real estate—"a postage stamp of soil," to use Faulkner's familiar analogy—is nothing less than the microcosmic history of Texas, and of the American frontier. This is one man's perceived reality. Graves says, in a "note" that precedes his text, "this is not a book of fiction, [but] it has some fictionalizing in it." Graves does what all true artists do: he orders the chaotic events of our experience to create a meaningful interpretation of past and present. His myth, in particular, posits the inextricable destiny—and fate—of Texans and their land.

Finally, I want to offer a few remarks on the work of one of the most distinguished of recent Texas writers, the late Russell Gordon Vliet. No Texas writer, not even the ones I have discussed, set out more consciously and explicitly than did R. G. Vliet to prove the truth of James Folsom's contention, quoted earlier, that "man reflects in moral terms the physical nature of his environment." Since his father was a career medical officer in the U.S. Navy, Vliet was born in Chicago and as a youngster lived in many parts of the country and of the world. He graduated from high school in Texas City, Texas, and then attended Southwest Texas State University on a track scholarship. He became over the next thirty years a nationally recognized poet, playwright, and novelist. When he died in 1984, after a prolonged battle with cancer, he was residing in New England.

Vliet's *home,* however, in the most profound sense of the term, was Rocksprings, Texas. He lived in Rocksprings only one year, the academic year 1953–54, when he and his wife Ann taught in the public schools of that community. But the time spent in Rocksprings was, as one recent critic has put it, "the most artistically formative year of his life."[17] The county seat of Edwards County, Rocksprings is on the Edwards Plateau in southwest Texas, near the headwaters of the Nueces River and not far from the Rio Grande and the Mexican border. Rocksprings and environs gave Vliet a landscape and a culture that form the backdrop for many of his poems, all of his dramatic work, and the entirety of his long fiction.

The landscape is one of severe, even savage beauty. It is ruled by a cruel sun and by crueler vegetation. "That tall sun," muses a character in the novel *Rockspring* (1974), "this forever country. Country of the thousand thorns." The culture is pastoral, dependent on farming and herding. The first Anglo-Saxons who came to the region survived by imprinting the savagery of the land on their psyches. In one of Vliet's unpublished plays, a newcomer to the area says, "I've got to get a little prickly in the soul, like that brush out there; catclaw, cedar: they stick their needles through the air, they make their own shape."

In another unpublished play, a son speaks to the body of his deceased father: "You've got a lot of the land and weather in you, Dad, even strung out like you are. The scrub oaks look like they've winded clean into your skin and scratched them wrinkles. And the wind and the dust still crackin' your lips."[18] This is hard country indeed; ultimately, it is heartbreak country. The drifter Clare Borah, in the play "The Regions of Noon," says:

> what this land will do [is] drive you out or drive you crazy, one. Look at it. So smart, sometimes you can hear it think. . . . A man comes along, gets the lay of it, fits all his ways to it, prospers. Then the land changes its weather like a fence lizard its stripes, and a man's done for. Whipped.

In Vliet's fiction Rocksprings becomes Alto Springs, and his three published novels — *Rockspring, Solitudes* (1977; republished in a substantially revised edition as *Soledad, or Solitudes,* 1986), and *Scorpio Rising* (1985) — provide a fine, if fragmentary, history of the place. Somehow, in a single year of exposure, Vliet absorbed the very essence of the Edwards Plateau, right down to the rhythms and intonations of the English and Spanish that are commonly spoken there. In whatever form he was writing, Vliet remained a poet, expressing himself in a language at once lyrical and colloquial, appropriate to the history and the land it describes. In 1978, in accepting an award from the Texas Institute of Letters, Vliet recommended for a literature of the Southwest "a language as highly charged imaginatively as the landscape it comes from and as harsh musically and idiomatically as its natives' speech."[19] No Texas writer, in my view, has come closer to fulfilling that requirement than R. G. Vliet.

The books I have pointed to in the foregoing pages all fall into a genre that might be called "the literature of the soil"—what Larry McMurtry once derisively labeled "Country-and-Western" literature.[20] Seemingly this genre is old-fashioned, and thus vulnerable to ridicule by those who want Texas and southwestern writing to be as hip and up-to-date as the latest issue of *The New Yorker* magazine. Unquestionably the genre is conservative, even reactionary—reactionary not in a political sense, but certainly in an ideological sense: it attempts to preserve the land and the past. But in present day Texas, the past becomes increasingly difficult to discern, much less preserve. During the past half-century, the most important social and cultural movement in Texas has been from country to city, away from the land and the beliefs and traditions it nurtured. This movement has given birth to drastic and, to some extent, still unforeseeable consequences. One fact stands forth clearly, however: Texas is now predominantly urban, and many Texans have been forced over the past few decades to adjust to a pattern of life wholly different from the one in which they were reared. As people absorb the tempo and ambience of the city, memories of the land fade.

Writers, needless to say, mirror their environment; in the past most Texas writers have been rural in origin, and as a result they have written about their feeling for the land, about a past consciously kept alive and still vividly remembered. But in recent years the Texan's roots—and the writer's no less than his fellow's—have been wrenched from the soil and planted in concrete. Many Texas writers now seem bent on trying to understand the city, to assimilate the city's essential qualities and to incorporate those qualities into their books. Cityscapes become more compelling than landscapes. But the myth of the land is strong. More important, the land itself is strong. People shape, or at least rearrange, the land, but reciprocally the land shapes people; sometimes the shaping even seems like vengeance for sins against the environment. "The spirit of place," in prophetic Lawrentian terminology, *will* be "atoned for."

I myself have experienced a measure of that atonement in the form of a kind of irresistible atavism. The "landowner ethos," to invoke Fehrenbach's phrase, seems too deeply ingrained in the Anglo-Texan character to die easily or completely. As the state becomes inexorably more urban with every passing year, the recrudescence of the land as an enduring part of the Texas myth becomes more apparent. While money is made in the city, the goal of a large proportion of Texas city dwellers seems to be the country. It has long been the custom, of course, for Texas tycoons, as almost their first act, once their wealth is solidified, to purchase a large "spread" so as to validate their Texanness (and, as a bonus, to obtain a healthy tax write-off). Today, even middle-income Texans are fleeing the cities, if not permanently, at least for weekends. Having "a place in the country" is now an entrenched part of the ambition of many Texas families. A ranch would be heaven. A small farm would do. A couple of acres at eight to ten thousand per acre are, the bank and interest rates willing, the usual compromise. Farmers and ranchers and real-estate agents living within a hundred or so miles of the major Texas cities will readily tell you what this reverse movement — from city to country — is doing to the price of land these days.

I do not claim this phenomenon is peculiarly Texan — obviously it is not — but I believe there is a special intensity in the Texan's desire to reestablish contact with the soil. I teach in Stephenville, a town about seventy miles southwest of Fort Worth. Stephenville has a rich agricultural history, and the first thing I did when I moved there more than a quarter-century ago was to buy into that history. Despite my training and experience as a youth, my wife and I purchased a house and a few acres of land outside town. I wanted to see if I could make "country living" more satisfactory than it had been when I was a child. I tried raising vegetables and discovered that I do not possess a green thumb. Now and then I have run a few head of cattle, usually with disastrous financial results. A dozen years ago we were burned out — and I mean burned out: one hundred percent total loss. Two years later we moved into a house rebuilt on the same spot where the other house had stood. I tried living in town and did not like it. There's something about living in the country you get addicted to. I, at least, just cannot seem to get enough of it.

I think a lot of Texans are like me. They grew up on farms and ranches or in the environs of small towns, but found it necessary to move to cities to make a living. They no longer possess the skills needed to survive in the country and should probably be content with the comfort and convenience of urban existence. But despite all evidence to the contrary, they are not. There's still an itch, the genetic inheritance of a long line of country forebears, to commune with the life-giving earth. They remember the stories told by their parents and grandparents, and they begin to recall the events of their upbringing with something resembling nostalgia. Myths are powerful determinants of human behavior; as long as there is a Texas land myth, there will be a special relationship between Texans and their earth.

CHAPTER 5

Texas Gothic

The South in Lone Star Life and Letters

East Texas in August is a long heat sandwich, days of
lassitude and dust pressed between slices of spongy night,
breathed and swallowed and digested by victims of the
climate until, gorged on sun and swollen with humidity,
no one can tell any longer what is real and life
takes on the aspect of a dream.

—TERESA KENNEDY,
Baby Todd and the Rattlesnake Stradivarius

The eastern third of Texas is the most southern part of the state. Apparently there is something in the murky atmosphere and brown, sluggish waters of East Texas that cultivates, in both life and art, the gothic and surreal. The area was settled in the nineteenth century primarily by Southerners who brought with them the plantation system, slavery, and the narrow moral and religious beliefs of their old home. Thus much of East Texas is indistinguishable, in landscape and culture, from Louisiana or Mississippi or Alabama. Cotton and timber have been the traditional cash crops, and race has always been central to the area's social and political processes.

I grew up in the 1940s and 1950s in rural south Tarrant County, on the fringes of rolling, treeless prairie. The route of the old Chisholm Trail had passed by a few miles to the west of our place. Over not too many hills in the same direction, the plains and cattle ranches of West Texas—the Texas of legend and myth—began. A big event in our household, to which my father always took me, was the Fort Worth Fat Stock Show and Rodeo, a historic stop on the professional rodeo circuit, recognized as the world's first indoor rodeo. Because of a quirk in district lines, I attended high school in the town of Mansfield, twenty miles east of my family's farm (while most of my childhood pals went to high school in Burleson, ten miles to the west).

Mansfield is tucked away in the southeastern corner of Tarrant County, and I quickly discovered that it lies in a different geographical and cultural zone than the one I became accustomed to as a child. I noticed immediately, for example, that even the air in Mansfield felt different from that of my native precincts. It seemed liquid and heavy, and I spent many an evening awash in that air, perhaps sitting on somebody's veranda watching the moon rise through the honeysuckle. I recall thinking, even at the time, that I may as well have been in Mississippi. In the 1950s Mansfield was a small, ingrown community that existed primarily as a trading center for farmers who tilled the rich black earth that surrounds it. Cotton was the crop that the black soil produced in greatest abundance, and many of the businesses along the highway that served as the town's main street catered to those who grew the cotton.

I liked most of the citizens of Mansfield that I knew personally, but when I began high school there, things began to register at some level of consciousness that I found increasingly difficult to explain to myself. I noticed that, as was true of virtually all southern towns in the 1950s, Mansfield was split into two spheres: white Mansfield and black Mansfield. (There were no black citizens at all in Burleson, which I considered my hometown, so I had little firsthand knowledge of racial arrangements of the sort.) In Mansfield, the relative quality of the dwellings and the state of repair of the streets of the two sections of town provided even the most unobservant with a clear line of demarcation. It was plain that Mansfield strictly guarded its rigidly segregated social structure, and even a hint of the possibility of change was enough to send jolts of hysteria pulsing through the white community.

I remember, as a measure of Mansfield's xenophobic rigidity, that all through my high-school years I heard whispered rumors about a strange man living on a farm just outside town. I eventually learned his name was John Howard Griffin and that he was a writer, someone who was obviously *different*. He was said to be a Catholic, and he had published in 1952 what many considered a "trashy" book, a novel set in France entitled *The Devil Rides Outside*. Later, after I had left Mansfield, I discovered that a couple of literary critics had proclaimed Griffin's work to be one of the best American novels to appear in the 1950s.

In the early 1960s, Griffin would anger white Mansfield to the point of apoplexy by having the pigment of his skin chemically altered and traveling throughout the South passing as a black man. The account of his painful journey, *Black Like Me,* published in 1961, would become a national best-seller. But in 1956 Griffin had done nothing, so far as I was aware, to challenge Mansfield's racial views; nevertheless, his mere presence seemed, to those who worry about such things, to threaten the comfortable status quo.

In 1956, however, the status quo in Mansfield was to be tested by forces that had their origins far beyond the town limits. It had begun in 1954, when the U.S. Supreme Court, in *Brown v. Board of Education,* ruled that the concept of "separate but equal" educational facilities for white and black youngsters is unconstitutional. "Separate educational facilities," the Court adjudged, "are inherently unequal." At the time twenty-one states, plus the District of Columbia, *required,* by law, segregated schooling; four other states permitted the practice. The Court instructed federal judges and officials of local school districts to take stock of their individual situations and to move toward integrated classrooms "with all deliberate speed" as soon as was "practicable."

The two earliest attempts to legally enforce the Court's decision occurred in 1956, when court orders were handed down from federal benches to the school districts of Clinton, Tennessee, and Mansfield, Texas (Little Rock, where federal troops were used to desegregate Central High School, would come one year later, in 1957.) Clinton and Mansfield, in late August, 1956, became the first flashpoints in the battle to desegregate public schooling in the South. The Clinton incident, which involved some vandalism and plenty of threatened violence, finally ended when Governor Frank Clement sent state troopers to the town to restore order. But even more instrumental in ending the demonstrations were the moderate voices of Clinton, who calmed the hotheads, and the significant number of white students — including the captain of the football team — who spoke out in favor of desegregation.

The story in Mansfield was somewhat different. By the summer of 1956, more than 150 school districts in the western part of Texas had voluntarily desegregated. (Few of these districts, it should be pointed out, had more than a handful of black students; some had none.) That summer a federal judge in Fort Worth heard a suit brought by the National Association for the Advancement of Colored People against the Mansfield school district. Essentially the district had no legal ground to stand on. Mansfield not only failed to provide equal educational facilities for black children; it provided no facilities at all. Black students were transported by bus to Fort Worth, where they attended school. Judge Joe B. Estes's only recourse was to order the Mansfield district to allow eight black high-school students to enroll for the fall semester. At that point, I knew trouble was brewing. White Mansfield would not accept so thorough and abrupt a change in its social and racial customs without a fight.

The scene I witnessed as I began my senior year in high school in late August 1956 was volatile and alarming. On Thursday, August 30, and Friday, August 31, days set aside for registration, mobs of up to five hundred people gathered on the spacious grounds in front of the old brown-brick high school. They were there to protest, by whatever means, court-ordered integration. I do not doubt that many outside agitators were in their midst (it was later claimed that such agitators were the cause of all the trouble), but I recognized lots of Mansfield folk as well. On Thursday effigies, which were left hanging for more than a week, were raised on a flagpole and over the entrance to the high school.

The worst of the protests occurred on Friday. The Tarrant County district attorney, down from his headquarters in Fort Worth, was pummeled by a swarm of angry men who openly threatened to use guns if necessary to prevent implementation of the court order. A photographer's camera was knocked to the ground and destroyed. An Episcopal minister, professing to offer "a Christian solution" to the problem, was roughed up by the crowd and quickly hustled away by law enforcement officers. The most dramatic — and appalling — event of the day took place in the afternoon when several hundred protesters barged into the school and marched noisily down the hallways. Within a couple of days Mansfield — to sum up the seriousness of the situation for our media-conscious age — had got itself on national television and on the front pages of the *New York Times* and other newspapers across the country.

Over the long Labor Day weekend following registration, Mansfield simmered in the late summer heat and in the tense expectation of what might happen when school convened the following Tuesday. On Monday, Labor Day, a climax of sorts occurred. Governor Allan Shivers dispatched a telegram to the Mansfield school board instructing that "any students who might be the cause of the difficulties" be registered, then immediately transferred to schools in "adjoining districts." The effect of Shivers's telegram was to nullify the federal court order. The governor also sent a half-dozen Texas Rangers to Mansfield to maintain, he said, "law and order and the general welfare."[1]

When classes began after Labor Day, restless crowds continued to gather, but the crisis was, for practical purposes, at an end. The eight black students who were eligible to enroll in Mansfield High School quietly registered at all-black I. M. Terrell High School in Fort Worth. The NAACP, which had brought the suit to desegregate Mansfield High in the first place, grumbled a bit but declined to push the matter further, given the probability of mob violence. After a week or two tempers cooled, members of the mob either drifted away and went back where they came from or became ordinary Mansfield citizens once again, and for a while anyway Mansfield settled back into the rhythms of segregated life that it had known for close to a century.

Mansfield was a mere blip on the radar screen of racial unrest and violence that emerged from the 1950s and 1960s, but to this day I carry vivid images of that time and place in my consciousness. I had wandered through the crowds in a daze. What I saw was ugly and scary. I recall signs everywhere questioning the parentage of the black young people audacious enough to want to enter the sacred confines of Mansfield High. I observed angry, red-faced men and women gathered in small clusters, shouting at each other seemingly just for practice. Weapons were not hard to spot — nor was the undisguised hatred for reporters and photographers that emanated from the crowd in spasmodic outbursts. Rumors of impending violence against the town's black population floated through the crowd like a poisonous fog.

I would like to report that I stood up in 1956 and spoke out for decency and justice — as did the captain of the football team in the town in Tennessee. But I did not. Though I recognized, even as a teenager growing up in a racist society, the lunacy of what was happening, I was passing through a particularly troubled stage of adolescence at the time. I lived with my parents and my sister (who was a freshman at Mansfield High that year) on a farm many miles away, and except as occasional bystanders we were not involved in the mob scene. I decided — subconsciously, I suppose — to keep a low profile and hope the crisis would slide quietly by so that I could get on with my life. There was always another day when things would be better, both for the society and for me personally. Surely there was no way I could have affected the outcome of anything that occurred in Mansfield in late summer of 1956, but I still feel twinges of guilt that I didn't do *something* — even if had been merely to make a token gesture.

The passions that moved the normally peaceable citizens of Mansfield are, in my memory, immediate and real, and yet they seem incomprehensibly remote within the context of the fast-changing history of our era. In 1967, eleven years after the events I have described, the Mansfield board of education, primarily for economic rather than legal reasons, completely integrated the town's schools. A few years later the high school hired a popular and successful black basketball coach, and there have been, in addition, a number of other black teachers in the system.

Today Mansfield is a bustling, prosperous bedroom community. Not many farmers live in or around Mansfield these days. At present the area's biggest cash crop is suburban housing. According to the chamber of commerce, Mansfield's population has topped 20,000. It seems more an adjunct of Fort Worth and Dallas than an autonomous city. It has shopping malls and multi-screen movie theaters; chain stores and restaurants sprout in profusion year by year. The prong of a freeway from Fort Worth slices across the east side of town. Few memories remain of the turbulence of the 1950s. But there are many towns in East Texas that have not changed as dramatically as Mansfield, and the menacing cloud of racial misunderstanding and conflict still hovers over the region.

Writers, of course, absorb the concerns and interests of the place from which they spring. Living in — or near — a town like Mansfield, drenched in racial anxieties throughout the 1950s, undoubtedly had something to do with John Howard Griffin's decision to pass as a black man in the Deep South and to write about his experiences in the book *Black Like Me*. William A. Owens's account in *This Stubborn Soil* (1966) of the lynching of a black man in a small East Texas town, an event he observed as a boy, is still shocking nearly a century after the event occurred. Race, then, is an element of southern society so deep-seated it appears tightly, almost invisibly, woven into the cultural fabric. So are family and class. The region's writers seem compelled willy-nilly to incorporate these elements into their work. In Texas literature I know of no writer who has dealt more provocatively with this triad of southern culture — race, class, family — than Katherine Anne Porter, in the short story sequence she called "The Old Order."

The work is generally thought to be autobiographical, though just how reliably autobiographical has been brought into question by Porter's biographer, Joan Givner; as Givner has clearly shown, Porter, for whatever reason, frequently lied about her upbringing, and gullible critics for a long time swallowed these stories hook, line, and sinker.[2] But that's another story for another time. "The Old Order" is about the Rhea (pronounced "Ray") family. The Rheas, originally from Kentucky, migrated after the Civil War to Texas, by way of Louisiana. The family includes a domineering grandmother; Harry, the feckless father (one of a long list of ineffectual males who appear in Porter's fiction); and three young children, Maria, Paul, and Miranda. Miranda, the youngest, is supposed to be a fictionalized version of the author.

Though living in somewhat straitened circumstances, the Rheas are from an old aristocratic southern family, and they are careful to distinguish themselves from what Porter once called the "plain people" — that is, poor white trash. They have faithful family servants, Aunt Nannie and Uncle Jimbilly, both former slaves who had accompanied the grandmother all the way from Kentucky. In the absence of strong leadership from the father, the grandmother, by sheer force of will, holds the motherless family together, as does, less obviously, Aunt Nannie whose hard work and organizational skills are the bedrock of family unity. The grandmother and Aunt Nannie are friends, in a sense, but the barriers of race and class are always present between them.

I, as a white person, often wonder how realistic portrayals of characters like Aunt Nannie and Faulkner's Dilsey (in *The Sound and the Fury*) really are, especially since those portrayals are by white authors. I can only say that Aunt Nannie is a memorable individual, as both a black person and a woman. When the grandmother dies, Aunt Nannie decides it is time for her to lay down her burdens. She orders Harry to prepare a little house across the stream for her "retirement"; Harry, who as an infant had been suckled at her breast, is not strong enough to deny her request. With the commanding presences of the grandmother and Aunt Nannie both gone, the family begins to disintegrate, the victim of centrifugal forces they cannot control. A question suggests itself: Who is the slave? Aunt Nannie? Or the family, who have become so dependent on her they cannot function without her? For her part, Aunt Nannie sticks to her guns; she firmly declines to return to the big house. When Uncle Jimbilly tentatively tries to move into her cabin, she forcibly rejects him. "I don' aim to pass my las' days waitin on no man," she says. "I've served my time, I've done my do, and dat's all."

The theme of family is treated most saliently in Porter's short novel "Old Mortality" (which is not part of "The Old Order" sequence, but features the same cast of characters). The tale, filtered through the consciousness of Miranda, follows her efforts, over nearly two decades, to detach herself from her family and become a fully functioning adult. The stronger the family, the more difficult the detachment becomes, and indeed Miranda finds the tyranny of family myths and family expectations a powerful force to combat. The role of family in shaping destiny is examined from every possible angle, culminating in Cousin Eva's diatribe: "Ah, the family. . . . the whole hideous institution should be wiped from the face of the earth. It is the root of all human wrongs." Miranda understands that Cousin Eva's judgment is no more true than the romantic family myths she had been fed as a child. Ultimately, though, the family leaves her nothing to cling to, and she must embark on her quest for autonomy alone, "in her hopefulness, her ignorance." The irony at the close of "Old Mortality" is both understated and masterful. Miranda will never escape the hold her family has on her, but her youthful optimism impels her forward on her quest.

Given the conditions of southern life and the grotesqueries that those conditions sometimes engender, it is perhaps not surprising that so many of the region's writers should adopt the gothic mode. It cannot be said that Katherine Anne Porter wrote in that mode — though even Porter in a story such as "He," a tale of the "plain people," could deploy gothic conventions. Still, much of the literature of East Texas, in its lush, overripe style and gothic subject matter, is quintessentially southern. Probably the master of East Texas gothic was the late William Goyen, who wrote an excellent novel, *The House of Breath* (1950), and a handful of memorable short stories, but was hardly the literary genius the French proclaimed him to be. (The French appear to have a weakness for Jerry Lewis, Jack London, and just about any writer from the American South who enters their field of vision.)

An all-too-typical Goyen tale is "Arthur Bond," in which the title character lives for forty years with a large worm in his thigh. He picks up the worm in a Louisiana swamp, and the parasite is particularly aggravated by the presence of women and liquor. The worm torments Arthur Bond to the point that he finally kills himself by drinking rat poison. Like most of Goyen's fiction, the story is set in *mondo bizarro,* and the reader, upon finishing it, feels the need to hose himself down, just to wash away the slime. It is, of course, an allegory of the kind of pinched, destructive moral code that permeates East Texas culture. Goyen himself once admitted that he was irreparably wounded by his East Texas upbringing, and he departed for more tolerant intellectual landscapes as fast as he could. Interestingly, though, he continued obsessively to write about his native region.

One of the most promising writers to emerge from East Texas in recent times is Carol Dawson, who grew up in Corsicana, southeast of Dallas — not deepest East Texas admittedly, but close enough to be bathed in the surreal ambience of that singular locale. Her first novel, *The Waking Spell*

(1992), is an autobiographical narrative that angered some of the longtime citizens of her hometown. (A scheduled book signing in Corsicana had to be canceled.) A subsequent novel, *Body of Knowledge* (1994), is a gothic tale set in the town of Bernice, probably a thinly veiled Corsicana. This novel, however, failed to stir up animosity of the sort the first book provoked. *Body of Knowledge* chronicles the history of a doomed Faulknerian family so strange and star-crossed that it is unlikely to have any grounding in fact; the tale, Dawson has been quoted as saying, is purely the product of her "prolific imagination."

Inevitably, a couple of reviewers speculated on the novel's debt to "magic realism" and Gabriel García Márquez's *One Hundred Years of Solitude*. To me, however, *Body of Knowledge* is good, old-fashioned East Texas gothic. (There is no reason, of course, why the book could not owe something to both literary traditions.) The story, at any rate, is narrated by Victoria Grace Ransom, the last of the Ransom line and heiress to a fortune. Victoria's corpulent flesh, because of glandular damage from a childhood case of the measles, has ballooned to six hundred pounds. She lives in the family mansion, "a palace of white rock" standing three stories tall, outside Bernice. Special furniture to support her enormous weight is necessary, as well as a steel-reinforced toilet seat. An elevator had been installed years before to allow her to reach her bedroom on the second floor.

One of Victoria's few viable pastimes is to speculate on her peculiar fate. Calling herself at one point the "Great White Whale," she believes that she "contain[s] the entirety" of her family's turbulent history. Thus she sets out to reconstruct that history and to learn its meaning: "Truth can be a solace. There is consolation in knowing your own function, in discovering what you really are." Much of the factual history must be dredged up from stories told her by Viola, the black woman who had come to the Ransom household as an orphan girl and had stayed on to rear three generations of Ransom children.

The animating element of the history is a feud between the Ransoms and the Macafees. The foundation of the Ransom fortune was Garner Ransom's decision, in 1908, to open icehouses in parched Bernice and surrounding communities. The success of these ventures provided capital for forays into oil exploration and automobile dealerships, and eventually the accumulation of great wealth. Garner Ransom's first backing had come from Archibald Macafee, and their partnership in the RanMac Chill Company had formed a successful business union. Personally, however, Macafee resented the haughty disdain of Ransom's wife, Arliss. This initial split is made permanent in the next generation by the instinctive antipathy of William Ransom and Grant Macafee.

Grant, against his will, is attracted to William's beautiful sister, Sarah, who in turn is fascinated by Grant's fanaticism, the cornerstone of his character. Sarah becomes pregnant by Grant, but refuses to marry him. Instead, she runs off to California, where she is murdered — a crime that is never solved in the novel. Grant marries Sophie, with whom William is in love. When Sophie becomes pregnant with William's child, Grant is enraged. He attempts to kill the baby, even holding a mock funeral with a jazz band brought in from New Orleans. Through a set of bizarre circumstances, the infant is adopted by William's other sister, Mavis, a hunchbacked gnome whose only fulfillment in life is to rear and to love her brother's child.

At this point, Grant Macafee's baleful hatred is directed at all Ransoms; he places a "curse" on the family, the cumulative weight of which finally destroys the clan. Strange, and usually fatal, things seem to happen to Ransoms. William's illegitimate son, known only as Baby Boy, is killed in an odd automobile accident near Grant Macafee's farm. Mavis falls off a statue onto her head and is reduced to a drooling stump for the rest of her life. Bert, one of William's twin sons, is murdered, possibly by Macafee's niece. The other twin, Willie Junior, loses an arm in a hunting accident, an expedition on which a Macafee relative had been present.

Finally, William, an old man no longer capable of dealing with family tragedy and Grant's implacable hatred, beheads himself with a buzz saw. Victoria even becomes convinced, toward the end, that the Macafee curse may victimize her as well. In a somewhat improbable conclusion, however, the two families are brought together in harmony by the only surviving descendants of the warring clans, and Victoria, knowing finally that she is loved, achieves a serenity and peace of mind she has never before possessed. She even begins to lose weight.

As the foregoing summary probably suggests, the plot of *Body of Knowledge* is much too convoluted and dependent on coincidence. Still, the author's skills in storytelling — an honored art form in southern culture — almost surmount the weaknesses of structure. Despite recurring disbelief, the reader often finds himself caught up in the narrative for long stretches at a time, admiring the dense, elegant prose and wondering what horror will befall the hapless Ransoms next.

But Dawson's real triumph in the novel is her character development. The people in the book are vividly drawn and thoroughly believable. Even minor characters like Mavis come alive on the page. Hunchbacked Mavis, who wilts in comparison with her lovely sister Sarah, learns to gain attention with a kind of waspish persistence. She blossoms when her brother's child is, almost literally, left on her doorstep, then crumbles emotionally when the boy, as a teenager, dies mysteriously, perhaps as the result of Grant Macafee's machinations.

Grant seems to me an Arthur Bond-type character, tormented, not by a worm in his thigh, but by a stern Presbyterian conscience and an Old Testament eye-for-an-eye world view. At one point, Victoria studies a photograph of Grant as a young man, "enclosed, already bearing the bitter, indelible marks of his imprisonment, and wearing an expression of surprised self-reproach."

Unable to control his passion for Sarah, Grant "is aghast at his own renegade emotions; his asceticism rails against him. Lust has made him a puppet." Ultimately Grant's malevolence is focused outward, on the Ransom family: "he was deranged with the notion that true evil lay here [in the Ransom house]. Decay, he called it. Inwardness and corruption." While he is not as exaggerated a character as Flannery O'Connor's God-haunted grotesques, Grant is a personality recognizable to anyone familiar with life in the South in the early decades of the present century.

Grant's enemy and his peer in age is William. The two are thrown together early on because of their fathers' business connections. They even attend Yale together. But their characters are so totally different, they are bound to clash. William is gentle and scholarly. He is tolerant to a fault of other people's behavior. He turns away wrath with a soft answer. He leaves others alone, and wishes to be left alone himself, left to retreat into his library where he spends most of his time reading history and philosophy. He showers his family with benign neglect and a kind of abstracted love; he is everybody's ideal of the perfect grandfather.

The character who steals the show, however, is Viola Lewis, the black servant. Viola, needless to say, is a character cut from the mold of Faulkner's Dilsey and Porter's Aunt Nannie. Over the years, she cares for a half-dozen Ransom children. She is described, by a minor character in the story, as "a true, old-style mammy." Dandy, a friend of Viola's who is also a servant, says of her, "ain't nobody kinder to her white folks." Indeed, Viola, as a resident in the Ransom household for over half a century, measures her self-worth by being one of the high-and-mighty Ransoms. Uncle Shine, an old black man with whom she sometimes trades banter, gently rebukes her, "Sometimes it seem like you believe they're *your* family."

Despite her loyalty to the Ransom family, Viola's emotions are a plausible mixture of love and bitterness. In some sense the Ransom children are hers, and yet with no biological children of her own, she is left with nothing in her old age. "All those years, sweating for this family," bring her only a rocking chair in the kitchen on which to rest her arthritic bones. Viola is crucial to the story, since she becomes for Victoria a historical source, a link to the past, the transmitter of family legends. "She had made me what I was," Victoria concludes: "a repository of all the events left behind her and relived, an archive of her own acts and feelings."

Flannery O'Connor once said something to the effect that the South is the only region of America where evil is still a reality. Thematically, I think, *Body of Knowledge* attempts to explore the nature of evil. For Grant, the Ransoms are the very embodiment of evil. But, while no one is guiltless, William is clearly more victim than victimizer, and Grant is the one — "with his do's and don'ts and long lean slitty eyes" — whose rigid code takes on the color of evil. Throughout, it is Viola who recognizes the diabolical aspect of Grant's motives. She refers to him at one point as "that devil man" and elsewhere as "a miserable hunk of hell"; "that man," she insists, "have the devil in his soul and breath."

"Ain't nobody cunning like the devil," Viola says. "He look like a clean, fine, upstanding man. He's real good at fooling who he need to fool. He lives like a Christian. Oh, yeah! Don't ever lie. Not so folk hear him at it. Nome, he's too cunning. But then he snake around in the dark, and he wait in the trees, spying to see who's ready." Viola instinctively recognizes the spuriousness of Grant's righteousness: "He'll do anything that suits him, if he think it's going to keep from dirtying his name or his righteousness. Righteousness!"

Perhaps the point is that evil is very personal and very immediate. We all face, from time to time, what we perceive as evil incarnate — "evil according to nature," as Melville put it. The question becomes, How do we respond to that evil? And in this regard, William is woefully lacking; in fact, he is, in a sense, responsible for his own suffering. When Baby Boy, the child William fathered with Grant's wife, is found dead near Grant's property, everybody — Viola most vehemently — believes Grant is the author of the boy's death.

When Viola demands to know what William is going to do about Baby Boy's death, William says, "The best we can do is to leave each other alone." True to his character, he will do nothing. He will hope Grant changes, that the enmity between the families evaporates. Instead, the enmity takes on a life of its own; the string of violent events in the Ransom family history, with their inevitable association with Macafees, becomes self-perpetuating, as the anticipation of the next calamity partly causes it to occur.

The chain culminates in William's suicide, "his one response to his enemy." Meditating on her grandfather's death, Victoria scans the beloved books in his library: "for *this*," she concludes, "he allowed the sacrifices, for his pathetic peace he had let it happen." The narrative spans a good part of the twentieth century, including the century's four major wars. In particular, many of the story's defining events take place in and around World War II.

In the late 1930s, just before his death, Baby Boy attempts to talk to his father about world politics. He says, "when I understood what Hitler was proposing to do, it came to me suddenly, clear as clear. 'This is evil. This is what it means.' . . . It's there, staring us in the face." Again, true to his nature, William refuses to discuss the matter, pretending not to have heard the comment. The lesson appears to be this: there are times, at both the personal and collective levels, when evil must be actively opposed, else it will engulf and overwhelm. If this is indeed the message, it comes close to being an affirmation of the old southern principle of defending one's honor, no matter the cost.

The South has a grand and glorious literary tradition, and at least some of that tradition has sloshed over into the backwater of East Texas. The Texan character, in ways both good and ill, partakes of southern attitudes and beliefs, and nowhere more obviously than in the easternmost reaches of the state. As a cultural barometer, the literature of East Texas faithfully mirrors the region's anxieties and values, its obsessions and conflicts. Writers such as John Howard Griffin, William A. Owens, Katherine Anne Porter, William Goyen, and Carol Dawson did not set out with the intent of drawing a roadmap of a region's culture, but given their experiences and conditioning, they could do nothing else.

CHAPTER 6

The Way West

The Frontier in Texas Fiction

*Fort Worth is still not much more
than a cattle stockade in Indian country.*

— GLENYS ROBERTS, *London Express* (May 11, 1986)

Conspiracy theorists — James Ward Lee, a native of Leeds, Alabama, is one — believe that prior to the middle decades of the present century Texas was a southern state to the core and was so perceived by the rest of the country.[1] It was only, asserts Lee, as a result of a carefully planned and orchestrated publicity campaign by J. Frank Dobie and his gang of cultural hijackers that Texas came to be seen, by most Americans, as a western — or at least a southwestern — state. This is an interesting and thought-provoking thesis. The only problem with it is that it is willfully wrong-headed.

True, Texas was one of eleven states of the Confederacy. It is still frequently classified as southern, especially when the reason for classification is politics. But it has been, from the beginning, as much a part of the old West as of the old South. The myth of the West, still a powerful presence in the national (and worldwide) psyche, emerged in the latter part of the nineteenth century, in large measure out of the immense popularity of dime-novel westerns. These were formula stories devoured by millions, and many of them featured a Texas backdrop. By the turn of the century Texas, in the popular imagination, was synonymous with the wild West. It is no accident that Stephen Crane's well-known story "The Bride Comes to Yellow Sky" (first published in 1898) is set in West Texas. Crane's tale gently satirizes and pokes fun at key elements of a myth that had already become part of the nation's cultural capital.

It is self-evident, I submit, that the Texas myth — a curious hybrid, to be sure — owes much more to the myth of the West than to the myth of the old South. The Southerner's bittersweet fascination with tragedy and defeat seems wholly foreign to the typical Texan's exuberance and expansiveness. In particular, the Texan character issued out of the nation's frontier experience. The South had a frontier, of course, but it was pretty much at an end by the early nineteenth century. It is to the western frontier — the last three or four decades of the nineteenth century, the cowboys-and-Indians period of American history — that the Texas myth is primarily indebted.

The American frontier vanished over a century ago; it was closed, by bureaucratic fiat, in 1890. But the influence of the frontier experience has lingered on long after the actuality of that experience evaporated in the mists of time. It remains a popular notion that the American character was shaped, in large measure, by the inexorable process of westward expansion and by the presence of large chunks of virgin soil that served as an escape hatch for those infused with the pioneer spirit. If that idea is at all true with regard to the American character generally, it is even more true of the "Texan character."

Traits we usually associate with the American pioneer — individual initiative, openness, generosity, heartiness of spirit — were incorporated into that image of the typical Texan that long ago invaded the American consciousness. Icons plucked from the frontier's most celebrated hero, the cowboy boots, jeans, ten-gallon hats — are familiar accoutrements of the daily garb of many (male) Texans. That these traits and icons have in some cases been debased and corrupted in twentieth-century Texas is beyond question. (*Dallas*'s J. R. Ewing and Robert Caro's Lyndon B. Johnson are fictional Texans that illustrate the near-limitless possibilities of such corruption.[2]) The point is, however, that the appeal of the frontier, over a hundred years after it ceased to exist, continues to exert a powerful influence on the beliefs and behavior of Texans.

It should surprise no one, therefore, that the frontier myth dominates the imaginations of so many Texas writers. Even a European-oriented *New Yorker* staff writer like Jane Kramer found herself, in the late 1970s, in the Texas Panhandle studying the recrudescence of frontier values and traditions in the present. The result of Kramer's investigation was published under the title *The Last Cowboy* (1978).[3] Larry McMurtry, in his now-famous 1981 rocket-launching in the *Texas Observer,* accounted for the many failings of recent Texas literature by pointing to the enduring lure of what he called the "cowboy myth." And yet McMurtry was, manifestly and spectacularly, unable to kill off the myth—witness his own Pulitzer Prize-winning foray into that territory of the mind and emotions, *Lonesome Dove* (1985).

Why is the frontier myth or cowboy myth (or whatever one wishes to dub it) so attractive to so many Texas writers? To say simply that they are obsessed with the past is not an adequate answer. Not all past events interest them equally. Few Texas writers, for example, have shown an inclination to deal with the state's participation in the Civil War or with the beginnings of the oil industry in the early twentieth century—important occurrences certainly in the nation's, as well as the state's, history. It seems to me that the appeal of the frontier era—not just to Texans but to Americans—lies in the fact that it is perceived as *the* epic moment of our national experience. In his classic essay "The Significance of the Frontier in American History" (1893), Frederick Jackson Turner describes the frontier as a moving line, "the outer edge of a wave—the meeting point between savagery and civilization."[4]

The implications of this metaphor are worth thinking about. In Turner's intellectual scenario, the frontier was visualized as a terrain on which two kingdoms of force—"savagery and civilization"—stood toe to toe contending for supremacy. As long as neither held dominance, there was danger, but there was also boundless freedom. Into this landscape came the archetypal American, an American who was free in a way that no American has been free since; free to choose patterns of conduct from an infinity of choices, free to move easily back and forth across the line which separated savagery and civilization, free to take the best from the wilderness and the best that civilization had to offer, free to create his *self* from the materials of a totally unrestricted environment. The frontier was the Eden of our history.

That, at least, is the frontier "myth." Whether or not the myth bears much relation to the reality is unimportant. What is important is that Americans have believed—and continue to believe—that there was once an Edenic period in our history, a time of unequalled promise and possibility. This belief echoes resonantly through our nation's literature. Certainly it echoes through Texas literature. Here are quotations from the work of two recent Texas writers. The first was penned by Larry McMurtry, in an essay published in the 1960s:

> If one loves the West it is sometimes deeply moving to drive along one of its rims and sense the great spread of country that lies before

one: West Texas, New Mexico and Colorado, Wyoming, the Dako-
tas, Utah, Arizona, Montana and Idaho, Nevada, Oregon and Washington, and the long trough of California. . . . On the rims of the
West — and perhaps, in America, only there — one can still know for
a moment the frontier emotion, the loneliness and the excitement
and the sense of an openness so vast that it still challenges — in Gatsbian phrase — our capacity for wonder.[5]

The second quotation, somewhat more playful, is from a magazine piece
by Larry L. King. He describes a stretch of "lonely windblown ranch country, between San Angelo and Water Valley," to which he has returned
many times:

Never have I rounded the turn leading into that peaceful valley with
the spiny ridge of hills beyond it, that I failed to feel new surges and
exhilarations and hope. For a precious few moments I exist in a time
warp: I'm back in Old Texas, under a high sky, where all things are
possible and the wind blows free. Invariably, I put the heavy spurs to
my trusty Hertz or Avis steed: go flying lickety-split down that lonesome road, whooping a crazy yell and taking deep joyous breaths,
sloshing Lone Star beer on my neglected dangling safety belt, and
scattering roadside gravel like bursts of buckshot. Ride 'im, cowboy!
Ride 'im.[6]

"Loneliness" and "excitement" and a "sense of openness" are indeed
emotions we associate with the frontier. And "surges and exhilarations and
hope." And each of these emotions, I believe, has its origin in our un-
quenchable belief that the American frontier was a place where "all things
are possible." It seems to me altogether natural and desirable that at least
some Texas writers continue to explore the shadings and gradations of the
state's frontier heritage. If Frederick Jackson Turner was mistaken in his
root premises (and there are plenty of revisionist historians these days who
dismiss the Turner thesis as the foundation of an outmoded "triumphalist"
view of American history), he was surely right in at least one major thrust
of his argument: the frontier has had an enormous, perhaps inordinate,
influence in shaping our self-definition as a people — Texans even more,
perhaps, than Americans in general. Interestingly, most of the attempts
at self-definition have occurred in the twentieth century, rather than the
nineteenth. The Turnerian hypothesis, therefore, may now have more rele-

vance to a study of twentieth-century American culture and literature than it has to a reconstruction of the actuality of the nineteenth-century frontier.

I want to discuss, at any rate, a handful of attempts by Texas writers to come to artistic and imaginative terms with the frontier experience and its legacy. The works I will discuss are all set in West Texas; thus they relate to the influence of the West on Texas literature. All are works of fiction and are of fairly recent vintage. All represent variations on a single theme: the frontier and its impact on human lives, past and present; the nuances and variations issue from the imaginations and artistic visions of the individual writers.

If the frontier was a place of limitless freedom, hope, promise, and possibility (or even if we in the twentieth century only believe that it was), it follows that with the closure of that period in our history something was lost. Inevitably, then, the literature of frontier Texas — and of the frontier West — is pervaded by a sense of loss: the old ways and the old values have faded and with them something fragile and precious and irrecoverable has disappeared. For the writer the trick is to convey this idea without slipping into the worst excesses of nostalgia and sentimentality. F. Scott Fitzgerald, of course, turned the trick at the close of *The Great Gatsby*. Many Texas writers have not been similarly successful, but some have.

Of those who have succeeded, I think first of John Graves. In his memorable short story "The Last Running," Graves writes of a scraggly band of Comanches in the early twentieth century, down from their reservation in Oklahoma, who beg from old man Charlie Goodnight a scrawny buffalo. Running the buffalo before them, the Indians whoop and holler, eventually killing the animal with lances and arrows in the traditional way. All that is left for these human relics is one last ritualistic reenactment of the old free times. To me, the story presents an unforgettable image of time and change and loss. Given the surcharged emotionalism of his materials, it is a near miracle that Graves manages to avoid the stickier forms of nostalgia. If the author indulges in nostalgia in the story (and probably he does), it is a tough-minded nostalgia that assesses the high cost of change and "progress," without advocating a reversal of time — an advocacy that would be doomed in any event.

The most sustained and consistent — and, to my mind, successful — attempt by a contemporary Texas writer to deal with the state's frontier history is that of Elmer Kelton. Kelton has published at least two dozen superior westerns, all of which feature authentic historical backdrops and skillful manipulation of basic fictional formulas that have often been used by writers of westerns. However, critics do not generally hold the western, as a genre, in high esteem. To call a work a "superior western," therefore, is to damn with faint praise. Fortunately, Kelton has produced several "serious" novels that merit consideration as works of high literary art: four of the best are *The Day the Cowboys Quit* (1971), *The Time It Never Rained* (1973), *The Good Old Boys* (1978), and *The Wolf and the Buffalo* (1980).

The chronological settings of these novels range from the 1870s to the 1950s. They are connected, however, by a framework of related thematic concerns. As Kelton has said, the theme that is woven through all these stories is that of "change, and the way people meet or resist change."[7] With change, of course, comes loss. People must adjust to change—or be destroyed. But human nature being what it is, they usually find it difficult, or impossible, not to lament the loss of the old ways.

Of the four novels the most ambitious and probably the most successful as a work of art is *The Time It Never Rained*. The Kelton novel that treats most poignantly and suggestively the theme of lost values and traditions, however, is *The Good Old Boys*. The book's title derives from Boy Rasmussen, a character who appears only briefly in the narrative but is nonetheless of considerable significance to the story. Boy Rasmussen had been a cowboy who had gone up the trails to Kansas and beyond; he had roamed the open range from Montana to Mexico. In 1906, the year in which the novel is set, he is a pitiable old man who rides a gaunt, aged cow-pony, an ancient ghost who haunts the countryside doing odd jobs and begging food and whiskey and tobacco. One day he apparently dies of a heart attack while bending over to open a gate. His body is found lying beside his horse, the lapels of his tattered coat flapping in the prairie wind. The cowboys who pay for his burial raise a toast in the local saloon: "To *him,* and to all the other good old boys!"

Boy Rasmussen, as a living—and dying—emblem of what happens to those who stay too long at the fair, provides an unsettling object lesson for Hewey Calloway, the novel's protagonist. Hewey, a "fiddlefooted" cowboy in his late thirties, discovers in the course of the narrative that time is running out—has perhaps already run out—on the footloose life he loves. As I said, *The Good Old Boys* is set in 1906, a time of transition; the frontier past is still vividly remembered, but a mechanized, urban future can be unmistakably, if only dimly, discerned. For Hewey it is a time of personal transition as well as of social and historical change. Hewey has chosen to spend his youth wandering across the West, drifting from transient job to transient job, always shunning the position of foreman because "too much responsibility went with it." But he has seen Kansas City and Fort Worth, automobiles and telephones: "I've seen streets so strung up with wires," Hewey says, "that you couldn't see the sky through, hardly. I don't understand it. I can't take a-hold of it. It scares me so bad I can't hardly wait to saddle up and get back into the open country where you've got to look a man in the face to talk to him."

In 1906 Hewey returns to the West Texas homestead of his brother Walter and sister-in-law Eve. He finds the property mortgaged to the hilt to C. C. Tarpley's bank, and in danger of foreclosure. The complications of the plot concern, mostly, how that danger is surmounted. In the course of helping his brother's family out of a tight spot, Hewey meets Spring Renfro, the local school teacher. Since Spring and Hewey are attracted to each other, it seems evident to everybody else, if not to Hewey, that it is time for him to settle down, like his brother. Hewey wrestles with the temptation that Spring represents, but at novel's end he is back on the trail. A cowpuncher friend has convinced him to take a herd of horses to Mexico — a new frontier. Mexico, his friend tells Hewey, is "big and wild and wide open. It's like Texas was before they commenced puttin' fences across it. . . . It's like goin' back to when we was young." Whether Hewey returns to Spring or ends up a wasted wanderer like Boy Rasmussen or whether some intermediate fate awaits him is left for the reader to decide.

The Good Old Boys is an impressive novel. Its artistry is understated; you have to look hard to see the care that went into its creation, but the inquisitive eye begins to pick out signs rather quickly. The style, for example. Kelton has mastered the West Texas cowboy's laconic, pithy way of speaking better than any writer I know of. That manner of speech is best illustrated in the colorful dialogue. But even in the third-person narration enough of it is injected to suggest the flavor of the region — without becoming annoying dialect. I could quote passage after passage to illustrate my point, but really the entire book should be read for the cumulative effect of Kelton's marvelous style to be appreciated.

The novel's plot, too, is the product of sound craftsmanship. The narrative flows smoothly and briskly. On the surface, of course, the story is familiar enough. It is a version of a classic formula of western fiction: cowboy rides into town, cowboy helps the good guys defeat the bad guys, cowboy rides off into the sunset (or, in this case, the sunrise). We even have here one of the most common of western stereotypes, the schoolmarm. And yet there are enough subtleties and reversals of the formula and of the stereotypes that it never seems, even for a moment, that we are reading just another "cowboy novel." Indeed the novel succeeds, finally, because of the force of the story told, familiar though it may be, and because of its believably drawn characters. Even the schoolmarm comes across as an individual rather than a type.

But it is in the character of Hewey that the larger meanings of the novel are embodied. Hewey is a man faced with a closed frontier, a personal dead end, the need to adjust to a world increasingly hostile to the skills and values by which he has lived. Hewey finds it difficult not to cling to what he has lost. Perhaps the ambiguity of the novel's ending begs the question of Hewey's fate. But I find the ending effective; for a man living out of his time there may be no answers, only questions.

If the theme of loss pervades literature about the Texas frontier, then so does the theme of betrayal. For some writers the legacy of the frontier is not so much values lost as values betrayed, even perverted. From the beginning the frontier experience had its dark underside. Those qualities that we associate with the frontier—openness, generosity, freedom, individualism—were reserved largely for white males. Mexican Americans, blacks, Indians, and women, among others, were usually excluded, either totally or in some degree, from participating in the benefits of frontier "freedom." Recently, and rightly, representatives of some of the groups named have begun to question the supposed advantages of our famed frontier heritage.

In the twentieth century even white male Texans have discovered that the frontier legacy is a two-edged sword. The government may stifle individualism, but so may a billionaire oilman or a giant corporation speaking in the name of individualism. Rural West Texas was settled by people attracted to the openness and freedom of the land; yet in the twentieth century the area has been dominated by a rigidly conformist society that has taken a fearful toll of psychological and emotional suffering from those who declined to conform. That, at least, is the report of some who have written on the subject. Those of us who have lived in rural West Texas for a good part of our lives can attest to the accuracy, by and large, of such reports.

The essential distinction to be made here, of course, is between the land, the wilderness, which in Turnerian ideology bestowed the gifts of freedom and opportunity, and the embryonic society that sprang up on the land, a society that often abused and betrayed those gifts. In *The Wolf and the Buffalo*, Elmer Kelton writes of a black man, an ex-slave from Louisiana, who in West Texas manages to rise to a position of leadership in the U.S. Army. "Out there," muses Gideon Ledbetter, "he seemed set free from the constraints of his blackness. The land made equal demands upon all men and neither gave credit nor demanded extra for their color." But if the harsh conditions of the wilderness imposed an initial equality among men, allowing them to succeed or fail according to their merits rather than by preordained standards of class and skin color, the social entities that the pioneers built on the frontier certainly have not exhibited a similar tolerance.

In my view the Texas writer who has dealt most trenchantly with the perversion of frontier values in modern times is Larry McMurtry in his early fiction. In that work, certainly, McMurtry sometimes waxes nostalgic in his portrayal of cowboys and frontiersmen, particularly old ones. One thinks of Homer Bannon in *Horseman, Pass By* (1961) and Roger Waggoner in *Moving On* (1970) as wonderfully sympathetic characters who embody all of the frontier virtues. With his creation of the character Uncle L in *All My Friends Are Going to Be Strangers* (1972), however, the author appears to have consciously purged himself or any lingering personal nostalgia concerning the cowboy and his vanishing way of life. Old Uncle L is as crazy as a bedbug, a certifiable lunatic, no doubt, were he to be examined by a psychiatrist. Such is the fate, McMurtry seems to be saying, of those who try to live within an anachronistic tradition.

McMurtry shows in his early novels that he can be a wickedly effective social critic. In *The Last Picture Show* (1966), for example, a small Texas town, Thalia, is indicted in about every possible way for deadening and constricting the lives of its citizens, for making those lives as drab and gray as the West Texas sky during a spring sandstorm. In Thalia in the 1950s, the frontier imperative to establish a moral order in the wilderness has resulted in the imposition of a social and ethical code that allows little or no room for even minor rebellion. The cowboy's famous (or notorious) attitude toward women — a kind of respectful uneasiness — has evolved into sexual misunderstanding and repression that inflicts terrible emotional wounds on both sexes. For old and young alike, the soured residue of frontier values in the middle of the twentieth century is a bitter draught to swallow — though they drink it, for the most part, without realizing there are alternatives.

Though McMurtry has consistently denigrated his first novel as "a piece of juvenilia,"[8] I maintain that, all things considered, *Horseman, Pass By* is still the writer's most polished work of fiction. Without a doubt it is his most illuminating and suggestive gloss on what has happened to the frontier tradition in modern times. The three major characters in the novel —

eighty-six-year-old Homer Bannon; thirty-five-year-old Hud, his stepson; and seventeen-year-old Lonnie, Homer's grandson — are three versions of the cowboy at different stages of life. What they have in common is that they live in the twentieth century at a time when the cowboy way of life is all but dead; a major concern of the narrative is to show how each reacts to this fact.

Homer had been born in the 1860s and had grown up in the old times — had once been known as "Wild Horse" Homer Bannon. He had built a ranch and accrued a considerable herd of cattle and a large stake of West Texas rangeland. He is a man of honor and principle who loves the land and the animals he works with. He refuses to allow oil wells to be drilled in his beloved soil, since that would be contrary, he believes, to nature's intention as to how the land ought to be used. He is obviously a man living out of tune with his times. Fittingly, at the close of the novel Homer's cattle are destroyed and he dies, one last remnant of the frontier passing from the scene.

Hud, Homer's stepson, is a frustrated frontiersman who, living in the mid-1950s, has no geographic frontiers left to conquer. So, for Hud, sex becomes a frontier. He invests most of his time and energy in sexual conquest. In Hud the lone wolf of the nineteenth century becomes just a wolf in the twentieth. Hud is inconsiderate, selfish, and cynical. He bulldozes and uses other people to get his way. He is more than a touch mean. In Hud, then, the aggressive self-sufficiency of the frontiersman has been transformed into single-minded viciousness. At novel's end Homer Bannon's ranch apparently has been passed on to Hud. Though we do not know for sure, we assume that, now that Homer is out of the way, oil wells will be punched in the land. Perhaps Hud is destined to become an eccentric oil tycoon. Probably he will move to Dallas and change his name to J. R. Ewing.

For Lonnie, the youngest of the three, living on the land, as his grandfather had done, is never a possible alternative. Lonnie admires his grandfather, and he is fond of the ranch and the horses and cattle it harbors. But he realizes his future lies elsewhere. Since Lonnie is the narrator of the story, we see everything that happens through his consciousness. Some of McMurtry's sharpest social satire, therefore, is filtered through the perceptions of young Lonnie. His description of his grandfather's funeral, for example, underscores (with unnecessary malice perhaps) the hypocritical morality of small-town preachers and undertakers.

Lonnie's ruminations on the significance of the banal lyrics of country-

and-western songs to the lives of modern-day cowboys and cowgirls represent a striking perception of West Texas kicker culture:

> The band was playing one of those songs of Hank Williams', the one
> about the wild side of life, and the music floated over the car tops
> and touched me. . . . It fit the night and the country and the way I
> was feeling, and fit them better than anything I knew. What few sto-
> ries the drinking people had to tell were already told in the worn-out
> words of songs like that one, and their kind of living, the few things
> they knew and lived to a fare-thee-well were in the sad high tune. City
> people probably wouldn't believe there were folks simple enough to
> live their lives out on sentiments like those — but they didn't know.

For Lonnie frontier simplicity has become a trap; it is simplicity without
possibility and thus must be escaped. Opportunity now lies in the city, not
in the distant plains and mountains. From time to time in his narration
Lonnie recalls a brief trip to Fort Worth, his lone taste of city life to this
point. He remembers wandering through the streets after dark, enjoying
"the shatter of those nights: things were moving around me, and it was
exciting." At the end of *Horseman, Pass By,* Lonnie has left the ranch, his
grandfather dead, Hud now in control. His future is far from settled, but
we are fairly certain that it will be spent in cities — Fort Worth, perhaps;
Houston; Washington, D.C. Since Lonnie is an intelligent, sensitive young
man, he may well become a professional writer.

In this fictional study of three generations of a West Texas family, we
have a vivid allegory of the fate of frontier values in the twentieth century.
Homer doggedly holds on to the values because he is too old to adapt to
any other way of life. Hud betrays the values, perverts them, out of spite
and ignorance; in a way, he is as much a man living out of his time as is
Homer. It is Lonnie, sensing rather than intellectualizing the perversion
that Hud represents, who rejects the sad, undernourished life that the frontier has spawned on the prairie. Lonnie, because of his youth, is only partly
aware of his dissatisfaction with the repressive society of rural West Texas,
but he knows that, for him, the frontier must be a realm of the mind and
spirit rather than of the land.

Although most Texans — and Texas writers — have viewed the state's
frontier period positively, nostalgically even, have regretted its passing and
mourned the loss of the values it engendered, popular American attitudes
toward the frontier have always been characterized by ambivalence. In his

well-known study *Virgin Land: The American West as Symbol and Myth,* Henry Nash Smith shows how Americans of the eighteenth and nineteenth centuries saw the frontier as, at one and the same time, a hospitable garden and a hostile desert.[9] These seemingly conflicting images of the West were promulgated simultaneously in popular literature of the time. Indeed the idea of the West has always been a mercurial concept. The frontier, to some, was an invigorating moral landscape, clean and uncorrupted because of its very wildness; to others, it was morally ambiguous, promoting human degradation, even brutalization. If the frontier was a place of freedom and unlimited opportunity, it could also, because of an absence of moral order and social discipline, generate terrifying loneliness — and aloneness.

A recent Texas writer who provocatively juggles these ambivalent ideas about the frontier is R. G. Vliet. Specifically, Vliet's first two novels, *Rockspring* (1974) and *Solitudes* (1977), are set in frontier West Texas. While *Rockspring* is a lyrical love story (in a way, an inversion of the tale told in *Solitudes*), the latter novel projects the most suggestive treatment of this theme. *Solitudes* is a narrative, a "western" of sorts, about a wandering cowboy — a "lonesome cowboy," to use an appropriate cliché — traversing the landscape of Texas in the 1880s.[10] It is, however, a western with a difference. Any moderately informed reader of the genre knows that something is up when a western begins with an epigraph from Wallace Stevens: "We live in an old chaos of the sun." The epigraph should be a tip-off that the reader is about to enter into one of the world's few existentialist westerns. *Solitudes* is, as one reviewer put it, "a philosophical Western, as though Camus had been grafted onto Zane Grey, with a touch of Walt Whitman thrown in for good measure."[11] (The literary sophistication of Vliet and his fiction, incidentally, would seem to belie a charge made by some critics that Texas writers are poorly read and uninformed as to cultural trends in the rest of the world.)

The protagonist of *Solitudes* is a twenty-four-year-old cowboy who is known variously as Claiborne Sanderlin, Claiborne Arnett, Clabe, and Red — the uncertainty of his name presumably suggesting his uncertain sense of identity. Rounding up cattle in a norther, Claiborne shoots and kills a tall stranger, a Mexican, he later learns, named don Alvaro Reyes Ibarra. He had been disturbed by the stranger in a way he does not understand; and further disoriented by what is apparently an epileptic seizure, he reacts violently. He takes from don Reyes's body only the smudged photograph of a young woman in a white dress. Thus begins Claiborne's search for the woman — and for his own soul.

His quest carries him through Central and West Texas in the spring and summer of 1881. The historical reality of frontier Texas of a century ago is recreated in the novel with wonderful precision and care; pains were obviously taken to make place names and even the smallest of background details right. But Claiborne's journey is more spiritual than spatial. He is free in that the law will never punish him for his violent act; he is also alone, and in his freedom and aloneness he discovers fear, alienation, even a kind of terror. The landscape the novel explores, therefore, is not so much that of late nineteenth-century Texas as it is the landscape of Claiborne's mind. His search for the woman in the photograph is ultimately a search for absolution — and an attempt to create order and a sense of his existential self from the moral chaos of frontier Texas below and the sun above.

Claiborne eventually discovers that the young woman in the photograph is don Reyes's granddaughter, Soledad. He finds her and falls in love with her. After one brief experience of sexual abandon, however, Soledad, needing her hatred more than love, sends him away. Claiborne thus becomes another of those cowboys who ride off into the sunset. He does not, however, ride toward a beckoning horizon; he is consumed instead in a void of aloneness. On the last page of the novel Claiborne relates, through his thoughts, what he has learned of the meaning of human existence:

> Here's the stars ain't got no word for us. Here's your sky-blue heaven empty of comfort as ice up a man's ass. . . . Here's the wall that says we got to die, where folks tack up the word "God" to hang their hats onto, but a man walks across the dirt ground that's gonna soak him up quick as piss. There ain't nowheres a body can make a deal. It don't quit. A man is so damn alone he might could be on the moon.

Claiborne learns other things as well from his experiences. He never solves the mystery of his "fits," as he calls them — his seizures — but he does conclude that he killed don Reyes because he saw *himself* in his victim and was struck by an unnameable fear: "It was myself I seen," Claiborne decides, and it was himself he feared and tried to destroy. Claiborne reasons that Soledad cannot forgive him for his crime; God will not forgive him; so he must forgive himself. When Claiborne attains a state of qualified self-forgiveness at the close of the novel, his quest for absolution, at least, is complete. In the end one of the most important things Claiborne learns is that he prefers being alive rather than dead; he is glad to be himself rather than don Reyes. "I ain't about to trade places," he concludes. If the presence of existentialist angst in a story that is, on one level anyway, a recognizable version of the traditional western formula seems amusingly improbable, I urge you to read *Solitudes*. It is a powerful and provocative novel.

I have focused here on fiction by Graves, Kelton, McMurtry, and Vliet, but I could have easily gathered in works by at least a half-dozen other writers who have dealt imaginatively with the frontier experience in Texas. Tom Lea's *The Wonderful Country* (1952) is an adventure story set in far West Texas toward the end of the nineteenth century. It has all the usual background props: marauding Indians, cavalry, Texas Rangers. But the book's precise, controlled style and structure raise it far above the aesthetic level of the typical formula western. Benjamin Capps is another Texas writer who deserves more than passing mention. Capps has written a series of novels that successfully portray various aspects of late nineteenth-century Texas history. Among his best efforts are *The Trail to Ogallala* (1964), an exceptionally vivid and realistic narrative of a trail drive from South Texas to Nebraska, and *Sam Chance* (1965), the story of the rise of a Texas cattle baron. Robert Flynn's fine, underrated trail-drive novel *North to Yesterday* (1967) projects an ironic vision of the frontier past that nonetheless helps keep the myth alive in literature.

What I like about the fiction of these writers and of still others whose names might justifiably appear on this fragmentary list is that they expand, in important ways, the literary possibilities of Texas's frontier heritage. I agree with McMurtry that Texas is now an urban state and that Texas literature, to be vital or even viable, must reflect that fact. I do not agree with the corollary assumption that we — writers and readers alike — must reject the "cowboy myth," as he calls it, and the values that the myth promotes. A people's self-definition inevitably flows from their past, and like it or not, Texas's sense of itself — at least to this point in time — has been shaped by the legends and myths that evolved out of its frontier experience. What is needed is not a self-imposed ban on literary treatment of the myth; what are needed are *better* and more *imaginative* transmutations of the myth in art. Fortunately there are still a few Texas writers attempting to fill that requirement. For them let us be thankful.

CHAPTER 7

Texans at War

The Military Experience in Texas Letters

*Prior to [World War II] Texas was probably the least
isolationist state in the union, and certainly the most inter-
ventionist in the West. So many Texans went to Canada to
enlist before Pearl Harbor that Montreal wags talked of
"the Royal Canadian Texan Air Force."*

— JOHN GUNTHER, *Inside U.S.A.*

A crucial facet of the stereotypical male Texan is that he is a fighter. This
element of the Texan's character has consequences that are both good and
bad. At his best, the typical Texan is viewed as a man who takes seriously
his duty to protect, by violence if necessary, his honor and the safety of his
family and nation. At his worst, he is seen as a trigger-happy thug who
shoots first and asks questions later.

For fighting men, whether they are good guys or bad guys, there are
likely to be occasions when battles escalate from the personal level to the
collective level — that is, when they must submit themselves to the demands of concerted military action. Texans have never been slow to volunteer for such action. Throughout our history, America's relations with
other countries, as Peter Aichinger says in *The American Soldier in Fiction*,
have been governed by a "traditional isolationism and neutrality,"[1] a position severely compromised in the decades following World War II by the
expansionist activities of Soviet communism and by our own ambitions in
the world. Unquestionably, however, in this century in the years preceding
both World War I and World War II, American public opinion was on the
whole isolationist — in some regions, decidedly so.

But not in Texas. It was no accident that Teddy Roosevelt came to San

Antonio at the close of the nineteenth century to recruit his Rough Riders for service in the Spanish American War; the majority of Roosevelt's volunteers, consequently, were Texans and Southwesterners. Of all the states of the union, the vocal sentiment for intervention before the two world wars was demonstrably strongest in Texas. Moreover, a large percentage of American troops that served in the Vietnam War — many of them Mexican American — were Texans. More second lieutenants who were graduates of Texas A&M University suffered casualties in Vietnam than did the graduates of any other university in the nation.

Texans, then, are fighters, and historically much of their fighting has been done within the context of organized military campaigns. But right off I must enter a disclaimer: if there is such a thing as a military tradition in Texas culture, it is considerably more individualistic and quirky than most professional military men would no doubt prefer. In this regard, however, the Texas military tradition is only a mirror image — in a slightly distorted or exaggerated form — of the *American* military tradition. John Bainbridge, in *The Super Americans* (1961), has argued that the importance of Texas lies in the manner in which it anticipates and exaggerates tendencies in the United States as a whole.[2] A case in point, I believe, is Texans' ambivalent attitudes toward the military.

Because our nation emerged from a revolution that consciously violated "due process of law" and, even more, because its expansion was effected by wresting land from Indians and Frenchmen and Mexicans by means not always strictly legal, Americans have never had much respect for institutionalized forms of law and order such as the military. More than one American folk hero, historians tell us, was little more than a shady character whose actions, as Aichinger puts it, "were legitimized because he fought in what appeared to be a good cause."[3] (If this is true of America's legendary heroes, consider the heroes of Texas: the defenders of the Alamo, for example, most of whom were adventurers that were somehow transformed in the public mind into valiant and doomed "soldiers.") When one recalls that as late as 1960 one of America's greatest generals and a two-term president of the republic, Dwight D. Eisenhower, warned his fellow citizens against the dangers of the "military-industrial complex,"[4] the recurrent American animosity toward militarism and a professional military establishment comes more sharply into focus.

If Texans, free-spirited and freedom-loving individualists that they are supposed to be, sometimes chafe under and even burst out of the constraints of the military code, they are only asserting their credentials as

Americans — or "super Americans." Certainly Texans have never adjusted well to the lockstep. I find it interesting that a well-known Texas writer, George Sessions Perry, could publish in 1951 a history of what was then known as Texas A&M College that contains only two brief references to the Reserve Officers Training Corps. Perry talks at length about football and engineering and agriculture, and he spins many yarns about "Aggies I have known," but he scarcely mentions the corps at all. Any graduate of Texas A&M of 1951 or earlier, I wager, would cite the corps as a major element of university life during those years. Perry saw action during World War II as a magazine and newspaper correspondent, an experience that apparently initiated his downward spiral into alcoholism and mental illness and ultimately, in 1956, suicide. Probably he witnessed too much of war and killing and, in *The Story of Texas A&M,* simply chose to ignore that institution's role as a military school. Perhaps also Perry was consciously cultivating the mildly rebellious attitude toward military discipline that Texans have ordinarily adopted.

Traditional attitudes and beliefs, in any event, emerge from a people's collective experience, and Texans' attitudes toward the military are no exception to the rule. There are several fairly clear-cut events and periods in the history of Texas when the military and military action have come to the fore: the 1836 War of Independence; the Civil War; the Indian wars of the late nineteenth century; and the four wars in this century in which the United States has become involved. A handful of works of literature has dealt provocatively with Texans' participation in these bloody events.

One of the earliest Texas novels — or at least one of the earliest novels set in Texas — a book titled *Mexico Versus Texas,* published in Philadelphia in 1838, treats the Texas Revolution from an unusual perspective. In the first printing the author was identified only as "a Texian," though later editions suggested that his name was A. T. Myrthe, a Frenchman and a Catholic priest and missionary who had once been assigned to a post in Texas. The novel's dedication, to General Sam Houston, is a fair sample of the book's prose style:

> To whom with more propriety than your Excellency can I inscribe a work whose principal theme consists of the glorious and successful struggles by which your fellow citizens attained their independence? It is, under God, to your valor, prudence and humanity they are indebted for their success, and now you stand before the world as one

of those master-spirits by whom mighty changes are wrought in the economy of human affairs.

As might be expected in a work by a priest, there is a good deal of religious conflict and turmoil—specifically between Catholics and protestants—in *Mexico Versus Texas*. But the novel's most unusual aspect is that it is told from the vantage point of a young Mexican army officer who has an Anglo-American mother and a Spanish father. The officer possesses a degree of sympathy for the Texans' cause, and perhaps as a result of his conflicting feelings, he is treated kindly when he is captured at San Jacinto. Despite an interesting premise, *Mexico Versus Texas* is marred by the florid sentimentality that characterizes most minor American novels—or romances—of its period.

Two other nineteenth-century novels of some note that use the Texas Revolution as their background are Augusta J. Evans's *Inez* (1855) and Amelia E. Barr's *Remember the Alamo* (1888). Both tales treat, for the most part, turbulent historical events of the time from the perspective of female characters. And both suffer from the aesthetic flaws that tend to weaken popular fiction in any era. Here, for example, is Augusta Evans's overwrought description of Fannin at Goliad:

Rumors of the fall of the Alamo, the overwhelming force of Santa Anna, and his own imminent danger, had reached Colonel Fanning [sic]. In vain he entreated reinforcements, in vain urged the risk hourly incurred. The Texan councils bade him save himself by flight. "Retreat, fly from the post committed to my keeping!" The words sounded like a knell on the ear of the noble man to whom they were addressed. He groaned in the anguish of his spirit, "I will not leave this fortress—Travis fell defending with his latest breath the Alamo! Oh, Crockett! Bowie! can I do better than follow thy example, and give my life in this true cause?"

In the twentieth century there have been surprisingly few attempts by Texas writers to deal imaginatively with the Texas Revolution and its topsy turvy outcome. In her novel *Star of the Wilderness* (1942), Karle Wilson Baker writes creditable historical fiction that, in its final chapters, provides an honest and generally believable account of the main events of the Revolution; and J. Y. Bryan's *Come to the Bower* (1963) is a rousing tale of that epoch. Otherwise, except for a few works of popularized history, such as

Thirteen Days to Glory (1958), Lon Tinkle's narrative of the fall of the Alamo, pickings are slim. James A. Michener's bloated *Texas* (1985) contains a long, confused (and confusing) rehash of the three major battles of the Revolution: the Alamo, Goliad, and San Jacinto. A recent, rather odd addition to the literature of the period is Michael Lind's *The Alamo* (1997), an epic poem of 6,006 lines that casts William Barret Travis as its hero.

Overall, literature, like film, portrays the Texas Revolution, especially the battle of the Alamo, in a melodramatic and superficial manner. In the writing dealing with this event, no sense of an embryonic Texas military tradition emerges. The Texans are usually shown to be patriots, volunteers, and citizen-soldiers who have banded together to resist intolerable Mexican oppression. They must fight Santa Anna's dandified and Europeanized army, and they do so more with extreme, even suicidal acts of bravery than with military strategy and organization. Soon enough, of course, motivated valor wins out over superior force and merely mechanical military planning.

Another historical event that has received but scant attention in Texas literature is the state's participation in the Civil War. Texas was settled primarily by Southerners and upon entry into the union in 1845 was recognized as a slave state. Despite opposition from Sam Houston (himself a slaveholder) and some scattered grumbling along the state's northern and western frontiers, Texans in 1861 voted overwhelmingly for secession and alliance with the Confederate States of America. Few armed conflicts took place on Texas soil during the Civil War, but thousands of Texans fought elsewhere for the Confederacy, most with honor and some with distinction.

The one certified (though minor) literary classic about Texans' military participation in the Civil War is John W. Thomason Jr.'s *Lone Star Preacher* (1941), subtitled, "Being a Chronicle of the Acts of Praxiteles Swan, M. E. Church South, Sometime Captain, 5th Texas Regiment, Confederate Provisional Army." Thomason grew up in Huntsville, a southern town if ever there were one, and he became a career military officer who reached the rank of lieutenant colonel in the United States Marine Corps. During his lifetime he was also a well-known writer, a protegé of famed Scribner's editor Maxwell Perkins. (Perkins was credited with discovering such major-league literary talents as F. Scott Fitzgerald, Ernest Hemingway, and Thomas Wolfe.) Thomason's gifts as an artist and illustrator almost matched those he demonstrated as a writer; reviewers often commented that Thomason's illustrations were among the most enjoyable aspects of his works. He published several books in addition to fulfilling his military duties; one of these, *Fix Bayonets* (1926), is a collection of stories about the adventures of American military men around the globe.

Thomason's best work by far, however, is *Lone Star Preacher*, which is, more or less, a novel. I say "more or less" because the volume's various chapters were originally self-contained stories published in the 1930s in the *Saturday Evening Post* and other popular periodicals. In the book the tales are brought together and strung along a loose plot line. Thomason describes his hero, Praxiteles Swan, as a "hot-headed and desirous young man, combatant officer in a most accomplished fighting army, and all his life a soldier of the Cross," who "did in every essential aspect exist, and move, and have his being in the southern regions of these United States, within the memory of living men."

Praxiteles Swan, born in Virginia, an ordained Methodist minister, is sent by his church in the early 1850s to the village of Washington-on-the-Brazos in southeast Texas. Primarily an adherent to the God of the Old Testament, he is not averse to occasional instructive violence. In fact, Swan makes his first mark in Washington by whipping the town bully in a fist-fight. "The engagement," the narrator observes, "was like San Jacinto fight in its brevity and violence and its astonishing and improbable outcome." In the course of a few years, Swan marries, starts a family, and establishes himself as a successful minister and prosperous farmer.

When the Civil War begins, Swan suffers a brief pang of conscience. He does not support secession, but his loyalties to the South are too strong to allow him to stay home while others march off to battle. On his way to war Swan encounters Sam Houston, who has been removed from the office of governor of Texas because of his refusal to take an oath of allegiance to the Confederacy. Old Sam Houston's prophecy is as ominous as that of an oracle in Greek tragedy. "As Gadarine swine," he tells Praxiteles Swan, "you rush on destruction! And you who live will see your substance wasted, your women and children homeless, your very social order destroyed." Swan does not heed the warning.

He joins Hood's Texas Brigade, which throughout the war was attached to Robert E. Lee's Army of Northern Virginia. Swan is the brigade's chaplain, but it is not long before he is involved in the fighting, eventually achieving the rank of captain. He is portrayed as a fierce warrior. At Gettysburg,

He rose to his knees and raised his immense voice—"Fifth Texas—Hood's Texans." . . . An anger surged through him. He stood erect, and looked around. "We air going," he announced, "to take that there hill. Come on." He began to walk towards the hill. . . . A sort of moaning sigh ran from one man to another. A few of them got to their feet, and a few more, and then all of them.

In the advance on the hill, Swan urges the men on with a kind of song: "Come on, Fifth Texas, / Come on, Fifth Texians—/ You boys from the Brazos / and the Trinity." As the war drags on and bone-weariness and hopelessness begin to undermine the will of the southern army, Praxiteles Swan never loses his optimism and exuberance, and even more remarkably he somehow retains his sense of rough-and-ready humor.

Lone Star Preacher has a kind of antique air about it. It springs from a simpler, more naive time, when war and fighting were deemed to be glorious occupations, when the stacking of the dead and even the certainty of defeat could not quench a man's thirst for battle. In this regard, the fictional Swan in the 1860s and the real-life John Thomason in the 1920s and 1930s seemed to share a common view. Both lived and fought, of course, before the mass, anonymous slaughter that began in the final stages of World War II, before the advent of the ineffable horror of the possibility of nuclear destruction. Praxiteles Swan, in any event, is a memorable and representative Texan.

Moreover, in helping the reader to fix the shape of the Texas military tradition, *Lone Star Preacher* sketches out some of the contours of that tradition about as well as any book I know. The Confederate army, in Thomason's rendering at least, was a Texan's kind of outfit. It was, writes Thomason, "as little bound by doctrine as any ever mustered for war, and the militia soldiers looked with cold suspicion upon anything emanating from West Point." The typical Confederate soldier, he continues, "was an individual, distrustful of anything that smacked of regimentation; jealous and ardent for his sectional ties; and peculiarly susceptible to leadership." Here, it seems to me, is the Texas military philosophy conveniently summarized: a Texan will follow a brave leader against the demons of hell if necessary, but he resists regimentation and maintains his individuality at all costs.

A period of Texas history in which the military played a prominent role and which has received a fair amount of coverage in the state's writing is the 1870s. At the beginning of the decade, Texas, like other southern states, was occupied territory. Union troops were present, in large measure, to enforce what Anglo Texans and other Southerners viewed as the harsh rule of Reconstruction. Unlike other southern states at the time, Texas had a blazing frontier, and Texans' attitudes toward the military were consequently somewhat ambivalent. If most Texans saw the army troopers as hated reminders of their bitter defeat, some — those living on the West Texas frontier, in particular — welcomed the military as a guard against the depredations of hostile Indians. And indeed by the close of the 1870s the threat of Indian raids in Texas had been virtually eliminated, largely through the efforts of frontier cavalry units.

The most artistically accomplished work of Texas literature to treat the military during this time is Elmer Kelton's *The Wolf and the Buffalo* (1980). Kelton, who has published more than two dozen novels laid in nineteenth-century Texas, features in his books vivid characterizations and plotting, as well as settings authentic in every detail. *The Wolf and the Buffalo* is set in an around Fort Concho, near present-day San Angelo. At the beginning of the narrative in the early 1870s, the feared Comanches are still making bloody forays onto the southern plains with impunity. The Comanches are generally contemptuous of the U.S. Cavalry, since the soldiers "are slow to get started. And unless they had the aid of good trackers . . . were usually not hard to shake off the trail."

The main character of *The Wolf and the Buffalo* is Gideon Ledbetter, a former slave from Louisiana who joins the army following the Civil War because there is nothing else for him to do. Gideon becomes a "buffalo soldier," one of those black troopers stationed in West Texas during the 1870s who acquired their name from the Indians because their curly black hair resembled that of the buffalo, or bison. Gideon discovers that, despite the useful function he and his fellow African American soldiers serve on the frontier, he is not welcome in West Texas:

> To ex-Confederates, a black man in a blue uniform represented authority, a swaggering symbol of a lost war. To Northerners moving in to seize upon rapidly opening business opportunities, Negroes were a social and economic burden. In a subtle way they also goaded the conscience, a reminder that much of the inspirational wartime talk about freedom and brotherhood and equality had come from the mouth and not from the heart.

But in the field Gideon prospers. He becomes increasingly confident of his ability to pit himself successfully against the land and the elements. Early on in the story he is tested and blooded as a leader of men: "He had tasted the land now. For all its strangeness, its continuous threat of disaster, it produced a stimulation he had never known before. . . . The land made equal demands on all men and neither gave credit nor demanded extra for their color." By novel's end, Gideon has been promoted to sergeant, about the highest rank a black man can aspire to, since all the officers are white.

Gideon's immediate superior, the white Lieutenant Hollander, is an honorable man who nonetheless understands and accepts the violent and vengeful nature of his duty. "It is not army policy," Hollander tells his troop as they are about to attack an Indian village, "to brutalize these people, but it *is* army policy to see that every transgression is punished." The troopers, black and white, recognize that in a way they are just mercenaries, paid to perform an unpleasant task and then to move on. "The soldier never gets to keep what he wins," a buffalo hunter tells Hollander. "We are tools of destiny, you and me and your darkies here. We'll do our bit and drift away with nothing to show for it." Hollander later says to Gideon: "We made the land safe for civilized people. Now the danger is gone and we're in the way just as the Comanche was."

The inevitable resentment, even hostility, the army (mostly white officers from the North and black horse soldiers) and civilians (mostly Southerners) feel for each other is never very far from the surface. "The army cannot watch over every outlying cabin of every ex-Confederate foolish enough to expose himself to the hazard of Indians," grouses a snippy Yankee major when the troopers come upon a farm family slain by Comanches. A former Confederate, Pat Maloney, who scouts for the army patrols, carries on a half-mocking, half-serious debate with the cavalry officers. Once Maloney, along with Gideon and a couple of other buffalo soldiers, is trailing a party of Comanches, and Maloney comments on the "glory" they will share should they find the Indians. "They ain't goin' to let you and us have no glory," Gideon says. "We're too dark, and you're a Texican."

Interpolated into the story of Gideon Ledbetter are episodes from the life of a Comanche warrior named Gray Horse. The fate of Gray Horse is representative of that of all plains Indians in the late nineteenth century. As the buffalo are slaughtered by white hunters, as the cavalry by sheer weight of numbers slowly forces the nomadic tribes onto the reservations in Oklahoma, as Anglo settlers make their way onto the plains, the old free life of pre-white times all too quickly comes to an end. Frustrated and confused, Gray Horse makes a foolhardy assault on an army patrol, only to be killed, ironically, by Gideon. The supreme irony of this symbolic scene is, as Kelton has said, that in "essence it was the black trooper's role to take the land away from the red man so the white men could have it."

The Wolf and the Buffalo takes place before the Comanche wars are completely resolved. A novel that explores the final eradication of the Indian menace on the West Texas plains in the mid-1870s is Max Crawford's *Lords of the Plain* (1985). Crawford's James John McSwain, commander of the Second Cavalry, is apparently a fictionalized version of Colonel Ranald S. Mackenzie. Crawford portrays McSwain as a Custer-like figure who entertains political ambitions. In real life Mackenzie appears to have been a decent, practical man and a superb commanding officer. In 1873 Mackenzie was commended in a joint resolution of the Texas legislature for pursuing and punishing "a band of Kickapoo Indians who . . . have for years been waging a predatory warfare upon the frontiers of Texas." Thanks, the resolution continues, are due Mackenzie and his men "for their prompt action and gallant conduct in inflicting well-merited punishment upon these scourges of our frontier." In 1874 Mackenzie became the hero of the Battle of Palo Duro Canyon, in which his troops routed a large band of Comanches and Kiowas camped in the canyon, captured many of them, and slaughtered more than a thousand Indian ponies. Some saw the killing of the horses as a draconian measure, but it had the intended effect of severely diminishing the Comanches' mobility and, therefore, the threat they posed to Anglo settlers.[5]

Lords of the Plain, in any event, is narrated by Captain Philip Chapman, a proper Bostonian who serves under Colonel McSwain. Chapman, as an outsider, describes the Anglo Texans he meets along the way with the scientific detachment of an entomologist examining some exotic new species of insect. Most of these Texans turn out to be very odd creatures indeed — violent, bigoted, often half-crazed by loneliness and isolation. As in *The Wolf and the Buffalo,* relations between frontier Texans and the cavalrymen — most, like Chapman, from the North — are shown in *Lords of the Plain* to be tense at best.

Yet another noteworthy Texas novel that takes as at least one of its subjects military operations against hostile Indians is Tom Lea's *The Wonderful Country* (1952). This tale is set near the close of the decade of the 1870s, and the only Indian problems remaining in Texas are in the far western part of the state. The buffalo soldiers have been moved westward from Fort Concho to places like Fort Jefflin (Fort Bliss), near Puerto (El Paso). Indeed, there is a character in *The Wonderful Country,* a black sergeant named Tobe Sutton, who, although not as fully or believably developed as Elmer

Kelton's Gideon, resembles Gideon in many respects. In Lea's version of history, the buffalo soldiers perform honorably in their campaigns against the Apaches, and their white commanding officer, Major Starke Colton, is somewhat foolhardy but nonetheless courageous. Dying, Colton asks to be remembered by the following epitaph: "when I found the enemy, I engaged him."

The Wonderful Country tosses a new element into the fictional history of the Indian wars of the 1870s: the Texas Rangers. The Rangers, who in this novel anyway are depicted as a semi-military organization, have produced over the years a stormy and controversial track record. Their demeanor has not always been in the best military tradition. For example, by all accounts they were almost uncontrollable during their service in the Mexican War in the 1840s, and they were participants in several grisly incidents that live in legend in Mexico to this day.[6] Apparently, however, the Rangers were very effective — more effective than the regular army — in negating the guerilla warfare tactics of the plains Indians. In *The Wolf and the Buffalo,* for instance, the Comanche Gray Horse fears "the implacable . . . Texas Rangers — men always angry and always ready to travel."

The protagonist of *The Wonderful Country,* Martin Brady, eventually fulfills his ambition to become a Texas Ranger; he joins Captain John Rucker's Company E, Frontier Battalion, headquartered at Puerto at the tip of far West Texas. Rucker is a wise man and a good leader, and his company takes part in a joint military operation on Mexican soil — involving the Rangers, the U.S. Army's Tenth Cavalry, and the private army of the governor of Chihuahua, Mexico — to flush out of their mountain stronghold the renegade Apache, Fuego, and his band of followers. The Mexican army does most of the fighting — and annexes most of the credit — a circumstance that does not sit well with the Rangers. "The wind kind of missing from my sails," one of them complains, "coming home from Mexico without a scrap." In general, though, the Rangers accept their disappointment with good grace. *The Wonderful Country,* then, tends to perpetuate the myth of the Texas Rangers as first-rate fighting men who work well together while retaining their frontier individualism.

Indeed, the Ranger myth has a long literary history, stretching back to the popular dime novels of the late nineteenth century. And it has made innumerable appearances in works of literature in the twentieth century. One of my favorite fictional treatments of the mythical Ranger temperament is Larry McMurtry's trail-drive novel, *Lonesome Dove* (1985). The prime mover behind the drive is Captain Woodrow Call, a retired Texas

Ranger. Call is a competent, controlled man — a brave man who lives comfortably with danger. In fact, he is much more at home with physical danger than with emotional discomfort. He is the most interesting character in *Lonesome Dove,* but in some ways he is also a stereotype — for better or worse, the quintessential Ranger.

After the 1870s, most of the forts in Texas were closed and the cavalry moved even farther west, to New Mexico and Arizona, though a few army bases, such as those at San Antonio and El Paso, continued operations and became important American military installations. For the most part, Texans of the late nineteenth and early twentieth centuries turned their attention to matters of economic survival, activities that had nothing to do with military life: raising beef cattle and getting them to market; growing cotton; and, after 1901, extracting oil from the earth. Pro-war sentiment was strong in Texas during the brief Spanish-American War and, as mentioned earlier, prior to United States involvement in World War I. In all American wars of this century, large numbers of Texans have eagerly disrupted the normal pursuits of their civilian lives to volunteer for military service.

A literary work that covers the twentieth-century spectrum — from World War I to the Vietnam War — of Texans and their relation to the military is a thought-provoking and thoroughly remarkable novel by Andrew Jolly, *A Time of Soldiers* (1976). The tale follows the fortunes of three generations of a Texas military family, the Lears. In the first generation, as represented by Jack Lear, the flame of idealism burns with a hard intensity. Jack Lear is a New Englander by birth who marries the daughter of a German saddlemaker from San Angelo. But he is really married to the army. Jack Lear believes that the soldier's calling is akin to that of the priest. Lear writes a book, ostensibly a study of the interrelation of warfare and religion among the Apaches in the nineteenth century. It is titled *War and Faith,* and its first two sentences read: "War is an act of belief on the part of a people in their conception of the meaning of human life. The way in which people make war is influenced by this conception."

Jack Lear once told his friend the El Paso newspaperman Stefan Graf that "he had become a soldier not to be only his own self alone, and in his romantic view the soldier was the incorruptible guardian of the City of Man and at the same time a part of that City." Lear's belief in the nobility of America's mission in the world seems unshakable: "if the profit motive is the bedrock of the nation's morality," he declares, "then I am only a hired killer, and I decline to accept that judgment." Graf sees in Jack Lear the embodiment of "some profound innocence and purity which could be murderous, bloody, and destructive. I thought of Lee and Stonewall Jackson and Lamar and Houston and Washington and of all those other saintly soldiers, and I felt that the enigma of our country sat before me."

Jack Lear becomes a kind of hero during the Punitive Expedition against Pancho Villa in northern Mexico. However, he antagonizes the "horse generals" by advocating greater and more imaginative use of technology and, during World War I, is consigned to a series of demeaning tasks. Eventually, in the 1930s, he is sent to the mountains of southern New Mexico to help train a group of quasi-religious counterrevolutionary Mexican nationals who call themselves the Cristeros. In due course, policy changes dictate that Lear be ordered to abandon the mission. Instead of obeying orders, Lear chooses to stand with the Cristeros when they are attacked by the U.S. Army in the valley of La Luz in the Sacramento Mountains of New Mexico. He is one of first to be killed.

Why this suicidal gesture? In Graf's view, Lear had lost his idealism, his faith in his country and the sanctity of his vocation. While training the Cristeros in the mountains, Graf says, Lear "must have halted upon some height within his mind and reasoned backward from technique and weapon and strategy to the faith from which he had himself asserted they sprang and to which they bore witness, and he must have seen that there was no faith at all, only a clutch of pure and mindless techniques in place of a common set of assumptions about the goodness and purpose of human existence, and that his beloved country was not a noble Idea but a savage giant of a child, Browning's Caliban randomly smashing crabs on Setebos." Lear, Graf concludes, "had left to him only the gift of command. He must have thought that it was time for soldiers to protect whatever they could of the City by the naked example of command until some new civilizing faith should appear among men."

Jack Lear's son, Ben, is also an idealist and "a passionate man" who is betrayed at both the collective and personal levels. After serving honorably in World War II, Ben returns to a nation reveling in a "self-indulgent mood." He is repelled by the country's loose attitude, but "he did not know to what purpose he should discipline himself." His homecoming is made even more difficult by his wife, Kathleen, the only child of a famed history professor at the University of Texas at Austin. Ben wonders "whether it had always been this way for the soldier to come home to pick up the threads of his life for which he had fought only to find that it had changed through the very act of defending it."

His wife's promiscuity, which is somehow linked in Ben's mind with his nation's promiscuity, is so dismaying to Ben that he kills her. He is not convicted of murder — Kathleen had been in bed with her Mexican lover at the time Ben shot her, and no jury in Texas in the 1940s would convict a man of killing his wife under those circumstances — but his promising military career is effectively ended. At the close of the novel, however, in the late 1960s, Ben is still searching for "'the just war,' 'the good killing,' 'the pure act of service.'" He is a mercenary fighting in Africa, or at least somewhere in the Third World: "It was not money and adventure that drove him but some kind of translation into a different quest of the love he had had for his wife who had . . . defiled it. Like a lover looking for a perfect beloved, he went about the world in search of the perfect cause for which to risk his life."

The third generation of Lears is embodied in Doniphan, Ben's son, in whom the springs of idealism have dried up and been dusted over with the bitter ashes of cynicism. Graf tells Doniphan that his father and grandfather were "heroes and nobody gives a damn and never will in this forsaken country because any instance of the heroic is an unwanted reminder that there may be greater possibilities in life than stuffing your gut and making money and screwing your wife, or, better still, someone else's wife, and amassing things for which one has no taste or use, because, by God, the heroic is a call to order, to sacrifice, to honor — the dirty words of this sullen age."

Graf's outburst occurs in a Juárez restaurant the evening after Doniphan has been decorated for bravery in Vietnam. He has also been crippled in the fighting and must walk with the aid of a cane. Doniphan's disability is a none-too-subtle symbol of the severe disadvantages under which the aspiring idealist must exist in modern America. Doniphan is confused and uncertain about his motivation in going to Vietnam. He recalls "shooting down women and children running over the bridges of the sluggish brown streams in a far land out of love of country, or freedom, or family, or honor, or some goddamned thing he could not remember anymore, which was just as well because it was not the truth since the mysterious passion that burned in his father and his father's father had never come to him at all so that he could not say he had done anything out of love of God, or country, or woman." Graf tells Doniphan: "I mean no offense when I say the serious business of your generation is to learn to live as a nation of cripples. You have less passion and therefore less meaning than your fathers and your sons will have less than you."

A Time of Soldiers is, as I have said, a remarkable book, not really a war or military novel, but a novel of ideas, a philosophical novel. It takes seriously the concept of a "warrior class and its special code of behavior," and it assumes that faith and idealism must be the driving forces in the creation of such a class. Though it is set in Texas, mostly in El Paso and Austin, and focuses on a family of Texas military men, I am not sure the book helps to define a Texas military tradition. But it does trace the experiences of a trio of Texans who, in their different ways, fought their country's wars, only to have their country reveal itself as corrupt and not worthy of their sacrifice.

A Time of Soldiers grapples with the individual responses of military men to the philosophy of war and of a professional military. Only obliquely does it comment on the rightness or wrongness of America's wars in this century — or even the corruption and moral rot that, in Graf's view, have rendered the nation incapable of waging a "good war." Certainly Doniphan takes no pride in his service in Vietnam, as his father and grandfather were proud of their participation in battle. By the 1960s Americans, even many Texans, were increasingly cynical concerning the country's foreign policy and the reasons for having 400,000 fighting men in a small nation in southeast Asia. Many were downright hostile to the idea of American military action there and, as a result, saw the United States as the blackguard villain in the drama unfolding in Vietnam — an arrogant superpower attempting to expand its empire at the expense of a small, backward country struggling for the right to determine its own destiny.

While *A Time of Soldiers* projects the high motives that have often propelled Texans into battle, its bleak ending brings to the surface the dark side of the Texas military experience. This duality apparently is inescapable. A recurring and familiar figure in twentieth-century war novels and movies is the fighting Texan. He's brave, he's mean — and sometimes he's more than a touch crazy. A writer who has exploited this stereotype to the hilt is Norman Mailer. Mailer, a card-carrying member of "the New York literary establishment," might plausibly be considered an honorary Texan — even though he usually does not have very flattering things to say about Texas and Texans.

During World War II, Mailer served in the 112th Armored Cavalry Regiment, which entered the war as a Texas National Guard unit. Most of Mailer's comrades in arms were Texans. After the war Mailer's sister recalled:

Norman would occasionally mention the men he was overseas with — which ones drank, which ones would fight, how they treated the . . . Jewish boys. He puts on his Texas accent now, but he didn't have it before he went in the army, and when he came back something was lost. A certain kindness, his softness. Because those Texas men were wild. . . . [The] army will never be out of his system. It scarred him.[7]

Mailer's portrait of the typical Texan gone to war is Sergeant Sam Croft in *The Naked and the Dead* (1948), a novel set in the South Pacific in the waning days of World War II. Croft is a fighting machine. Brown, one of Croft's fellow soldiers, describes him:

Listen, he's made of iron. He's the one man I'd *never* cross. He's probably the best platoon sergeant in the army and the meanest. He just doesn't have any nerves. . . . Out of all the old guys in recon, there ain't one of us whose nerves ain't shot. . . . But Croft—I tell you Croft loves combat, he *loves* it. There ain't a worse man you could be under or a better one, depending on how you look at it. We lost eleven guys out of seventeen in the platoon, counting the Lieutenant we had then, some of the best guys in the world and the rest of us weren't good for anything for a week, but Croft asked for a patrol the next day.

Croft is portrayed as a sadistic authoritarian who derives satisfaction and a considerable personal magnetism from his capabilities as a killer. He is an expert at what he is supposed to do—disposing of the enemy—but clearly he takes too much pleasure in fulfilling that role: "but why *is* Croft that way? Oh, there are answers. He is that way because of the corruption-of-the-society. He is that way because the devil has claimed him for one of his own. It is because he is a Texan; it is because he has renounced God. . . . He was born that way."

Croft is prejudiced and creates division in the ranks by criticizing and irritating the Jewish soldiers in his outfit as well as the Mexican American, Martinez—who, incidentally, is also a Texan since he comes from the barrio in San Antonio. In one episode, Croft indirectly causes the death of Roth (a Jew), who suffers a fatal fall as the men traverse a mountain trail. Roth's fear of Croft makes him attempt a jump across a gap in the trail, a jump Roth knows he cannot accomplish. Roth is aware that Croft will be furious if the men do not quickly leap across the ravine and continue toward their destination without delay. Roth's death upsets other men in the platoon, but Croft is unconcerned about anything except completing the mission at hand.

Thus Croft is shown to be merely an instrument of the officers, particularly the mean-spirited General Cummings. In Mailer's political morality, Croft is evil since he uses fascist methods to implement the general's fascist program. A more generous view of Croft might see him as, whether good or bad, a *Texan* — not really a military man at all, but an extreme individualist; a gunslinger; not a military strategist, but a relentless frontiersman who leads by example.

In any event, *The Naked and the Dead* was hardly Mailer's last word on the Texan at war. In 1967, at the height of United States involvement in southeast Asia, Mailer published a novel titled *Why Are We in Vietnam?* The author attempts to answer the title's question by telling the story of a group of Texans who are in Alaska on a bear hunt. The three main characters are Rusty Jethroe, a wealthy corporation executive from Dallas; Rusty's sixteen-year-old son, D. J.; and D. J.'s friend Tex Hyde. Present time in the novel is actually two years after the bear hunt, and the setting is a dinner party in north Dallas in honor of D. J. and Tex, who are about to depart for military service in Vietnam. Most of the narrative is a kind of stream-of-consciousness recollection by D. J., interspersed between the various courses of the banquet, of the events of the hunt two summers back.

Rusty's reason for participating in the hunt is, simply, to confirm his manhood. Rusty is a Texan (mythical mode) nonpareil: "His cells are filled with the biological inheritance and trait transmissions of his ancestors, all such rawhide, cactus hearts, eagle eggs, and coyote." He is so competitive that once, in a game of one-on-one football with his son D. J., he becomes "insane . . . with frustration," lunges at D. J., and bites him on the neck, bringing forth a spurt of blood. In Alaska, Rusty declares, "I want to behold Bruin right in his pig red eye so I'll never have to be scared again, not until I got to face The Big Man."

For D. J., the hunt is of even more significance. In a way Mailer's *Why Are We in Vietnam?* is a kind of mean parody of William Faulkner's great short novel *The Bear,* which is also about a bear hunt. Traditionally, the hunt has been a coming-of-age ritual by means of which a boy meets in a mystically charged encounter a legendary animal, and as a result of his experience he becomes a man. Further, the hunt, because it excludes women, is ordinarily an exercise in what pop anthropologists call "male bonding." To D. J., then, the bear hunt is a means of initiation into adulthood.

Tex Hyde does not require initiation, since he was born with "that mean glint in the eye for which Texans are justly proud and famous." The party of Texans, and particularly D. J., is instructed in the rules of the hunt by the world-famous guide and hunter, Big Luke Fellinka, who is described simply as "a *man!*" Tex and D. J. each bag a "grizzer" fairly early in the hunt, but it is not until they leave behind their guns and supplies and trek into the mountains to face the grizzly unprotected that their mystical revelation occurs. In the wilderness there is a brief instant of sexual attraction that passes between them, an impulse they quickly reject. Instead, they share an epiphany, a vision of God, who turns out to be "a beast, not a man, and God said, 'Go out and kill—fulfill my will, go and kill!'" From that moment they become "twins, never to be near as lovers again, but killer brothers, owned by something, prince of darkness, lord of light, they did not know."

Some of the surface parallels of the bear hunt with the then-current Vietnam War are fairly obvious. The Texans in the hoodoo land of Alaska are like invaders from an alien culture—like, you guessed it, Americans in Vietnam. The expedition, which includes, in addition to the three main characters, several of Rusty Jedhoe's corporate underlings, carries a veritable arsenal of sophisticated weaponry, which is described in lengthy and loving detail. The "grizzers" are hunted from a helicopter—a favorite mode of transportation for American troops in Vietnam. After a couple of days of hunting, the body count is impressive: "twenty-five assorted grizzly, moose, ram, goat and caribou." There is no way the hunters can use all the meat, but the slaughter continues apace.

The point is, of course, that it is an *attitude,* a mind-set, that motivates Americans to invade places like Alaska and Vietnam. At novel's end, Tex and D. J. are eager "to see the wizard in Vietnam." Says D. J.: "Vietnam, hot damn." Mailer seems to be saying that America's frustrated sexuality—both hetero and homo—crystallizes in a frenzied desire to impose our will on others, to dominate and conquer, that we force feed the rest of world as foreign policy. And, as usual, the Texan is seen as the super-American—possessing typically American traits in exaggerated form. The Texans in Mailer's novel are examples of a type—"the ugly Texan," Don Graham has called him[8]—that was pervasive in American popular culture in the years following the Kennedy assassination in Dallas and during Lyndon Johnson's increasingly controversial escalation of the war in Vietnam. For Mailer, the inevitable equation is that "the kink which resides in the heart of the Lone Star" is what got the United States into Vietnam. Whether or not there is any truth in such an explanation (Mailer's version today seems fatally flawed by 1960s simple-mindedness), it was, and probably still is, a widely shared perception among Americans — especially American intellectuals — living outside Texas.

It appears to me we Texans have taken a bum rap in having to shoulder most of the blame for the Vietnam fiasco. We undeniably produced Lyndon Johnson, with all his weaknesses and insecurities, but not John Kennedy, who left a considerable mess in southeast Asia upon his death; nor did we suckle and nurture Ronald Reagan whose commitment to military build-up in the 1980s bordered on the fanatical; but then we do have to take at least partial responsibility for George Bush, who gave us a one-hundred-hour war in the desert that, nearly a decade after its successful termination, already recedes from memory. It seems fair to say, by all accounts, that the Texas military tradition is a two-edged sword. Texans' readiness to fight for their rights and beliefs can result in heroism, the subject of much Texas military lore, or, in the cases of the Texas Rangers during the Mexican War and (if we may infer) Tex and D. J. in Vietnam, in unbridled aggression and mindless violence. As is true of most things in life, the Texans' famed fighting abilities are a mixed blessing. At worst, they have put us — and, if we are to believe Norman Mailer and others, the rest of the world — in some awkward and dangerous situations. At best, they are instruments by which tyranny and oppression are resisted in the name of honor and individual freedom. Literature, as a mirror of a people's culture, reflects these two sides of the Texas military experience with provocative fidelity.

CHAPTER 8

A Prairie Homestead

Texas Writers and the Family Romance

*Country music singers have always been a real close family
But lately some of my kin folk have
disowned a few others than me.*

— HANK WILLIAMS JR., *"Family Tradition"*

The house of literature on the Texas plains is not a stately mansion, nor does it have many rooms. It is a compact, serviceable structure built in the 1920s. At most, three generations of writers have resided there, finding shelter from the chill winds of public indifference and even hostility. In thinking about Texas writing, one immediately seizes upon the analogy of the family. Texas writers are a close-knit family—in some ways, a shockingly close-knit family. Everybody knows everybody else—or at least everybody knows *about* everybody else. For more than half a century the Texas Institute of Letters has fostered an in-group psychology among the state's literary community—a kind of us-against-them defiance of the pragmatic, commonsensical values of traditional Texas culture. When challenged by the philistinism and know-nothingism that surround them, Texas writers tend to close ranks in furtherance of a common cause. In less trying times, however, the bickering and squabbling within the household are often fierce.

Without question, the big daddy of the family at the moment is Larry McMurtry. From the beginning McMurtry's public relations with his fellow Texas writers, however cordial in private, have been peculiar. McMurtry's first novel, *Horseman, Pass By,* published in 1961 when he was twenty-five years of age, was awarded the Texas Institute of Letters' annual prize for fiction. The young author responded to the award by publicly trashing the TIL as a provincial, third-rate collection of writers, critics, and assorted literary hangers-on. That rampage won McMurtry the sobriquet enfant terrible, a phrase that has been used far too often over the last thirty years to suggest the contemptuous sneer that became the trademark of the writer's public persona. (I promise not to use it again since it is an egregious cliché, and anyway McMurtry is now well past the *enfant* stage.) At periodic intervals since 1961 McMurtry has launched what James Ward Lee labels his "decadal diatribes" against the shabby state of Texas writing.[1] In fact, the last of these diatribes appeared in the early 1980s, so with the passing of every day, we are overdue for another one; somehow, I doubt there will ever be another.

Many have been appalled by McMurtry's denigration of the literature of his home state; others applaud him for his sincerity and high standards. However correct McMurtry's judgments may or may not have been in, say, his controversial 1981 essay, "Ever a Bridegroom: Reflections on the Failure of Texas Literature," I see his condemnations of Texas writing as a combination of insecurity and ambition masquerading as honesty and plain-speaking. Now let me concede right off that, while I cannot say much in favor of insecurity, there is nothing inherently wrong with ambition. Writers and artists must possess considerable ambition — even to the point of egotism — in order to accomplish anything worthwhile. Their creative energies, in most cases, are fueled by competition. Surely the careers of, for example, Ernest Hemingway and Norman Mailer teach us this simple but enduring lesson. And while McMurtry's manners have been perhaps slightly better than those of Hemingway or of Mailer, his aggressiveness and combativeness, at least in print, have been no less keen. Dare we call him the Tonya Harding of Texas letters?

I believe McMurtry's behavior may be explained, in large measure, by what Professor Harold Bloom of Yale University has famously called "the anxiety of influence." Bloom contends that "strong poets" misread "one another, so as to clear imaginative space for themselves."[2] (Bloom uses the term *poet*, incidentally, in the old-fashioned sense, meaning any writer; he appears also to include literary critics in this catchall category, definitely a postmodern aberration.) As part of his theory Bloom invokes the Freudian concept of the "family romance," involving generational conflict, symbolic patricide and matricide, and sibling rivalry.

Over the years there have indeed been some strange goings-on in the little house of literature on the Texas prairie. Let's start with generational conflict and patricide. Whatever one thinks of J. Frank Dobie as a man and writer, he was undeniably the father of Texas literature. In the 1920s, before Dobie began to publish the results of his folklore-collecting forays through Mexico and the American Southwest, there was precious little Texas writing that could justifiably be called literature. Dobie changed all that in significant ways. His main importance lay in the fact that he was a pioneer, a trailblazer. He taught Texans and Southwesterners how to succeed at the culture game.

By "succeed," I mean making money. In the 1920s Dobie frequently sold articles to *Country Gentleman,* the *Saturday Evening Post,* and other mass-circulation, high-paying periodicals. From the 1930s until well after his death in 1964, the Boston publishing house of Little, Brown and Company brought out his books with clockwork regularity and to good sales. By the early 1930s, according to his biographer Lon Tinkle, Dobie was making considerably more money from writing than from teaching in the English Department of the University of Texas at Austin.[3] Dobie often turned over his classes to others, to graduate students and sometimes to his wife, Bertha. By 1947 he was so bored with teaching that he more or less provoked the notorious controversy that resulted in his dismissal from the university. In short, he no longer needed teaching as an economic crutch; he had attracted a large reading audience, national in scope, and as a man always careful with a dollar, he enjoyed financial security in his middle and old age.

As I said, Dobie set the example. Billy Lee Brammer, whose polished and sophisticated fiction could scarcely be different from Dobie's style and subjects, once remarked that when he was growing up in the Oak Cliff section of Dallas in the 1940s, reading Dobie "made [me] realize . . . that the Texas experience . . . could be transformed into literature."[4] McMurtry claims not to have read Dobie — or Dobie's friends and colleagues Walter Prescott Webb and Roy Bedichek — until he was past thirty. Nevertheless, as a young writer, he felt them as "Presences." "The writer my age," McMurtry ruminated in an essay published in 1968, "who wishes to write about this state must relate himself one way or the other to the tradition they fostered, whether he reads the three men or not."[5] McMurtry then proceeded to flay the Holy Old-timers unmercifully. His last word on Dobie to date was penned in 1981: "Dobie's twenty-odd books," McMurtry wrote with serene confidence, "are a congealed mass of virtually undifferentiated anecdotage: endlessly repetitious, thematically empty, structureless, and carelessly written."[6] Perhaps McMurtry should try reading some of his own recent books. So much, in any event, for Papa Frank.

If J. Frank Dobie was the father of Texas literature who established one paradigm for budding Texas writers to follow — that is, stay home and till one's own literary and cultural soil — Katherine Anne Porter was, I submit, the matriarch of Texas letters. Porter's life and career provide yet another paradigm for Texans who wish to succeed in the literary arena. She decamped from Texas early, in her twenties, and remained a voluntary exile for the rest of her life; many Texas writers and intellectuals, needless to say, have followed in her footsteps. In the drama (some might say melodrama) of her life that she assiduously constructed, Porter cast herself as the lonely but dedicated artist. She threw in with the so-called Modernists, who believed Art (with a capital *A*) was a substitute for religion. She once wrote that art is "The substance of faith and the only reality." That is about as succinct a statement of the Modernists' credo as one is likely to find.

Though she renounced her Texas citizenship as a young woman, Porter was apparently concerned about her place in the literary history of her native state. She told an interviewer in the 1950s, "I am the first and only serious writer that Texas has produced." Later, in 1975, she would claim, "I happen to be the first native of Texas in its whole history to be a professional writer."[7] Actually Porter made her living more from her reputation among intellectuals than from her writing. The textbook I use to teach American literature to college sophomores contains the following capsule summation of Porter's significance as an American writer:

> The reputation of Katherine Anne Porter in contemporary literature probably has no parallel. All her published fiction comprises but one novel, five novelettes, and three volumes of short stories. She never had a popular following; yet nearly all discriminating readers are acquainted with her work; and she exercised a considerable influence on many serious younger writers.[8]

Porter seems to have decided early on to target a tiny but highly influential reading audience: the educated elite. In the 1920s and 1930s, many of her stories appeared in *Century* magazine, edited by scholar-critic Carl Van Doren; she also published fiction in small experimental journals such as *transition* (with a lower-case *t*) for little or no pay. She cozied up to and made friends with powerful New Critics such as Robert Penn Warren and Cleanth Brooks, who found her symbol-laden tales and burnished prose style congenial to their mode of literary criticism. In the long run Porter's campaign of self-promotion was highly successful—among the American literati, if not among Texans.

One of the more scandalous chapters in the checkered history of the Texas Institute of Letters occurred in 1940, when the group gave its annual award to Dobie's *Apache Gold and Yaqui Silver* rather than to Porter's masterful *Pale Horse, Pale Rider,* a collection of three of her short novels. Porter was, justifiably, enraged by the decision. From today's perspective, such a choice is inconceivable. But if we attempt to put ourselves in the members' positions back in 1939, it is somewhat easier to understand. Dobie was making a great deal of money from his writing and had attracted a large national readership; Porter subsisted primarily on grants from foundations, and her published works at that point were far from best-sellers. Thus the TIL decision was not just a matter of rewarding a good old local boy and snubbing an uppity woman who had abandoned Texas two decades earlier, but also had to do with perceived clout on the national literary scene. Of course, the perception was disastrously flawed, but that, in a way, is beside the point.

In any event, Porter had her revenge. By the time of her death in 1980, her stories were routinely included in anthologies of American literature, introducing her name and her writings to new generations of American readers, while nobody outside Texas—and fewer and fewer inside Texas— had ever heard of J. Frank Dobie. I might add, as a kind of footnote, that the new, much-discussed anthology of American writing published by the D.C. Heath company, which purports to significantly revise and enlarge the canon of American literature, particularly with regard to the inclusion of more women and minority authors, reprints three of Porter's stories, which in number of pages equals the space allotted to the work of Ernest Hemingway and William Faulkner combined.

And what does Larry McMurtry have to say about Porter's fiction? Reading through the *Collected Stories,* he adjudges, "one is forced to think that all but the best of her work—perhaps half a dozen stories—is . . . the work of a half-talent." And there's more: "Gertrude Stein, whom Miss Porter did not like, once made a famous remark about . . . Oakland, California. There was no there there, she said. I feel very much the same way about the fiction of Katherine Anne Porter. The plumage is beautiful, but plumage, after all, is only feathers." So much for KAP. The anxiety of influence indeed! When the competitive juices are flowing, generosity does not come easily. Speaking personally, I would not swap Katherine Anne Porter's compact and brilliant "Noon Wine" for a dozen of McMurtry's bloated, meandering chronicles, but I do understand and appreciate the psychological imperative at work here: that, as Harold Bloom puts it, the writer must clear "imaginative space" for himself by killing off the symbolic father and mother.

What about siblings in this "family romance"? Were there brothers and sisters — fellow Texas writers — who posed a threat to the up-and-coming champ? A couple of specific examples must illustrate the point. In 1961, when McMurtry's first novel, *Horseman, Pass By,* was published, the Dobie-Webb-Bedichek era was rapidly coming to a close. Texas writing was changing shape, but the new outlines were still fuzzy. Another first novel by a Texas writer also appeared in 1961: *The Gay Place,* by Billy Lee Brammer (in truth it was published under the more respectable and thoroughly bogus name *William* Brammer). Brammer was a politico-turned-journalist-turned-novelist. He had been an aide to Lyndon Johnson when Johnson was Senate Majority Leader in the 1950s; he had lived in Washington and was an old hand in the Austin political arena as well.

The TIL awarded its prize for the best Texas novel of 1961, as noted earlier, to *Horseman* rather than to *The Gay Place.* (Gossip has it that John Graves, McMurtry's friend and mentor and at the time his English Department colleague at Texas Christian University in Fort Worth, had more than a little to do with the choice.) In many ways, however, in the early 1960s Brammer seemed a much more promising writer than did McMurtry — especially to readers and critics living outside Texas. Brammer had a large fund of practical information about modern life that McMurtry, a young man with West Texas sand still in his boots, lacked. Brammer's novel possesses a surface sheen, an elegance that makes McMurtry's early efforts appear gawky at best; it is worldly and city wise and politically hip — something definitely new in Texas writing. *The Gay Place* was a succès d'estime — that is, it didn't sell very many copies, but the critics loved it and hailed Brammer as a strong new voice in American letters.

In one of his essays from *In a Narrow Grave,* McMurtry says that he and Brammer were briefly roommates in 1963, when both were living in Austin. McMurtry comments, rather peevishly, that at the time Brammer was "the local culture hero."[9] The implication is that McMurtry was almost totally ignored by the groupies who hammered incessantly at Brammer's door. (The snub may account, in part at least, for McMurtry's oft-expressed dislike for Austin.) But Brammer, after *The Gay Place,* did not complete another book. He was given a large advance by a New York publisher to write a biography of Lyndon Johnson, to be titled "The Big Pumpkin," but the project never came to fruition. Moreover, he is credited with applying a steady hand at the helm when *Texas Monthly* hurtled from the launching pad in the early 1970s. But he could never muster the sustained energy and focus to finish another manuscript. As the pleasures of the Austin scene took their toll, as drugs and apathy clouded his existence, as his two marriages failed and his personal life continued its downward spiral, Brammer found the wellspring of his imagination clogged and his typewriter silent. He died in 1978, at age forty-eight, of a drug overdose. In 1978 Larry McMurtry turned forty-two, published his eighth novel, and began to get his second wind as a writer. McMurtry, no flash in the pan, proved that patience and stamina, in literature as in other areas of life, usually win out in the long haul over flash and glitter.

Other potential rivals — "brothers and sisters," as it were — from McMurtry's generation of Texas writers might well be cited. I am thinking, for instance, of Larry L. King. King, like Brammer, started as a politician (he was an assistant to a West Texas congressman in the 1950s) and turned to free-lance journalism in the mid-1960s. He got off to an excellent start: as part of a stable of talented writers, mostly Southerners, that sometime-Texan Willie Morris assembled at *Harper's* magazine. Eventually, though, King found it necessary to move on to more remunerative literary occupations. Over the last thirty years he has, by his own admission, made three-quarters of a fortune selling some fanciful versions of the Texas myth to gullible Yankees.[10]

Still, he never succeeded in transforming his name, as McMurtry has managed to do, into a household word. For most people, *Larry King* conjures up images of a TV talk show host rather than thoughts of a noted author and playwright. Moreover, it is somewhat shocking to survey the corpus of King's work and to note how slight and evanescent it is: a less-than-mediocre novel called *The One-Eyed Man;* a few plays, the best-known of which is *The Best Little Whorehouse in Texas* (a concoction McMurtry rightly compares with "cotton candy"); and a handful of magazine pieces, the most memorable of which is "The Old Man," a moving account of the writer's relationship with his father. This is, in its own way, almost as minuscule a quantitative yield as Katherine Anne Porter's collected works.

No, Larry McMurtry is the undisputed king of literary Texas. To employ a gunfighter analogy (and to mix metaphors), he is the top gun in town. His grand strategy, his dogged determination have paid off. He has made more money, in real dollars, than J. Frank Dobie ever dreamed of making. Beginning in the mid-1980s, there were lucrative contracts with book clubs and publishers, screenwriting deals, movie and TV adaptations of several of his tales. A signal that McMurtry had become a genuine, certified gold mine was the announcement, in 1985, that Irving "Swifty" Lazar had become his agent. Furthermore, McMurtry has charmed the pants off the New York literary establishment, even more successfully than did Katherine Anne Porter in the 1920s and 1930s. In early 1986 his epic *Lonesome Dove* won a Pulitzer Prize in fiction (the only other Texas writer to win a Pulitzer in fiction was Porter for her *Collected Stories* in 1966). McMurtry's works were subsequently reviewed in the *New York Review of Books,* the high church of American intellectuals; the review was accompanied by a much-coveted David Levine caricature. In 1989 McMurtry began a two-year term as president of American PEN, acronym for "Poets, Essayists, and Novelists," an international association of writers whose purpose is to combat censorship. He succeeded Susan Sontag in that post; before Sontag, Norman Mailer had been president. McMurtry has outlasted and outstripped and outwritten the Billy Lee Brammers and Larry L. Kings of this world, becoming in the process a force in national and international literary matters.

As far as the Texas literary scene is concerned, the late 1980s and early 1990s witnessed the emergence of a new, looser, even jovial Larry McMurtry. No more aloofness, no more snide disdain. Secure at last in his impregnable position, McMurtry in the 1980s stopped saying those nasty things about the Texas Institute of Letters and became an active member of the organization, even serving a term as president. Assuming the role of smiling, benevolent family elder, he began to give younger Texas writers avuncular pats on the head instead of tire-irons to the kneecaps. Today, as he serenely scans the horizon, there are no challengers in sight, no apparent threats to his hegemony. He can relax for the moment, his purpose fulfilled. But the ground shifts beneath one's feet. As we all know — at least those of us who still watch old cowboy movies know — there's always a young gun out there somewhere, eager to test his fast draw and itchy trigger finger. Perhaps someday, at some point in the future, we will think of Larry McMurtry as we currently think of J. Frank Dobie, as a man whose once-impressive reputation was shot full of holes and reduced to rubble by a spiritual offspring whose eyes were on the prize.

CHAPTER 9

Doing Without

Larry McMurtry's Thalia Trilogy

All of them wanted more and seemed to end up with less;
they wanted excitement and ended up stomped by a bull or
smashed against a highway . . . whatever it was they wanted,
that was what they ended up doing without.

— LARRY MCMURTRY, *Horseman, Pass By*

In the early summer of 1961, when Larry McMurtry's first novel, *Horseman,*
Pass By, was published, I was preparing to enter Texas Christian University
in Fort Worth as a graduate student in English. Since I had recently begun
to develop an interest in the literature of Texas and the American Southwest, I rushed out and bought a copy as soon as it went on sale. The hard-
back, as I recall, sold for $3.95. I could not resist the story of the narrator,
a young man — not a whole lot younger than myself at the time I first read
the book — growing up in the 1950s on a West Texas ranch, as I had grown
up on a farm near Fort Worth. I did not find the book a tale of charming
local color, as I suspected I might, but a work very grim and very different
from most of the Texas fiction I had read to that point.

As it happened, McMurtry was an instructor of English at TCU during
the academic year 1961–62. I was introduced to him once or twice but cannot say we formed even a superficial acquaintance. His manner seemed
aloof and distant; it may have been, as some were quick to assert, the result
of shyness, but it did not invite idle chitchat, at least not from strangers.
According to some students in his classes that I questioned, he was engaging enough in the classroom, apparently wanting to talk mostly about
movies, even in the surveys of British literature he was assigned to teach.
During the year, needless to say, I heard a good deal of gossip about the

young instructor from students and faculty alike. (None of the gossip, I hasten to add, was salacious.)

There was the story, for example — a story that has now become firmly embedded in Texas literary folklore — of Mabel Major, a senior professor of English at TCU and a pioneer scholar of southwestern literature, checking out the library's copy of *Horseman, Pass By* on faculty loan and refusing to return it. "TCU students," Major is supposed to have huffed, "ought not be exposed to such trash." I cannot personally vouch for the truth of this story, but I trusted — and trust — the source from which I heard it.

Another tale that made the rounds also had to do with McMurtry and the library. One weekday evening, it was said, McMurtry returned to Fort Worth from Archer County, after having hauled a pickup load of hay to his father's ranch. Before going home, he stopped at the college library, where a librarian found him, clad in soiled blue jeans and a tattered leather jacket, sitting on the floor between shelves, reading. The librarian booted him out of the building because of improper attire — and, no doubt, insufficient respect for library decorum. Remember, this was 1961.

I heard other stories as well, but will spare the reader further — possibly apocryphal, certainly self-indulgent — recollections. It is a fact that McMurtry left TCU for Rice University in Houston after a single, rather bumpy year on its faculty. Perhaps the relevant point to be made here is that, even though in 1961–62 he was twenty-five years of age and had published only one book, the legend of Larry McMurtry was already building a head of steam. That legend has always, it seems to me, been surrounded by an aura of mystery. McMurtry from the beginning has been not anti-social but a very private person.

Jay Milner's *Confessions of a Maddog* (1998) is a highly diverting memoir of literary goings-on in Texas in the 1960s and early 1970s. Milner was a minor literary figure of the time and a prominent member of a troop of merry pranksters — comprising the likes of Billy Lee Brammer, Edwin "Bud" Shrake, Gary "Jap" Cartwright, Larry L. King, Dan Jenkins, and others — who headquartered in Dallas and Austin. McMurtry, who lived in Texas (and for a while in Austin) until 1969, when he removed himself to Washington, D.C., was considered one of the gang. Yet the interesting thing is that, as Milner tells it, he was almost never around. He checked in now and then from Archer City or from the road, but rarely attended the endless parties at which the esteemed authors passed their nights and days.[1]

Of the millions of words McMurtry has written during his long career, few reveal (at least not directly) anything of the man himself. As is true of all popular writers who try to protect some part of their privacy, the effort only whets the public's appetite for information. If verifiable information is not available, questionable information will do. And even in 1961, when he first bobbed into my field of vision, it was widely believed that McMurtry was a young man to be reckoned with on the Texas—and, perhaps, national—literary scene. Thus the curiosity about Larry McMurtry the human being was expressed by readers and commentators early and often.

I hope the preceding comments sufficiently establish my bona fides as a longtime McMurtry watcher, so that I may offer a few observations (some of them grounded in inferences and guesses) on his career as a writer. To begin, I think the career may be divided into three—or, unfortunately, four—fairly distinct periods. The first, from the late 1950s to the late 1960s, encompassed the composition and publication of his first three novels, plus the 1968 essay collection *In a Narrow Grave: Essays on Texas*. McMurtry himself has said that 1968 is a clear line of demarcation in his life and literature: "*In a Narrow Grave* was my formal farewell to writing about the country."[2] Though *Lonesome Dove* (1985) and several other later works would seem to invalidate this statement, it was no doubt, in 1981, sincerely offered.

The second stage of McMurtry's career began in the late 1960s, when the writer moved to Washington, D.C. This was the period when he consciously turned to writing about city life: in the 1970s Houston, Hollywood, and Washington served as settings for McMurtry novels. For whatever reason—many claimed it was because he had abandoned his "true" subject—McMurtry's talents as a writer seemed all through this decade to dwindle book by book. In the early 1980s the author himself was glum about the quality of his accomplishment. "It took me," he said at the time, "until around 1972 to write a book that an intelligent reader might want to read twice, and by 1976 I had once again lost the knack."[3] Something that was overlooked in the controversy surrounding McMurtry's 1981 essay "Ever a Bridegroom: Reflections on the Failure of Texas Literature" is that he appeared, if one reads between the lines, even more convinced of his own "failure" than that of his fellow Texas writers.

Oddly, the breakthrough book—the one that sent his career hurtling to the pinnacle of the mid- to late 1980s, the third and culminating phase—was *The Desert Rose* (1983). The story of an aging Las Vegas showgirl, *The Desert Rose* is, to put it charitably, a mediocre novel; for McMurtry, however, it was obviously an important work. He has claimed the novel "was written in three weeks."[4] Writing the book in such a burst seems to have unclogged the pipeline, so to speak—to have allowed him to regain the knack he thought he had lost. *Lonesome Dove* and the economic and other rewards that flowed from it quickly followed. '

The 1990s have proved, sadly, the epilogue of a notable career. Even as McMurtry has reaped millions of dollars in advance money from book contracts, the quality of his work has declined alarmingly. His modus operandi now seems to be to write sequels and prequels to his earlier novels — the device worked reasonably well in *Texasville* (1987), a sequel to *The Last Picture Show,* but has produced mostly embarrassing hackwork in subsequent novels. Moreover, McMurtry in a couple of his recent books has taken on a collaborator, Diana Ossana. This move has failed to produce a noticeable improvement in the fiction. Book review outlets that once faithfully gave major notice to anything McMurtry published have ignored several of his recent books.

I think it fair to say that the jury is still out on the dimensions of McMurtry's achievement. For one thing he is still writing and publishing, and while another blossoming of his talents — as occurred in the 1980s — seems unlikely, it is not impossible.[5] It is easy (and understandable) enough to become exasperated by the author's current output. But one must keep in mind that many writers — I am thinking, for example, of Charles Dickens and Mark Twain — turned out huge quantities of junk during their careers and yet are remembered today primarily for the best they produced, not the worst. It is entirely plausible that posterity will treat McMurtry kindly. And one of the reasons it will do so is the work he did in the first phase of his career.

McMurtry's publicly expressed attitude toward this early phase remains odd. For nearly three decades he has continued to make statements about the early novels — *Horseman, Pass By* (1961), *Leaving Cheyenne* (1963), and *The Last Picture Show* (1966), the so-called Thalia trilogy — that suggest he would gladly burn, if possible, all existing copies of them. He consistently denigrates the books. For instance, as noted earlier, he has dismissed his first novel as "a piece of juvenilia." Of Molly Taylor, the much-admired heroine of *Leaving Cheyenne,* he has said that she is "a male journalist's fantasy."[6] Other expressions of the author's contempt for the books could easily be assembled.

There are probably some understandable reasons why McMurtry feels this way about his early books. First, many readers preferred — at least up to the publication of *Lonesome Dove* in 1985 — *Horseman, Pass By* and *Leaving Cheyenne* over any of the writer's subsequent novels. McMurtry has frequently complained of this (in his view) unreasonable preference. Despite his complaints many of us staunchly maintained over the years an admiration for his first two novels. We failed to appreciate the psychological principle that was the subtext of McMurtry's disdainful comments: few writers can continue to struggle with their craft if they become convinced their powers are diminishing rather than growing. In praising *Horseman, Pass By* and *Leaving Cheyenne,* we were telling McMurtry his best work was behind him, a judgment he rightly disputed.

Second, considerable evidence suggests that getting the early novels published caused the young writer a great deal of pain. In the case of *Horseman, Pass By,* there was, by his own admission, "editorial conflict over the book."[7] According to Charles D. Peavy, who has examined relevant correspondence and papers housed in the University of Houston library, the manuscript was rewritten at least five times. Style was revamped; dramatic scenes — such as a devastating "cyclone" — were deleted; and point of view was changed from third person to first.[8] The author eventually agreed to most editorial demands because he wanted the novel to be published, but he never came to believe in the rightness of the changes. Thus McMurtry's oft-expressed dislike for *Horseman, Pass By.*

It seems to me beyond question that *Horseman, Pass By* is McMurtry's tightest, most structurally sturdy narrative. I think all those revisions and rewritings — and probably most of the editor's suggestions as well — made it a better book. At any rate, by 1980 McMurtry would tell interviewer Patrick Bennett that he no longer had "editorial difficulty with anyone. . . . So little that one hardly knows if the editors are reading."[9] Such neglect is a shame because *any* writer can benefit from good editorial advice, from sympathetic — and, maybe even better, unsympathetic — readings of his or her manuscripts. McMurtry especially has never been a clear-eyed judge of what is good and what not so good in his own work. He has trouble knowing when enough is enough. Even *Lonesome Dove* could have been a better novel had some courageous editor firmly insisted the author discard about three hundred manuscript pages, thus eliminating at least one superfluous subplot. In any event, the documented conflicts with editors over the first three novels no doubt make the books something less than golden in the writer's memory.

I believe the third — and perhaps most important — reason McMurtry refuses to acknowledge the worth of his early novels is that they are plainly a young man's books. All three were written when he was still in his twenties. They are obviously the products of a precocious talent, but all show a young writer's groping for a subject and an appropriate vision through which to interpret that subject. Given the age of the author at the time of their composition, they also exhibit predictable attitudes: nostalgia, sentimentality, anger, a preoccupation with the past, both family and regional.

The sophisticated McMurtry who would later hobnob with the likes of Diane Keaton and Cybill Shephard and Virginia hunt-country aristocrats was probably more than a tad embarrassed by them. They no longer — nor should they have — reflected his world view. The point is, though, the early novels exist; the author, however much he might like to do so, cannot take them back. They are works of art (flawed, to be sure) that have a life of their own. Many readers, old an young alike, still respond to their power. Instead of sneering at them, the writer would do well simply to accept them for what they are and own up to them without embarrassment.

Certainly a strong case can be made in favor of both the historical and aesthetic importance of the early novels. Historically, they played a crucial role in the evolution of Texas fiction over the last few decades. Up until 1961, when *Horseman, Pass By* appeared, Texas writing had been rather reticent and genteel in its treatment of what most Texans considered unsuitable subjects. Billy Lee Brammer's *The Gay Place* was also published in 1961. Together McMurtry and Brammer dragged Texas literature, kicking and screaming, into the twentieth century. In language, subject matter, and thematic concerns, their novels are, for better or worse, thoroughly modern.

McMurtry, the boy wonder of Texas letters, and Brammer, the experienced journalist-politician, seemed to delight in shocking readers by telling the raw, unvarnished truth. They told us, for instance, what life in 1950s Texas had *really* been like. Between them they covered the demographic spectrum: from Brammer's jaded politicos and urban cosmopolites to McMurtry's West Texas swains and rural bumpkins. (When, as in *The Last Picture Show,* Thalia teenagers see Wichita Falls teenagers as the ultimate in worldliness and sophistication, we are clearly in the presence of serious social deprivation.)

Both McMurtry and Brammer brought news previous reports on life in Texas had usually left out: specifically that s-e-x was everywhere — city, small town, ranch. Many were horrified. No doubt they were mostly horrified at seeing the message boldly proclaimed on the printed page. For example, there is the story (told by Al Reinert in his introduction to the Texas Monthly Press edition of *The Gay Place*) of Lyndon B. Johnson's admonishing his one-time friend and aide, "Billy Lee, I tried to read your book but didn't get past the first ten pages because of all the dirty words."[10]

Mabel Major, if gossip is to be believed, was aghast at what she read in the pages of McMurtry's first novel.

J. Frank Dobie's reactions to McMurtry's and Brammer's novels are perhaps the best barometer as to how much of a threat to the Texas literary establishment the upstarts represented. In 1961 Dobie was nearing the close of a long reign as Texas's unofficial literary arbiter. (He died in 1964.) He owned copies of both novels and, according to Don Graham who has inspected them, peppered their pages with decidedly hostile annotations.[11] Apparently Dobie was offended by the language of the books and by their frank descriptions of the characters' sexual escapades. He no doubt believed that McMurtry, in particular, was impinging on his turf—ranching and its attendant way of life. In a sense Dobie was probably justified in his anxiety: after 1961 Texas writing has never been the same.

McMurtry's early novels are aesthetic as well as historical landmarks. They attain a level of artistry few previous works of Texas literature can match. While far from flawless, they are alive; they emanate passions the author undoubtedly experienced as he composed them: nostalgia, longing for an irrecoverable past, and, in *The Last Picture Show* anyway, bitterness and contempt. Since they were written by a young man, they feature, for the most part, young men as major characters. In fact, it is a commonplace among critics of the early novels that their primary theme is the initiation of those young men into adulthood. Peavy asserts, as an example of this view, that "the most important theme of the first three novels is the male protagonists' achievement of manhood."[12]

Peavy also notes, however, that when McMurtry's "male characters have left the precarious time of adolescence and have become, at least physiologically, adult men, they often remain psychologically fixed in an extended adolescence."[13] Precisely. The curious thing about the male characters is not their successful initiation, but their *failure* to achieve maturity. At the end of *Horseman, Pass By,* Lonnie Bannon is a confused seventeen-year-old, still befuddled by the enigma of Hud; we can only guess at his future, but it is clear he has a lot of growing up to do. Sonny Crawford, in *The Last Picture Show,* arrives at an alienation so acute it might almost be described as a psychosis. Gideon Fry, in *Leaving Cheyenne,* becomes a responsible adult in the eyes of the community. But it can scarcely be said he attains emotional maturity; his "adult" years are marred by misery and unhappiness, by feelings of love and guilt he is not capable of dealing with.

The question is, Why do these characters, as well as others in McMurtry's fiction, never become adults in any meaningful sense of the term? Is it simply that in the modern world most people — most Americans anyway — never "grow up"? That could well be part of the answer, but the full answer may be more complicated. The problem with the young men in McMurtry's early novels is that they lack a secure sense of identity, any semblance of self-definition; they have no feeling of belonging, of having a "place," emotional as well as social and geographical. Most of them are essentially parentless, and live in a fluid and uncertain environment. Displacement, both actual and metaphorical, supplies a clue, I think, to the characters' stunted growth.

Robert E. Park's well-known concept of "the marginal man" may help in understanding the protagonists' emotional deficiencies. The marginal man, in Park's formulation, emerges from the breakdown of a traditional society "as a result of contact and collision with a new invading culture." He is "a man on the margin of two cultures and two societies," and he is troubled by "spiritual instability, intensified self-consciousness, restlessness, and *malaise*."[14] By adding more stress to the usual burdens of adolescence and of life generally, the condition of marginality, which has frequently been used to illuminate the situation of minority groups in America, obviously retards emotional growth rather than assists it.

It is not surprising that McMurtry's young men, trapped between two cultures — between the mythic rural past and the rootless urban future — fail to grow and mature. (Even Gid, in *Leaving Cheyenne,* is torn asunder by the conflict between his own highly traditional views on sex and marriage and the kind of unconventional, "modern" love Molly offers him.) Inevitably the author's young men, displaced and on the margins of a brave new — and scary — world, fall victim to alienation and feelings of loneliness and aloneness. Lonnie, in *Horseman, Pass By,* more than once says he is "lonesome" or that he has "the blues." The very first sentence of *The Last Picture Show* strikes the same chord: "Sometimes Sonny felt like he was the only human creature in the town." Nothing in Sonny's subsequent experiences, not even his affair with Ruth Popper, alleviates his loneliness; in fact, in the end he comes to the full realization of "how hard it was to get from day to day if one felt hopeless."

The most pervasive and crippling emotion the characters from the early novels must come to terms with is, as several critics have remarked, a sense of loss. At one point in *Horseman, Pass By,* Lonnie tells Halmea, "Things used to be better around here. . . . I feel like I want something back." Halmea retorts, "You mighty young to be wantin' things back." Later, Lonnie, on discovering his grandfather is dead, says, "I needed him," and he asks Hud, "what will I do?" Hud's reply: "You'll do without like the rest of us." Hud's flip response conceals a perception of the world of the early novels that is of great importance: it is one of the modern individual's major tasks, the novels imply, to learn to do without that which has been lost.

But what, aside from unfulfilled personal desires, has been lost? What has been left behind? For many of the characters in McMurtry's early fiction, a stunning loss has been the frontier—or at least the living myth of the frontier and the freedom, openness, and opportunity the land had supposedly promised the pioneers who settled West Texas. "All through my youth," McMurtry once recalled, "I listened to stories about an earlier, purer, a more golden and more legendary Texas that I had been born too late to see."[15] As a young writer, conditioned by the tales of elder kinsmen, he embodied his nostalgia in the cowboys and frontiersmen—particularly old ones—who people the early fiction: Homer Bannon in *Horseman, Pass By*, Adam Fry in *Leaving Cheyenne*, Sam the Lion in *The Last Picture Show*, sympathetic characters possessing all the mythic virtues of the frontier.

In the early novels the land is still there, as are a few of the men of stature and integrity it shaped. However, living on the land, as *Horseman, Pass By* suggests, is an increasingly implausible alternative. At novel's end Lonnie recognizes the inevitability of his fate and leaves, the reader assumes, to pursue his future in cities. Furthermore, by the 1950s frontier freedom had given way to the constrictions of a rudimentary yet suffocating society that has superimposed on the wild country a set of rigidly conformist values and mores. The people in McMurtry's early fiction often suffer from a feeling of living in a lesser time, an age in which the frontier and its values have been betrayed, even perverted. *The Last Picture Show*, in particular, projects a wickedly damning critique of that betrayal.

Perhaps, finally, the greatest loss that McMurtry's young men must deal with is one they share with most people living in the modern industrialized world: the loss of stability and emotional confidence. The superficial (and sensational) significance to the state's literature of McMurtry's *Horseman, Pass By* and Brammer's *The Gay Place* is the open and—to some—outrageous manner in which both authors treated the hitherto taboo subject of sex. The books' really lasting significance, however, is much more subtle: they sounded a note that had seldom been heard in Texas writing before 1961. They implied that what has been lost is not just the frontier and its values, but all values—that the only principle by which one can now live is the assumption there are no absolute values.

It is hardly a startling revelation to say that the mode of thought predominant in modern European and American literature and intellectual life throughout much of the twentieth century has been, for lack of a better term, existentialism. Writers and thinkers often acquire their existentialist views secondhand, often in diluted or distorted form, but the idea of life and the universe as essentially absurd and meaningless is a common thread that runs through most important modern literature. A concomitant theme is that of coping with chaos, of "doing without" in the profoundest sense of the phrase, of the individual's escaping the abyss by generating purpose and meaning from hard-won interior battles.

Is this not the message of the great Modernist writers from earlier in the century? Eliot, Fitzgerald, Hemingway, and others? These writers saw the old world of faith and certainty lying shattered and broken at their feet and attempted to solve the riddle of how best to live in the new world of doubt and disorder. Eliot's answer was conservative, even reactionary; Fitzgerald and Hemingway faced the problem more honestly, bravely and with stiff upper lips, though, like the little boys they sometimes resembled, their lips trembled now and again.

Ideas often have a hard time making their way across the Red River, so it took a while for existential angst to ooze into the state's literature and culture. Once it did, however, beginning in the early 1960s, it quickly spread across Texas, if we may judge by relevant literary documents, from city to small town, even to isolated farms and ranches. Without pushing the analogy too far, it seems that Brammer and McMurtry were Texas's Fitzgerald and Hemingway at a time when we had little in the way of the modern literary spirit.

Clearly Brammer thought of himself and his work in Fitzgeraldian terms. (*The Gay Place* takes its title from a phrase in a little-known Fitzgerald poem.) Brammer's novel depicts Gatsbian decadence mired in despair as thick as molasses. For example, Neil Christiansen, the protagonist of the book's second section, contemplates the dissolution of his marriage:

[H]e was able, finally, to realize his loss, to feel the great gap in himself. Not so much long gone youth as adulthood never quite attained. For all his good intentions, there had been only a kind of chic faithlessness in between, randy and frivolous. . . . Moving into the center of the city he smoked the last of his cigarettes and thought about their deeply violated selves.

I could easily quote a dozen or more passages from *The Gay Place* that say essentially the same thing: once there was strong support for right conduct, but now the centrifugal force of modern life has splintered into an irresistible moral shiftlessness. A "lost generation" aura, undoubtedly a calculated effect, hangs over the novel. "You are all a depressed generation," says one of the characters in reference to the book's sizable cast of desultory hedonists, an obvious allusion to Gertrude Stein's description of American expatriates in 1920s Paris.

Rereading McMurtry's early novels recently, I could not help thinking of Hemingway. I do not mean to imply any specific debt on McMurtry's part to Hemingway's style, techniques, or subject matter, but there are nonetheless some striking correspondences. For instance, the rodeo in *Horseman, Pass By* functions in much the same way as the fiesta in *The Sun Also Rises:* as in interlude of ritual, tradition, and order in an otherwise random succession of monotonous and meaningless events. "Since it all came like Christmas, only once a year," says Lonnie, "I was careful not to let any of it pass me by." And is not the scene in *The Last Picture Show* in which terminally depressed Sonny sits with the waitress Genevieve in the all-night cafe reminiscent of "A Clean, Well-Lighted Place," one of the classic works of twentieth-century existentialist fiction? "The window by the booth was all fogged over, but the misted glass was cold to the touch, and the knowledge that the freezing wind was just outside made the booth seem all the cozier."

Whatever McMurtry thinks of them today, his trio of early novels remains a cornerstone of his reputation and achievement as a writer, and as I have tried to show, they are momentous events in Texas's literary history. Of the three, *Horseman, Pass By* is the best because it is the most tightly controlled and structurally sound. *Leaving Cheyenne* almost attains a similar high level of artistic power, but there are at least two weaknesses in the 1963 novel that diminish its aesthetic impact. The first is the uneven quality of the book's three segments. The second, related problem — and on this point I agree with McMurtry — is the character of Molly. Molly has elicited lavish praise from many critics, but I don't buy her for a minute. Indeed the middle section, which she narrates, is easily the least convincing part of the novel.

There are many believable and sometimes fascinating women in McMurtry's early fiction — Halmea, Ruth Popper, Genevieve, Lois and Jacy Farrow — but Molly is not among them. The fatal flaw of characterization is that she is basically a one-dimensional person, a "giver," as Adam Fry calls her, who gives far too much to "sorry bastards who don't deserve it." Even Mabel Peters (later Mabel Fry), who appears briefly in only a few scenes, is more believable, as a woman and as a human being, than is Molly. Still, despite Molly's lack of plausibility, *Leaving Cheyenne* is an impressive story, mainly because of its unifying theme: the myth of the end of the West.

Aesthetically *The Last Picture Show* is the poorest of the early novels. It is episodic and sprawling and as such anticipates the formlessness of much of McMurtry's later fiction. In this regard the movie version of *The Last Picture Show* is superior to the novel because it is more focused and powerful in conveying its message. Moreover, the depiction in the book of small-town Texas life in the 1950s wobbles unsteadily among realism, satire, and poison-pen caricature. At any given point in the story the reader is hard pressed to say which approach the author is employing.

The one element of the novel that seems exceptionally strong is characterization. While some of the people are stereotypes and Sam the Lion is something of a sentimentalized indulgence, many vivid and interesting characters emerge from the tale. The women in the narrative are well drawn, but then so too are the men: Abilene, Duane Moore, Gene Farrow, Lester Marlow, even Billy, the village idiot. The fate of Sonny, more or less the focal character of the story, is unfortunately all too believable.

At novel's end Sonny finds himself in a no-exit situation. He cannot join the army, like his buddy Duane, because of his injured eye, and he is much too passive to go out into the world to seek fame and fortune. He will remain in Thalia, but he feels that he has no connection to the town. Even the countryside—beloved by Homer Bannon and Adam and Gid Fry and Molly and Johnny McCloud—seems threatening and sinister. Driving in his pickup near the close of the narrative, Sonny becomes "scared. . . . As empty as he felt and as empty as the country looked it was too risky going out into it—he might be blown around for days like a broomweed in the wind." Sonny's existence has shrunk and diminished almost to the vanishing point. It is a sad, bleak story, but one that continues to be enacted even in the late 1990s.

None of McMurtry's early novels sold well, and yet they established him, almost immediately, as Texas's rising star in the literary heavens—an ascent culminated only in the 1980s. He was extraordinarily fortunate that all three were translated into motion pictures and that two of the three were both critical and popular successes. For close to a quarter of a century McMurtry was known to most literate Americans primarily as a writer who had produced fiction on which some good movies were based. A reconsideration of the early novels as literature, however, reaffirms their status as autonomous works of art. Despite their nostalgia and sentimentality, despite the fact their creator apparently would disown them if he could, they continue, as we bring the twentieth century to an end and confront a world far removed even from the one sketched in the novels, to speak to readers in a strong and passionate voice.

CHAPTER 10

Mac the Knife

Violence in Texas Fiction

*There's no such thing as life without bloodshed. I think the
notion that the species can be improved in some way, that
everyone could live in harmony, is a really dangerous idea.
Those who are afflicted with this notion are the first ones to
give up their souls, their freedom. Your desire that it be that
way will enslave you and make your life vacuous.*

— CORMAC MCCARTHY, *New York Times Magazine*

Violence, the cliché has it, is as American as apple pie. And Texans, of
course, as "super Americans," are supposed to be more prone to violence
than your average run-of-the-mill Americans. The propensity for violence,
the love of guns, the zealous preservation of the citizen's constitutional
right to own and bear arms—all of these are supposedly an outgrowth, at
both the national and state levels, of our frontier heritage. It is hardly surprising that the two best-known writers residing in Texas at the moment—
Larry McMurtry and Cormac McCarthy—have chosen as a major theme
of their recent fiction the persistence and intransigence of human violence.
Both writers deal with the subject in the context of "wild West" settings.
The two differ, however, in that McMurtry attempts, with minimal success,
to undermine the myth of violence in American culture, while McCarthy
tries to raise it to a quasi-philosophical level.

Larry McMurtry's *Anything for Billy* (1988) followed hard on the heels
of his 1985 smash hit, *Lonesome Dove*. These novels are very similar in many
ways. Both transport the reader back in time to the elusive, fabled old West.
Both attempt to examine the myth-making process and to distinguish between the myth and the reality of that unique landscape of American his-

tory. Indeed, both apparently were intended to subvert the myth of the West and to demonstrate its pernicious effects on the American psyche, past and present.

Lonesome Dove, the chronicle of a quixotic trail drive ramrodded by a pair of former Texas Rangers, Woodrow Call and Gus McCrae, clearly calls into question the myth of the cowboy. Clara, Gus's old girlfriend, no doubt speaks for the author when she gives Call a tongue-lashing that leaves him perplexed but unmoved. Clara, who loved Gus, had chosen a plodding, dependable man to be her mate and father to her children — a practical decision that highlights the disparity between the cowboy myth and the values of community and of family and child-rearing. Clara tells Call:

> I'm sorry you and Gus McCrae ever met. All you two done was ruin one another, not to mention those close to you. . . . I didn't want to fight you for him every day of my life. You men and your promises: they're just excuses to do what you plan to do anyway, which is leave. You think you've always done right — that's your ugly pride, Mr. Call. But you never did right and it would be a sad woman that needed anything from you. You're a vain coward, for all your fighting. I despised you then, for what you were, and I despise you now, for what you're doing.

Lonesome Dove offers many passages and incidents that illustrate the foolishness of the cowboy's ultra-masculine code of conduct. And yet McMurtry's characters in *Lonesome Dove* seem to have gotten away from him. In spite of the writer's best efforts, they appeal to readers as sympathetic, larger than life — in a word, heroic. Whatever McMurtry intended, for example, the scene in which Call goes berserk on the streets of Ogallala, Nebraska, is one of the most compelling episodes in the book.

Call is always on guard, always in control of his emotions, a man who never allows himself to be simply human. Until, that is, he observes some of his drovers being abused by an Army scout in Ogallala. His fury is awesome to behold. It's like a dam bursting, as the emotional restraints of a lifetime spill forth. The reader cannot help cheering Call's righteous anger and, beyond that, seeing him as an embodiment of the true western hero. Thus, for the myriad McMurtry fans, *Lonesome Dove* ended up reviving and enhancing the myth, rather than debunking it.

In writing *Anything for Billy,* McMurtry apparently determined early on to keep his characters firmly within his grasp. In this novel the author takes on the myth of the gunfighter, and he creates a western "hero" nobody can love. Billy the Kid is one of those protean figures who are the stuff of American legend. In song and story, on stage and on the silver screen, the Kid has been portrayed as everything from a saint to a psychotic. Obviously, somebody has been wrong.

Those who pick up *Anything for Billy* expecting the novel to illuminate the historical Billy the Kid will be sorely disappointed. Wisely, the author chose to ignore even the most elementary, agreed-upon details of the Kid's biography. No one, therefore, can claim the book is anything other than what it is: a work of fiction. Still, it supplies a credible, if sometimes confusing, portrait of the authentic Billy.

McMurtry's Billy is a grab bag of contradictions. He is seventeen years old, an unstable adolescent, and unquestionably a sociopath. At one point, for instance, he guns down a ten-year-old Indian boy without a twinge of conscience. Indeed, the narrator, Benjamin Sippy, compares Billy's conscience with "a blank domino." Sippy says elsewhere that "killing people just didn't bother him" and that Billy becomes "sulky" at the "merest hint that something as impractical as morality applied to anything he did." If Billy cannot feel for others, he sometimes slides into self-pity. More than once he moans that he is "alone . . . always alone." Billy is in delicate health, suffering from chronic headaches and "spells of weakness." He is superstitious and easily frightened, yet in an instant can be transformed into a loud-mouthed bully.

Billy worries most about his "reputation"; he lusts after fame, not fortune. When the narrator first meets Billy, the latter's reputation rests largely on gossip and exaggeration. Such is the burden of the reputation, however, that Billy soon becomes what he was supposed to have been all along: "a cold killer." His killings are for the most part senseless and are accomplished, since Billy is a poor shot with a pistol, by "volume, not accuracy." They do have the desired effect of dramatically enhancing his fame and of shoring up his fragile ego and minuscule self-esteem.

Billy is said to be tiny in stature, ugly, dressed in a filthy coat three sizes too large for him. Yet women—Katerina Garza, the beautiful bandit queen; the lovely Lady Cecily Snow—immediately fall in love with him. Lady Cecily says she is attracted to Billy because he's "not boring" like most other men. Billy's "lonely eyes" lend him a kind of anemic charisma, which hardly makes up for his nasty and unpredictable disposition. Inexplicably, he also inspires friendship and loyalty in the admirable Joe Lovelady.

In sum, McMurtry's Billy is plausible enough, but he is utterly banal.

Lady Cecily was wrong: Billy *is* boring. In accounting for the Billy of the novel, one thinks of Hannah Arendt's theory of "the banality of evil"[1]: that is, evil deeds are most often perpetrated not by mad geniuses, but by banal, dull, mindless people. Certainly the latter description fits Billy from head to toe.

Probably McMurtry's Billy is too real, too weak as a personality, and so distracting in his weakness that he deflects the reader's attention from the novel's most important character, Ben Sippy, the narrator. Sippy, a wealthy Philadelphian, acquires an interest in the West from reading dime novels, those paperback adventure tales of the late nineteenth century that were the first manifestations of American popular culture. Dime novels, initially mere entertainment, quickly become for Sippy a feverish addiction. His "mental malaria," as he calls it, results in his becoming a successful dime novelist himself, cranking out stories of exotic places he has never seen. Ultimately, at age fifty, a victim of romantic illusions, Sippy heads west, seeking excitement and fleeing his nine daughters and a coldly efficient wife. Improbably, he becomes Billy's companion on the owlhoot trail.

But instead of the land of his dreams — a realm of freedom and adventure — Sippy finds in the West a grubby reality that allows little room for romance. At the most mundane level he must cope with the "intense and tenacious appetite of the Western bug." Insects pose as great a threat to his morale as does violence, which he depicts as brutish and pervasive. "I was beginning," he concludes early in his narrative, "to have to reckon with the fact that I was riding around in a place where it was rather hard to last."

Most disillusioning to Sippy are the actual western gunfighters, who bear little resemblance to those in dime novels. He discovers that most gunfighters are "disappointed men. They spent their lives in the rough barrooms of ugly towns; they ate terrible food and drank a vile grade of liquor; few managed to shoot the right people, and even fewer got to die gloriously in a shootout with a peer."

The reader wonders why Sippy develops so strong an attachment to Billy. At one point he speaks of possessing a "fatherly" interest in the younger man. Later he describes Billy as "a little Western waif, with such a lonely look stuck on his ugly young face that you'd want to do anything for him." And again: "Despite all that he had done, I guess I just liked Billy." All such lame explanations fail to convince. Perhaps Sippy doesn't remember why he took a liking for Billy. Perhaps Sippy doesn't correctly recall a lot of things. The format of *Anything for Billy* is that of a memoir, an old man's recounting of colorful events from the distant past. Memoirs are one of the staples of western American literature, and like dime novels they played a part in creating the mythic West; by their very nature, they are susceptible to exaggeration and romanticizing.

A clear impression one takes away from a reading of *Anything for Billy* is this: the romanticized West of legend and myth, whether promulgated by the overheated imaginations of dime novelists or by the recollections of fading memories, is dangerously false — and almost impossible to kill off. The crowning irony for Ben Sippy is that, even as he attempts (he claims) to depict a real Billy in a real western landscape, he finds that he is only contributing to enlarging the mythic Billy. No doubt McMurtry sympathizes since, as a writer, he has suffered a similar fate. I believe, as suggested earlier, this is precisely what happened to McMurtry in the case of *Lonesome Dove*.

A problem that must be faced is whether or not McMurtry's version of the Billy the Kid saga (or, for that matter, the trail drive saga) is closer to the truth than the popular myth, since the myth itself is now, like it or not, part of western history. The Greek word *mythos* simply means "story." McMurtry has created a story. Since the reality of the old West cannot be reconstructed with absolute certainly, it is an interpretation of the facts, insofar as the facts can be ascertained. McMurtry has created a new myth, as it were, perhaps a better, "truer" myth, but a myth nonetheless.[2]

In many ways McMurtry's myth is more disturbing than the popular myth it is meant to supplant. The most characteristic element of life in the frontier West, as depicted in *Anything for Billy* anyway, was violence. Violence was apparently everywhere; it was random and sudden, literally popping up out of a dry wash on a seemingly level plain. Not only were near-demented thugs like Billy responsible for the violence, but so were wealthy, powerful ranchers like Will Isinglass. Judging by *Anything for Billy,* ninety percent of the inhabitants of the old West were capable of acts of desensitized brutality.

Over the years many commentators on American society have attempted to find a continuity between our violent past and our violent present. D. H. Lawrence asserted in 1922 that the "essential American soul is hard, isolate, stoic and a killer."[3] More recently Richard Slotkin has referred, in the title of his analysis of twentieth-century American culture, to a *Gunfighter Nation*.[4] The imagery of Slotkin's title is drawn directly from western history — and myth.

It may be argued that *Anything for Billy* is as much a picture of present-day America as it is of the nineteenth-century West. The spasmodic violence that punctuates life in America today is every bit at heartless and random and, in many cases, unmotivated as that of McMurtry's old West. Moreover, the psychological portrait of Billy—a dwarfed ego supported by an arsenal of weapons and a remorseless instinct to kill—is all too believable. Perhaps McMurtry is saying that our western heritage is in large measure responsible for an inclination to violence that threatens a society that no longer has a frontier to siphon off its dregs.

One does not often hear such lavish praise for an American writer. Saul Bellow gushed over the author's "absolutely overpowering use of language, his life-giving and death-dealing sentences." Shelby Foote wrote that the real hero of his novels "is the English language." "He must be acknowledged as a talent equal to William Faulkner," judged Madison Smartt Bell. *Newsweek* called him a "literary lion in the desert . . . the best-kept secret in American letters." *The New York Times Magazine* said he "may be the best unknown novelist in America."[5]

These and other encomiums were laid at the feet of Cormac McCarthy in the spring of 1992 upon the publication of *All the Pretty Horses,* the first volume of *The Border Trilogy.*[6] Like most stories of literary discovery and triumph, this one features plenty of twists and turns. McCarthy, who was born in New England and grew up in Knoxville, Tennessee, has lived for more than two decades in El Paso, Texas. So far as I know, New England does not claim him as a literary son, but the South certainly does. To be sure, McCarthy's first four novels—*The Orchard Keeper* (1965), *Outer Dark* (1968), *Child of God* (1974), and *Suttree* (1979)—are set in the Deep South. The majority of McCarthy's earliest reading audience—which came close to being a cult following—as well as his first champions in print came from the South.

Still, in his most recent novels, the author has been concerned with things southwestern (and Latin American) rather than southern. The shift westward was probably inevitable. "I've always been interested in the Southwest," McCarthy has said. "There isn't a place in the world you can go where they don't know about cowboys and Indians and the myth of the West."[7] McCarthy, therefore, must be considered a literary hybrid. In his formative years he was steeped in southern literature and culture, and the influence on him of southern writers like Faulkner—especially Faulkner—is clear.

The reader may be excused, therefore, for concluding that McCarthy's most recent fiction was composed by the illegitimate offspring of Zane

Grey and Flannery O'Connor — and that the Marquis de Sade was the delivering physician. Like Grey, the author of these books has a fine talent for painting western landscapes and action pictures in words. His resemblance to O'Connor seems twofold: first, there is a concern with the most vexing of metaphysical questions; and second, a taste for the flashier techniques of southern gothic. His debt to the Marquis de Sade is obvious: his novels contain some of the most graphic and shocking violence in modern fiction.

McCarthy's unrelenting realism in the depiction of violence makes Larry McMurtry appear positively squeamish by comparison. Certainly many episodes in *Lonesome Dove* and *Anything for Billy* suggest the violence and cruelty of the old West, but in subsequent books McMurtry's accounts of the western experience have grown ever more simplistic, sentimentalized, almost cartoonish. In *Buffalo Girls* (1990), for example, the West becomes a giant theme park. Calamity Jane is little more than a buffoon, a female Yosemite Sam. The characters wander on horseback across hundreds of miles, endure bone-chilling snowstorms, fall off horses, get into fights, and it all remains a B-grade movie: their pain and suffering never come across as real.

One of McCarthy's few literary friends — McCarthy is famous in American literary circles for his steadfast refusal to be part of those circles — was the late Edward Abbey. There are few technical parallels between their work, but philosophically these two writers are very close. Abbey wrote some good fiction, including *The Brave Cowboy* (1956; made into an exceptional motion picture under the title *Lonely Are the Brave*) and *The Monkey Wrench Gang* (1975), but he was best known as a polemicist and passionate environmentalist. In *Desert Solitaire,* Abbey's chronicle of "A Season in the Wilderness" (the subtitle) spent as a park ranger in Arches National Monument in southeastern Utah, he often decries humanity's anthropocentrism, our species pride.

McCarthy appears to hold a similar view. At one point the narrator of *Blood Meridian* comments:

> In the neuter austerity of that terrain all phenomena were bequeathed
> a strange equality and no one thing nor spider nor stone nor blade
> of grass could put forth claim to precedence. The very clarity of these
> articles belied their familiarity, for the eye predicates the whole on
> some feature or part and here was nothing more luminous than an-
> other and nothing more enshadowed and in the optical democracy

of such landscapes all preference is made whimsical and a man and a rock become endowed with unguessed kinships.

Nature's "democracy," in other words, is not a democracy among humans, but a democracy among objects and creatures.

In his nonfiction Abbey displays a special fondness for deserts, because they provide humbling experiences for humans. He sees the desert as a microcosm of the planet. The desert requires a rigid discipline of those who manage to survive in it. Any deviation from that discipline is disastrous; in the desert adaptation to existing conditions must be immediate and complete. For Abbey, the analogy between survival in the desert and our present precarious situation on earth is chastening and instructive.

Moreover, Abbey's world is one in which raw nature is often inimical to the interests of the human race. It is one in which violence and death are ubiquitous. Lethal violence may come suddenly and unexpectedly from a fellow human, or it may literally strike from out of the heavens. "A ruthless, brutal process," Abbey muses in *Desert Solitaire*, "but clean and beautiful."[8] In any case, humans, in the grand scheme of things, are puny and insignificant creatures who are hardly captains of their souls and masters of their fate.

At the close of *All the Pretty Horses,* John Grady Cole attends the funeral of Abuela, an old Mexican American woman who had worked as a servant for the Cole family for half a century. As he stands at the graveside, he thinks of "the world that was rushing away and seemed to care nothing for the old or the young or the rich or poor or dark or pale or he or she. Nothing for their struggles, nothing for their names. Nothing for the living or the dead." This epiphany — that the individual is alone in a cold, indifferent universe that can pass out of human consciousness in an instant — appears to be the sum of what John Grady learns from his experiences in the novel.

The passage is reminiscent of a similar commentary on life in Stephen Crane's story "The Blue Hotel": "One viewed the existence of man then as a marvel, and conceded a glamour of wonder to these lice which were caused to cling to a whirling, fire-smitten, ice-locked, disease-stricken, space-lost bulb. The conceit of man was explained . . . to be the very engine of life." The "conceit of man" is that he continues to pit himself against the power of the elements, to assert his will against the overwhelming force of nature. He continues to attempt to impose a moral order on a natural order in which morality is irrelevant.

McCarthy has shown himself to be a serious writer — "a novelist of religious feeling," as Robert Coles once said[9] — who explores in his fiction the most profound of philosophical questions. Is there an irreducible natural reality that continually undercuts human constructions of reality? To what extent is the individual's destiny the result of chance occurrences in a universe of chance? To what extent does it derive from the exercise of free will and free choice? Does God exist — and is there a pattern, a design at work, that lies beyond the ken of humankind? From the Greeks to Renaissance playwrights and poets to literary naturalists to existentialists, these are questions that thinkers have agonized over for centuries.

"Notions of chance and fate," the narrator of *Blood Meridian* observes, "are the preoccupations of men engaged in rash undertakings." For McCarthy, life itself is a rash undertaking. However, unlike Crane and the other turn-of-the-century naturalists, McCarthy does not posit a wholly deterministic universe. Humans do make choices — frequently bad choices, but choices nonetheless — that critically affect their destinies.

The environment in which McCarthy has chosen to raise these questions in recent novels — *Blood Meridian, or The Evening Redness in the West* (1985) and *All the Pretty Horses* (1992), the books I wish to discuss — is America's southwestern frontier. I use the word *frontier* in its literal sense: the settings of these tales are the marginal lands on either side of the U.S.–Mexico border. *Blood Meridian* begins in 1849; *All the Pretty Horses* in 1949. It is no accident that the separation is precisely a century. One of the purposes of the novels is to demonstrate a continuity in our history that time apparently is powerless to erase.

In *Blood Meridian,* the focal character leaves Tennessee because he has no family, no patrimony, no choice except to seek out a more promising homeland. In *All the Pretty Horses,* John Grady's father tells him, "We're like the Comanches was two hundred years ago." When the family ranch is sold out from under him, John Grady heads for Mexico, mainly because he feels Texas is too fenced in, too used up. McCarthy's characters, then, search out frontiers, those fluid zones of freedom and opportunity, of action and destiny that Americans traditionally have sought. What they often find is an actual and metaphysical horror.

In McCarthy's universe, humanity's "taste for mindless violence" is one of those facts of nature that may be lamented but cannot be denied. *Blood Meridian* is one of the bloodiest books ever penned by an American author. An Old Testament aura hangs over the novel, the narrative voice sometimes assuming prophetic dimensions. One reviewer compared the world of the novel to a Hieronymous Bosch painting; another suggested that Sam Peckinpah may well have choreographed the scenes of violence and killing.

Yet the story and even the characters of *Blood Meridian* are drawn directly from history; the novel follows, remarkably closely, the historical sources.[10] The protagonist of the tale is a fourteen-year-old lad known only as "the kid"· "He can neither read nor write and in him broods already a taste for mindless violence." Shortly after the end of the Mexican War, the kid leaves his home in Tennessee to wander south and west, landing finally in San Antonio. There he joins a party of filibusters, who say they are guided by the highest motives. "We are to be the instruments of liberation," one of them tells the kid, "in a dark and troubled land." Their real purpose is to seize choice grazing lands in Sonora.

In recent years a gaggle of revisionist historians of the American West has challenged the "triumphalist" view of American history. The revisionists claim that the history of the frontier, when seen aright, is characterized by unrelenting racism, sexism, naked imperialism, environmental madness. They would do well to take note of McCarthy's fiction; he appears to agree with them, though the spin he puts on such contrarian history is not necessarily that of the revisionists.

Somewhere in northern Mexico the filibusters are set upon by Comanches. The kid manages to escape, only to be taken in by another gang of opportunists — scalphunters who have been commissioned by the governor of Chihuahua, Mexico, to kill Comanches and Apaches, a bounty to be paid for each Indian scalp brought in. The oddest of the scalphunters is Judge Holden, an enormous fat man whose hairless body glistens eerily.

The judge, a man of eloquence, formulates the imperative of the Anglo-American conquest of a continent: "Only nature can enslave man and only when the existence of each last entity is routed out and made to stand naked before him will he be properly suzerain of the earth." In order for the earth to be his, says the judge, "nothing must be permitted to occur upon it save by my disposition." Milton's Satan and Melville's Ahab echo through the judge's arrogant and megalomaniacal monologues.

The scruffy band of scalphunters look "like cavefolk." They are barbaric, "tattered, stinking, ornamented with human parts like cannibals." Clad in animal skins, the bounty hunters seem like denizens of some prehistoric fen or bog as they set out on their journey across the Chihuahuan and Sonoran deserts, from West Texas through northern Mexico and then to California.

Pursuing their baleful mission, they are driven by animal instincts and plunge ever deeper into a vortex of killing and blood lust. When they meet a pack train on a precipitous mountain ledge, they push the mules over the side and calmly watch as the animals explode "in startling bursts of blood" on the floor of the canyon below. They become less and less selective about whose scalps they take; it doesn't matter as long as the scalps are from dark-skinned people.

Eventually they fall to fighting among themselves. "Here," the narrative voice comments, "beyond men's judgements all covenants were brittle." They are trapped, in drunken revelry, by Yuma Indians at a ferry crossing on the Colorado River, between Arizona and California. Most are killed, including the leader of the pack, John Glanton, but the kid—and a few others, including the judge it later turns out—escape.

The final chapter of *Blood Meridian* is brilliantly realized. The kid, nearly three decades after the start of the narrative, threads his way through ghostly piles of bones, the remains of tens of thousands of slaughtered buffalo—suggestive of the millions of bison killed for their hides on the southern plains in the 1870s, an ecological calamity so stunning as to be almost inconceivable—into Fort Griffin, Texas, north of Abilene. There, amid the gaiety of drinking and dancing and mating, he reaches the end of the line. He has cheated death for the last time, and he finally intersects, so to speak, with the bullet with his name on it.

His demise is presided over by Judge Holden, a bloated angel of war and death. The haunting ritualistic inevitability of the scene makes it one of the most memorable in McCarthy's fiction. The judge's extemporaneous commentary on fate and free will—on reality versus the representation of reality—employs the metaphor of dancing. The judge, despite his bulk, is an excellent dancer. As Yeats asks, "How do we know the dancer from the dance?"

"Why did you come here?" the judge asks the kid. "[T]o have a good time," the kid replies. But why didn't he stay in California? Why didn't he go anyplace else in the world? The springs of the kid's rootless, wandering existence were long ago activated. And yet specific choices and decisions were made that have brought him to this bleak corner of the earth. The inextricability of fate and free will has never been more vividly dramatized.

All the Pretty Horses is, as uncounted reviewers soberly noted, the "most accessible" of McCarthy's fictions. Its accessibility derives largely from a straightforward, linear plot line and from diction that, for McCarthy, is amazingly simple and direct. McCarthy's virtuosity with language is dazzling. Reading his books is like strolling through a museum of English prose styles. In *Blood Meridian,* his debt to the Elizabethans, to Milton, to Melville, and to Faulkner shines forth from every page. Yet the structure of *Blood Meridian,* reflecting the nineteenth-century novel of which it is (superficially, at least) an imitation, seems loose and baggy, and its style, though powerful, is somehow incongruous with the subject.

The Southwest demands a language that is simple and clean, yet musically idiomatic. The lean, sculpted prose of *All the Pretty Horses,* it seems to me, is more in keeping with the sparseness of the western landscape than is the decorous, antique style of *Blood Meridian.* The language of *All the Pretty Horses* — especially the wonderful dialogue — projects the laconic, understated lingo of the West Texas cowboy. The language also seems Hemingwayesque, as does the "masculine" subject matter of the book.

But then there is still Faulkner — with McCarthy, there is always Faulkner. Consider the following: "What he loved in horses was what he loved in men, the blood and the heat of the blood that ran them. All his reverence and all his fondness and all the leanings of his life were for the ardenthearted and they would always be so and never be otherwise." The Faulknerian cadences and rhythms of this passage — and of many others in the novel — are unmistakable.

On the surface the plot of *All the Pretty Horses* appears a variation on a story that has been told often in western literature. A wandering cowboy and his sidekick ride innocently into hostile territory. There ensue fights against insurmountable odds, the hero's romance with a lovely young señorita, chases on horseback through a harsh but beautiful landscape. Readers understand quickly enough, however, that this simple tale is but the vehicle on which they are to be taken on an excursion through the complex realms of philosophy.

First, we must consider the horses. John Grady and his pal Lacey Rawlins love horses more than anything else. When they get a job at La Purísima hacienda in Coahuila working with wild horses, they are pleased as can be. At one point John Grady observes the mustangs running in circles in their corral "like marbles swirled in a jar." Compare this description with Faulkner's in "Spotted Horses": "we could watch them spotted varmints swirling along the fence back and forth across the lot same as minnows in a pond."

For both Faulkner and McCarthy, horses are more incorporeal spirits than they are creatures of blood and bone. Faulkner's horses are malign; they are swarming Furies, sent by the gods to punish men for their folly. McCarthy's horses, however, represent the vital life force of the universe.

They stand for what *is*, pristine and unfallen nature in its most elemental form.

On several occasions John Grady dreams of horses:

> In his sleep he could hear horses stepping among the rocks . . . and in his sleep he dreamt of horses and the horses in his dream moved gravely among the tilted stones like horses come upon an antique site where some ordering of the world had failed and if anything had been written on the stones the weathers had taken it away again and the horses were wary and moved with great circumspection carrying in their blood as they did the recollection of this and other places where horses once had been and would be again. Finally what he saw in his dream was that the order in the horse's heart was more durable for it was written in a place where no rain could erase it.

The old *mozo* Luis tells John Grady that "the horse shares a common soul and its separate life only forms it out of all horses and makes it mortal. He said that if a person understood the soul of the horse then he would understand all horses that ever were." But according to Luis, "among men there was no such communion as among horses." The singularity and the problems of humanity, Luis suggests, stem from individual human consciousness. Only humans, of all earth's creatures, contemplate abstractions like truth and justice. Only humans are capable of viciousness, perfidy, evil. Only humans aspire — futilely — to build empires and lasting monuments, among the ruins of which horses contentedly graze.

All the Pretty Horses is a version of the familiar coming-of-age story. John Grady is sixteen when the tale begins. It is in adolescence, of course, that the issues of free will and fate are raised with greatest poignancy. In order for the young person to achieve a secure sense of identity, he or she must resolve the conflict between pressures from family and his or her desire for freedom and autonomy.

In McCarthy's novel mothers (and mother surrogates) make a poor showing. John Grady's mother turns a deaf ear to his plea to retain the Texas ranch; he rebels by running off to Mexico. The *dueña* Alfonsa, Alejandra's godmother and great-aunt, despite vivid recollections of her own youthful resistance to authority, attempts forcibly to direct the young woman's life. Fathers, on the other hand, are simply weak and ineffectual.

The relationship between John Grady and Alejandra brings all of these conflicts into sharp focus. Alejandra ends the affair because she is the daughter of her family, class, and nationality. The "sadness" John Grady sees "in the slope of her shoulders" is in recognition of the stoicism and fatalism of Mexico. She acknowledges the limitations on individual human action, the obduracy of centuries-old conventions and customs.

Whatever else he may be, John Grady in the beginning is an American — a *norteamericano*. He believes in individualism, free will, volition. He thinks every man born on this planet is an Adam, free of memory and external constraint, able to shape his illimitable "self" in any way he chooses. He is shocked when Alejandra refuses to break all ties and go with him.

Which is the dominant agent — free will or fate? Perhaps there is no either-or answer. In her final — rather improbable — conversation with John Grady, Alfonsa argues for a kind of modified predestination. The physical universe imposes certain conditions on the individual, including total unpredictability. But life is a shimmering web, and every time a strand is struck by an assertion of will, the web vibrates with consequences for all. Actually Alfonsa uses the metaphor of puppets. If one looks behind the curtain of a puppet show, she says, one finds puppets who control puppets who control puppets and on to infinity. There is, in other words, a vast interconnectedness of things, so that clear causal relationships are impossible to isolate.

By novel's end John Grady has fashioned a code to live by. It is a code of honor and responsibility — à la Hemingway — that has nothing to do with legality or traditional morality. It is an internal code and has been shaped by hard experience and the hard conditions of an indifferent universe.

The scene in the hotel room in Zacatecas — John Grady and Alejandra's last night together — is crucial. "He saw very clearly how all his life led only to this moment and all after led nowhere at all. He felt something cold and soulless enter him like another being and he imagined that it smiled malignly and he had no reason to believe that it would ever leave him." He immediately is invaded by what the Spanish call *la tristesa de la vida*. "He imagined the pain of the world to be like some formless parasitic being seeking out the warmth of human souls wherein to incubate and he thought he knew what made one liable to its visitations."

While the inflated rhetoric of these passages — at least the emotion is inflated — may be attributable in some degree to John Grady's adolescence, he has clearly undergone a very unpleasant initiatory experience. He is sadder but wiser, and wishes he was neither. On his way back to Texas, he watches a wedding ceremony being performed in the plaza of a Mexican village, and he listens knowingly as a store clerk tells him that "it was good that God kept the truths of life from the young as they were starting out or else they'd have no heart to start at all." John Grady is an old man at seventeen.

John Grady's seemingly capricious decision to return to Encantada to recover his and Lacey's horses, which have been appropriated by a local *hacendado,* may be seen as an attempt to impose order and justice on a world in which there is no inherent order or justice. It is also a direct response to what has happened in Zacatecas—a near-suicidal statement of grief and disillusionment. It symbolizes the lifting of the world's sorrows onto his own shoulders. He will never be a naive innocent again.

As is true of all McCarthy's fiction, *All the Pretty Horses* contains plenty of violent action, including a knife fight in a Mexican prison in which John Grady kills a man. Back in Texas, John Grady wanders the countryside, like a young Ancient Mariner, compulsively explaining to whomever will listen why he had killed his fellow inmate. In Mexico, John Grady had accepted the act without much thought; it seemed fated, part of a predetermined destiny. In the U.S.—the land of freedom—accountability and responsibility are the necessary complements of free will and volition.

As the narrative unravels, John Grady is sliced up in the knife fight in prison and receives a serious bullet wound in the leg—which, in a horrific scene, he cauterizes with the red-hot barrel of a pistol. His future seems headed towards ever-bleaker, ever-more-violent episodes. Like the kid's in *Blood Meridian,* the dynamic of John Grady's fate has been set in motion. It remains only for him to discover how and where his destiny will reach its bloody terminus.

CHAPTER 11

A Fan's Notes

Football in Texas Life and Literature

He was the pride of the backfield
Ahhh the hero of his day
Yeah he carried the ball for the red and blue
That won District triple-A. . . .

—TERRY ALLEN,
"The Great Joe Bob (A Regional Tragedy)"

I first became aware of sports in general and football in particular in the early 1950s when I was twelve or thirteen. I lived on an isolated farm without transportation and was largely unable to take part in organized sports at the high school I attended many miles away (though I was then and have remained most of my life a participant in pick-up football and basketball games). In lieu of partaking of sports in high school, I became a fan, a football fan for the most part. At the time college football was king. I followed the teams of the old Southwest Conference, made up of seven Texas schools plus the University of Arkansas. The Humble Oil Company sponsored radio broadcasts of conference games, and I never missed a contest called by renowned play-by-play man Kern Tips.

My favorite time of year as a football fan was mid- to late summer. When I was growing up in rural Tarrant County, late summer was a slow time—too hot and dry for anything to grow, too early for fall planting or harvest. Everybody was weary of the heat and eager for cool weather. This was precisely when the preseason football magazines appeared on the racks of drugstores and newsstands. I bought just about all of them. I recall many an August day, lying on my bed in my un–air-conditioned room, thumbing through the preseason mags, national as well as local. I admired the grotesquely posed photographs, memorized the schedules, read and reread every word. I learned who was supposed to be on top in the Big Ten and the Southeastern Conference, as well as how Hofstra was going to do that year, and Willamette College.

Outside the sun was blazing and the temperature 100-plus degrees, but in my head it was a golden autumn afternoon, and a halfback in a brightly colored jersey was carrying a pigskin down the sideline of an emerald green playing field. Needless to say, the reality of football—pulled hamstrings, torn ligaments, broken limbs, violent collisions that would put people in the hospital if they occurred on a highway—rarely intruded in my fantasies. Thinking back on all this from my perspective today, what I find noteworthy is that I never really dreamed of being a football hero. I felt vaguely deprived at not being able to try out for the high-school team, but never acutely so. Though I possessed moderate athletic ability, I realized from an early age that I was not extraordinarily gifted in that area.

No, I always wanted to be a sportswriter. Historically—and to a great extent this is still true—the best writing one is likely to find in a Texas newspaper is in the sports pages. Though some claim that football is the most revered of Texas pastimes, the top sportswriters in the state have never treated football—or any other sport—with very much reverence. It is in the field of society and politics that Texas newspaper folk have had to tread lightly, given the political biases of newspaper owners and editors. Texas journalists traditionally have found their greatest freedom of imagination and expression in sports reporting.

As a freshman in college at what is now the University of Texas at Arlington, I declared myself a journalism major, a first step toward achieving my goal of becoming a sportswriter. Various things happened, however, to convince me that I would probably never be a competent journalist, and I eventually settled for an advanced degree in English and the staid life of a college professor. But I have never got the romance of sportswriting completely out of my blood.

For me, the romance sprang from an accident of my youth. When I was a youngster, my family subscribed to the (now defunct) *Fort Worth Press*. The *Press* was a tabloid, part of the Scripps-Howard chain. As a news medium it was woefully inadequate. But in its sports pages in the 1950s and early 1960s a legend of Texas journalism was born. The list of sportswriters who worked for the *Press* during that period is impressive by any standard: Blackie Sherrod, Dan Jenkins, Bud Shrake, Gary Cartwright, Mike Shropshire, and others who went on to illustrious careers elsewhere.[1] Even as a teenager I had heard of Westbrook Pegler's famous description of a newspaper's sports section as "the toy department." But gosh, the *Press* gang seemed to be having a lot of fun. You name the technique, they used it deftly: irony, economy, humor, sublimity to honor the occasional sublime achievement. Employ irony in any other part of the newspaper, and it usually falls flat—I know because I've tried it. Sports fans are, above all else, sophisticated consumers of clever analysis.

If I have any facility as a writer today, I owe a great deal to those sportswriters of yesteryear who first drew my attention to the techniques by which words are arranged for maximum aesthetic effect. They were good mentors in that they implicitly offered much practical advice on using the language well. I could legitimately aim at being another Blackie Sherrod; being another Henry James or Ernest Hemingway seemed well beyond my reach. By the time I was in my late teens, I had given up reading preseason football magazines, since most of the forecasts turned out to be egregiously wrong. Still, today, as I sometimes leaf through the pages of such a magazine, pictures and prose are the agents of evocation. And it is not anger or dismay that is evoked, but other times and other places. The dream has dissipated, but the memory is ever bright.

My dream, like most dreams, had little grounding in actuality. Growing up in the 1950s, I did not know that many—perhaps most—athletes view sportswriters and other media folk with a mixture of contempt and loathing. In Peter Gent's *North Dallas Forty* (1973), the narrator, a professional football player, fulminates against sportswriters:

> Sportswriters were such assholes. They didn't know shit and acted as if they understood a game far more complex in emotion and technical skills than they had the ability to comprehend. They couldn't even transcribe my jokes correctly. That is why they were sportswriters, because they didn't know shit about anything.

That attitude, I believe, was not unusual among athletes in 1973, and it has grown progressively more hostile with the passage of time, as sports journalism (like sport itself) has become more a competitive business where too often the first casualty is truth. Nevertheless, sportswriters possess the power of the pen, and it is a considerable power. The view of a particular sport or a particular athlete held by a majority of fans is usually shaped by the scribes who write about them—and, more and more, by media gurus whose opinions flood the airwaves.

As a Texan, I came by my love of football — and, from that, my ambition to be a sportswriter — honestly. Texans — male Texans, at least — are, notoriously, football fans. Why? The standard explanations are predictable enough. Football is a violent sport, and Texans are prone to violence. Football is sexist, in that it segregates the sexes; boys are on the field playing the game, while girls are on the sidelines leading cheers and exposing their bodies. Texans love winners, and until very recently the only winning sports teams in the state with national reputations have played on the gridirons of a couple of major colleges and on the hallowed (artificial) turf of Texas Stadium, home of the Dallas Cowboys. Whatever the truth of the matter, the huge significance of football in Texas culture cannot be doubted.

Given that significance, the sport has provoked tons of journalistic coverage but surprisingly sparse literary treatment. And much of the literature that has derived from the game has been produced by sportswriters, some of whom were once employed by the old *Fort Worth Press*. Though many Texans are fanatical about high-school football, little of lasting value has been written on the subject. A book that caused a stir a few years back was H. G. Bissinger's *Friday Night Lights* (1990), the chronicle of "A Town, a Team, and a Dream" (the subtitle).[2] Bissinger, a Philadelphia journalist, went more or less undercover and spent a year in Odessa in the late 1980s observing the townspeople and their passionate attachment to the famed Permian High School football team. His account is penetrating and unsparingly honest — but also fair and objective and even, in a way, affectionate. It is an example of sportswriting that comes close to attaining the level of art.

Since high-school football is so important in creating a sense of community in most Texas towns, there is, for Texans, a special pathos in a prep star's failure to live up to his potential. Bissinger relates several such tales in his book. Probably the most celebrated running back ever produced by Texas high-school football was Joe Don Looney. J. Brent Clark's *Third Down and Forever* (1993) is a fascinating biography of a colorful "character" — football's original bad boy — whose disappointing career as a football player proves that truth is indeed often stranger than fiction.[3] After racking up dazzling statistics at a Fort Worth high school in the early 1960s, Looney went to the University of Oklahoma, where he ended up being kicked off the team for gross insubordination. As a professional he played at several venues, usually wearing out his welcome with any given team in a couple of months. The aptly named Looney clearly marched to a different drummer. A rebellious streak, partying, alcohol, steroids, psychedelic drugs, brushes with the law, and even oriental mysticism have been offered as reasons for his decline and fall. Looney died in a motorcycle accident in West Texas in 1988.

Joe Don Looney, then, was a real-life Joe Bob, the protagonist of Terry Allen's wonderful song "The Great Joe Bob (A Regional Tragedy)."[4] Joe Bob is "a panhandle prince . . . ahh/ Schoolboy football king. . . ./An there ain't nothin . . . as American/An clean." But inexplicably Joe Bob's life spins out of control. He is corrupted by women and booze. He slugs a coach and loses his scholarship to Texas Tech. He and a waitress hold up a liquor store, and Joe Bob lands in jail, his gridiron talents squandered: "Yeah so nobody understood it/When the great Joe Bob went bad."

High-school football crops up briefly in several works of Texas fiction, but can hardly be called the subject of that fiction. Ordinarily the sport is used as a barometer of communal values. An example is *The Blind Bull* (1952), George Williams's unjustly neglected novel of a young man's rise from poverty to power and position in modern-day Houston. A better-known example is Larry McMurtry's *The Last Picture Show* (1966), set in the small town of Thalia in the 1950s. In *Picture Show* McMurtry employs football as a framing device. As the novel begins, Sonny Crawford has just played in his last game for the local high school team. He is vaguely uneasy about this circumstance; it seems to him that a door has been closed. Near the end of the narrative, about a year later, Sonny returns as a spectator to the stadium where he had played for four years. He is allowed to assist in carrying the first-down markers. When the band plays the school song, he feels "as though he was part of it again, the high school, football, the really important part of life in the town." Soon enough, however, Sonny realizes he is not part of it: "He was an ex-student—nothing. . . . he felt like he wasn't even *in* town—he felt like he wasn't anywhere." Sonny's dreary epiphany at the football game is a major contributing factor in plunging him into near-complete alienation.

College football, like high-school football, is also a rather neglected topic in the state's literature. There has been an occasional exposé, such as *Meat on the Hoof* (1972) by Gary Shaw, a former player who purports to reveal the underhanded and unethical tactics of legendary University of Texas coach Darrell Royal.[5] Serious literary examination of Texas college athletics, however, is scarce. A glittering exception to this generalization is Don DeLillo's *End Zone* (1972), still a very funny and readable book despite the topical nature of some of its thematic concerns. DeLillo, one of the most distinguished of living American novelists, is a native of the Bronx and has never resided in Texas, but he has written a fair amount of fiction set in the state. *Libra* (1988), for example, an overly complicated conspiracy story centering on Lee Harvey Oswald and the Kennedy assassination, is laid in Dallas and environs. Dallas is also, in part, the backdrop of *Running Dog* (1978), and DeLillo slips Texas tidbits into several other of his novels.

The narrator of *End Zone* is Gary Harkness. After having been an all-state running back in high school in upstate New York, Gary had made several stops at collegiate football factories around the country. Now, his last chance to succeed is at Logos College, a small school on the baking plains of West Texas. The Logos coach, Emmett Creed—also down to his last chance, since he has been banned from the big time for punching one of his players—has recruited a band of "exiles" and "outcasts" to catapult Logos to the top of the small-college rankings. Gary sees Coach Creed as "a landlocked Ahab who paced and raged." A teammate of Gary's describes the coach as "part Satan, part Saint Francis or somebody." Creed's favorite maxim is, "It's only a game, but it's the only game." Creed remains throughout the tale an enigmatic presence; of all the coaches in the football books I read, he is the only one to rise above the stereotypical.

End Zone follows the unfolding of a season sometime in the 1960s, as the Logos Screaming Eagles (Creed had changed their nickname from the Cactus Wrens) attempt to put themselves on the college football map. The team's best player, Taft Robinson, a transfer from Columbia, is the first black to play for the school. Most of Logos's games are won easily, in effect before the first half is over. The only contest that is described in detail is the encounter with the Eagles' chief rival, Centrex Biotechnical Institute. Logos is thumped soundly, and dreams of a championship are punctured. Coach Creed, however, even though his health is failing, grimly begins planning for the next season, a new campaign.

End Zone is one of those books that is ostensibly about football, but is really about something else: the threat of nuclear annihilation and the failure of language to come to grips with reality. Gary likes "to read about mass destruction and suffering." He amuses himself by playing theoretical war games with an Air Force ROTC instructor. The narrative is laced with talk of thermonuclear warfare, a topic which Americans in the 1960s obsessed about. Indeed, this very aspect of the book is what makes it seem rather antiquated. At century's end the danger of nuclear devastation has hardly been eliminated, but the world's geopolitical landscape has shifted so radically that the possibility of an Armageddon in which two superpowers slug it out while millions die and the planet becomes uninhabitable now seems remote.

DeLillo, at any rate, suggests that football and nuclear warfare are violent "games" that appeal to atavistic impulses in the human psyche. They differ only in the degree of mayhem that is inflicted. The idea of football as a metaphor for war is virtually a cliché — indeed DeLillo makes fun of the concept. "I reject the notion of football as warfare," says a minor character. "Warfare is warfare. We don't need substitutes because we've got the real thing." But then Gary describes a couple of athletic department employees as "types familiar to football and other paramilitary complexes." The comparison is a cliché, I think, precisely because it is true. A football game is literally a battle, and a team, like an army, must execute its "game plan" to perfection in order to be successful. Game strategy, for good reason, is often described in military terms. Football demands teamwork and concerted effort, and a player must subordinate himself to the group. Much literature about football, like the literature of war, revolves around the conflict between an individual's desires and the needs of the team (as defined by coaches and generals)

Perhaps, from DeLillo's perspective, the most significant similarity between football and the nuclear-age military is that each has evolved a complicated jargon that comes close to being gibberish. It is a jargon that distances human emotions from the violent ends of the enterprise. It is, in fact, the activating agent which sets in motion the forces of conflict. "Each play must have a name," Gary says at one point. "The naming of plays is important. All teams run the same plays. But each team uses an entirely different system of naming. . . . No play begins until its name is called." For DeLillo, in *End Zone* and elsewhere in his fiction, the link between language and recalcitrant human nature is a conundrum to be pondered.

Douglas Terry's *The Last Texas Hero* (1982) is a novel that is not as elegantly written as DeLillo's, but in many ways is a subtler study of the culture of football. Terry, who played at Southern Methodist University in the 1970s, implies that on a college squad comprising upwards of a hundred men, earning playing time (to say nothing of stardom) means selling one's soul — or at least sacrificing one's individuality to a sometimes monstrous system devised by sadistic, self-aggrandizing coaches. The epigraph to Terry's novel is a quote from Jean Jacques Rousseau: "To renounce one's Liberty is to renounce one's quality as a man, the rights and also the duties of humanity."

The Last Texas Hero is narrated by Homer T. Jones, a kind of hick

Holden Caulfield. During his high-school days, Homer had been an all-state performer in Rutherford Park, Texas, where "the world is shaped like a football." He and his buddies Shad Sparks and Harold Sims are heavily recruited by college coaches. Recruiting has long been recognized as one of the more distasteful aspects of college football. Grown men must humble themselves before seventeen-year-olds, making unrealistic promises (and, according to the testimony of some, under-the-table cash payments, though there is no hint of this practice in Terry's account). Succumbing to the blandishments of Burt Carnegie, head coach of the Dallas University Wildcats, the three young men head for the big city, their heads filled with dreams of gridiron glory.

Once settled at Dallas U., they find a situation very different from what they expected. A caste system prevails on the team: at the top are the "jocks," those who actually play the games on Saturdays and thus have the best housing and the most privileges; then there are the freshmen, who have yet to win their spurs and are not likely to be given the chance to do so for a year or two; at the bottom are the "scouts," pathetic drones whose function is to simulate the upcoming opponent's plays during practice sessions and who are not even allowed to suit up for games.

Coach Carnegie rarely shows up at practices; his job is taking care of public relations and extracting money from wealthy alumni. The team is actually run by assistant coaches. One is a former Marine drill instructor who subjects the scouts and freshmen to dehumanizing, military-style exercises. The purpose of these exercises is supposedly to enhance team discipline and cohesion. Their practical effect, however, is to pit player against player, friend against friend; individual survival becomes the only goal. This brutal hazing has one of two outcomes: either players drop out of the program (in which case their scholarships can be used to lure fresh recruits) or their spirits are broken and they give themselves over wholly to the will of the coaches. The latter outcome is particularly relevant to the freshmen, since the scouts' spirits were broken long ago. "And they just keep on suckin' at you," Homer declares, "and keep on takin' till they get it all. Even your hopes and your dreams."

Homer arrives at college full of idealism and high expectations. He aspires to be not just a football hero, but a John Wayne-type hero "who stands for something worth a damn . . . something decent and honest." He immediately recognizes the injustice of what is occurring around him. He especially resents the defensive coordinator, Crazy Ray Cutler, a psychopath who demands violence and even "killing" (metaphorically speaking, of course) during practice and then sponsors a "fellowship of Athletes" that holds prayer meetings in the evenings. Homer fiercely resists being drawn into such an insane machine. He foments a brief mutiny among his teammates, only to end up a pariah, one of the contemptible scouts, the object of Crazy Ray's relentless wrath.

But the process can be seductive as well as brutal. If one technique doesn't get the desired result, another may. The novel's concluding chapter is completely unexpected, and unfortunately completely believable. Due to teammates' injuries, Homer is accorded a rare opportunity to play in a game. He responds by almost singlehandedly thwarting the opposing team's offense. Suddenly he becomes Crazy Ray's star pupil. Coach Carnegie takes him to an alumni luncheon at the Petroleum Club in downtown Dallas. The press announces that a new star has been born. All of Homer's altruistic motives vanish. Clearly fame, and the perks that go with it, have co-opted him into a cruel, Darwinian system he once despised. *The Last Texas Hero* is a powerful, disturbing book. As a fable, its implications extend well beyond the realm of college football. It is a shame that its author apparently has published nothing more since this first (and only) novel. Perhaps Terry, like his protagonist, knows only one subject: "when you take the game away," Homer says, "well, it's like stealing a violin from Vivaldi, or telling Liberace he can't play the piano any more."

The youngest variety of Texas football — professional football, which has been around less than four decades — has stimulated the most literary interest, and much of that interest has centered on one club: the Dallas Cowboys. The Cowboys were formed in 1960 as an expansion team in the National Football League. I was a college student at the time, and I have been a Cowboys fan from day one. It was not easy being a fan that first year, when the team finished 0–11–1. But over time the trio of general manager Tex Shramm, personnel director Gil Brandt, and head coach Tom Landry built the Cowboys into one of the most remarkable franchises in professional sports — America's Team, loved or hated but never ignored. In more recent years the tandem of Jerry Jones and Jimmy Johnson/Barry Switzer has added more Super Bowl wins — along with a large dollop of embarrassment.

The Cowboys, at any rate, whatever else may be said about them, are never dull, and they supply media types, sometimes on a daily basis, with reams of copy. A Dallas sportswriter, Skip Bayless, has written in the 1990s three books about the Cowboys, beginning with *God's Coach,* all published by Simon and Schuster, one of the largest commercial houses in the country. In 1997 alone three works detailing the club's history—Peter Golenbock's *Cowboys Have Always Been My Heroes,* John Eisenberg's *Cotton Bowl Days,* and Mike Shropshire's *The Ice Bowl*—were brought out by major publishers.[6] Obviously there are many people out there who want to read about the doings of America's Team. Currently Bayless claims to be writing something in a more literary vein: a novel with a professional football setting. Extant fiction about Texas professional football portrays an earlier generation of players and coaches and hangers-on and is now somewhat dated, though not necessarily out of date. Gary Cartwright's *The Hundred-Yard War* (1968), for example, is a sprawling train wreck of a novel that nonetheless projects interesting and informed observations of the professional game.

In the 1960s Cartwright covered first the Dallas Texans (now the Kansas City Chiefs) of the American Football League and later the Cowboys of the NFL for Dallas newspapers. His novel concerns the Dallas Troopers of the AFL, though to the degree the characters are drawn from real life the story appears to be more about the Cowboys than the Texans. The backdrop of the tale is the cut-throat competition between the two leagues (which eventually merged), involving the babysitting of players during the professional draft and the inevitable escalation of salaries. The narrative spans the end of a disappointing season, the off-season, and training camp and exhibition games preceding the next season. The story simply stops dead in its tracks just before the final exhibition game. I don't know if the ending was the author's idea or an editor's, but it is disconcertingly abrupt.

Though point of view shifts frequently, the focal character of the tale is the Troopers' quarterback, Rylie "Long John" Silver. Without question Silver is a fictionalized version of the Cowboys' first quarterback, Dandy Don Meredith, the most intriguing personality ever to play for the Dallas team. Meredith had been an All-American at SMU, and he came to the Cowboys in their initial season, 1960. He suffered through some dismal times, often playing injured and running for his life because the offensive line was so inept. Eventually he would quarterback the team in two league championship games against the Green Bay Packers. Dallas lost both games. The public perception of Meredith in Dallas in the 1960s is a good example of what I meant earlier when I used the phrase "power of the pen."

Cartwright, who covered the Cowboys for the *Dallas Morning News,* became convinced that Meredith was a "loser," and he confided his opinion to readers. In 1965 he wrote an oft-quoted lead to a story (Dan Jenkins uses a version of it in *Semi-Tough*) following a Cowboys loss to the Cleveland

Browns in which Meredith threw an interception just as it appeared the Cowboys would score and tie the game: "Outlined against a grey November sky, the Four Horsemen rode again Sunday. You know them: Pestilence, death, famine and Meredith."[7] Peter Gent, who caught passes from Meredith in the 1960s, told Golenbock, as reported in *Cowboys Have Always Been My Heroes* (an "oral history" of the team) that, following the newspaper story, "we had a private team meeting without the coaches over Cartwright. They all wanted to kill him [a severe physical beating was proposed], and Meredith kept saying, 'You can't. It's his job. He's just doing his job like we're doing ours.'"[8]

Don Meredith retired at the end of the 1968 season, probably before he really wanted to. But Coach Landry, who surprisingly often caved in to public opinion, declined to try to talk him into coming back, so the decision stuck. Meredith went on to become a popular analyst on ABC's *Monday Night Football* and a moderately successful movie and TV actor. Today he lives in seclusion in Santa Fe, New Mexico. In a recent *Texas Monthly* piece, Cartwright admitted that he had been wrong about Meredith: "Don Meredith was an extraordinarily gifted and complex man, at once whimsical and introspective, and no one ever worked harder or under more pain or pressure to prove himself as an athlete."[9] At the time he wrote *The Hundred-Yard War*, however, in the late 1960s, Cartwright had not yet arrived at such a balanced judgment.

The adjective that best describes Rylie Silver in the novel is *flippant*. He seems to suffer from a lack of high seriousness about football—or anything else. He wants to be a serious and sober leader, but various diversions—women and liquor and a "blind revulsion" against the demands of everyday life most prominently—undermine his best intentions. Ultimately he is a feckless human being whose moral limitations are symbolized by a tendency to throw interceptions in crucial situations. Coach Andy Craig, a cerebral Tom Landry-like tactician who believes players are interchangeable parts and it's the system that wins games, can accept Rylie's failings. Ward Dandridge, a stern Jimmy Johnson-like disciplinarian, cannot. When Dandridge replaces Craig at the beginning of a new season, Rylie is traded to another team because, as Dandridge tells him, he is a "loser."

As I said, *The Hundred-Yard War* falls considerably short as a work of art. But it does create a world—the world of a professional football team—from the perspective of somebody who knows a lot about what he's depicting, but is not an insider. (A character who pops up in the narrative now and then is a sportswriter named Pat Henderson, a likable and sympathetic chap.) One topic that Cartwright does not shy away from is race and the white/black divisions endemic to most professional sports these days. Troopers' management imposes an arbitrary quota to limit the number of black players on the team, and even a whisper about interracial sex is enough to get a player—a black player—traded. Cartwright, in sum, shows the pettiness, the brutality, the trafficking in human flesh that are an integral part of professional football. For management and coaches, players are indeed "meat on the hoof," and the death of a player from heat stroke and dehydration can be solemnly glossed over at a press conference and then forgotten.

If *The Hundred-Yard War* impresses with its gritty realism, Dan Jenkins's *Semi-Tough* (1972) is semi-fluff. To be sure, there are some very funny—and very salacious—scenes in the novel. Narrated by Billy Clyde Puckett (he is taping his ruminations on football and life for his collaborator on a book project), the story takes place mostly in Los Angeles during the week prior to the Super Bowl in which the New York Giants will play the "dog-ass New York Jets." Billy Clyde is the Giants' running back, and his buddy Shake Tiller is the feared wide receiver. After earning all-star honors in college at TCU, they had come to the Giants as a package. They hang out mostly with their pal Barbara Jane Bookman, who has known them since grade-school days in Fort Worth. Barbara Jane is now a model and actress in New York.

Jenkins, like Cartwright, addresses the problem of race in professional sports, but strictly for comic effect. Billy Clyde and Shake demonstrate they are actually enlightened on the subject by ostentatiously using the n-word whenever and wherever possible. The two friends share a Manhattan apartment, where they divide time between hosting wild parties and having deep philosophical discussions—about, for example, the attributes of the perfect woman:

> had to be extremely gorgeous in all ways from the minute she woke up . . . never got mad at anything a man might accidentally do, no matter how thoughtless or careless it might be . . . didn't care about having a lot of money . . . had to be good-natured and laugh a lot . . . could cook anything a man wanted fixed, quickly, and good.

Barbara Jane is almost a perfect woman, but not quite, since, as even Billy Clyde and Shake perceive, there is no "perfect woman." Twenty-five years after its publication, in a day of sometimes rancorous political correctness, *Semi-Tough* definitely seems a period piece.[10]

Jenkins introduces a supporting cast of zany characters: Coach Shoat Cooper, a Barry Switzer–like buffoon whose team is talented enough to win in spite of his half-baked ideas; Big Ed Bookman, Barbara Jane's father, a stereotypical Texas tycoon who is convinced God has chosen him as an arbiter of American political and social mores; T. J. Lambert, a defensive lineman, the butt (no pun intended) of many tasteless flatulence jokes; Elroy Blunt, a former player who has become a successful country-and-western composer and singer (one of his better efforts is called "I'm Just a Bug on the Windshield of Life").

The book is great fun, of course. But as far as supplying even a bare-bones sketch of what the life of a professional football player is really like, *Semi-Tough* is useless. There is much drinking, some dope-smoking, and plenty of recreational sex, but no inkling of the underlying reasons for such manic partying. The hedonism is front and center, but any hint of emotional complexity is absent. It is hardly surprising that *Semi-Tough* was excerpted in *Playboy* before its publication between hard covers.

The best of all Texas novels about professional football is Peter Gent's *North Dallas Forty*. Gent, who played six seasons for the Dallas Cowboys, writes with inside knowledge of the sport. To reread the book a quarter-century after its composition is to be reminded that scandals revolving around the Cowboys are an old story. All professional teams are aware of the necessity for good public relations; thus they attempt — usually unsuccessfully — to control their players' off-the-field behavior. Sports pages these days seem to have more police blotter reports than scores of games. Perhaps scandal is now an occupational hazard of professional sport. As Bill Russell, the great center for the Boston Celtics, once pointed out, professional athletes have been "on scholarship" since they were in the second grade; it's probably not realistic to expect them to grow up overnight and assume responsibility for their actions.[11] The Dallas Cowboys, in any event, have always seemed to have more than their share of difficulties in this area.

North Dallas Forty, in both its novel and movie versions, generated a bit of scandal itself. The scandal had mostly to do with drug usage, both legal and illegal, though the drugs in question are tame by today's standards: marijuana and painkillers. The story's narrator is Phil Elliott, who plays wide receiver for an unnamed Dallas professional team. After several years of being pounded by opposing defensive backs and sustaining multiple injuries, his body is beginning to balk at the demands he makes of it. He attempts to compensate by popping pills and staying high as much as possible. One thing Gent makes clear (something neither Cartwright nor Jenkins seemed to understand) is that the emotion that governs the pro player above all others is fear—fear of injury, fear of one's skills eroding, fear of losing one's job. Terry, in *The Last Texas Hero*, says much the same thing about the college player: abusive and exploitative college coaches are feared and obeyed because they are perceived as controlling the player's future.

Elliott's best friend on the team is Seth Maxwell, the quarterback—again, a character obviously based on Don Meredith. The relationship of Phil and Seth reminds me of that of Huck Finn and Tom Sawyer. Huck is an authentic rebel; Tom plays at being a rebel, but deep down he craves adult approval. In any given situation, Phil bucks authority. When the general manager, Clinton Foote, begins contract negotiations one year by mailing out a mimeographed message that begins "Dear player," Phil sends a mimeographed reply that begins "Dear general manager." The general manager is not amused. Seth, on the other hand, frequently parties and smokes pot with Phil, but then, to please Coach B. A. Quinlan, he delivers a pious speech to "the Society of Christian Athletes." Coach Quinlan, in return, supplies Seth with advance notice of major moves within the team, while looking on Phil with squint-eyed exasperation. (It is interesting that both Cartwright and Gent portray the Don Meredith character as something of a management fink.)

Phil is shown to be a man who truly loves the game of football. Apart from the money and the fame, he tells himself, there is the pure joy of the game itself: "the thrill of playing is no less real and that thrill is indescribable. Doing something better than anyone else in front of millions of people. It is the highest I have ever been." Phil is shocked to discover that his coach and quarterback are more interested in personal success than team success—or at least that they see team success as an avenue to personal success. There seems a large element of naiveté in such disillusionment. Phil suspects he is being cynically manipulated, and his paranoia is confirmed when he is cut from the team and banished from football ostensibly because he is caught using marijuana, but actually because he has been fooling around with the owner's son's girlfriend. (Gent's paranoia—its presence in *North Dallas Forty* is unmistakable—reaches full flower in the 1983 novel *The Franchise*.) When he discovers Phil has been cut from the team, his "friend" Seth drops him like a hot potato.

Most readers in the 1970s assumed that *North Dallas Forty* was a roman à clef. But is it based directly on real events and real people? Cowboys officials and even some of his former teammates accused Gent of twisting the facts to suit his own self-serving agenda — and that may well have been the case. Still, for me the tale has the ring of truth. The novel opens with a scene in which Phil and Seth have accompanied a couple of near-homicidal defensive linemen on a drunken dove-hunting expedition in the open country west of Fort Worth. Bob Lilly, the Cowboys' Hall-of-Fame defensive tackle, was notorious for bird-hunting forays on Monday mornings following a game. Is one of the fictional linemen a version of Lilly? Does every character and event in the story have to have a basis in fact in order for Gent's picture of professional football to be valid?

In my opinion, no. Gent's depiction, however much it is intended as self-justification, seems more true than not. Many pro football players are driven by fear and consumed by pain, both emotional and physical, that they attempt to blunt with large doses of booze, drugs, and sex. True, they are frequently coddled, and they are paid a good deal more today than they were in the 1960s when Gent played, though average salaries in the NFL remain much less than those in other major professional leagues; and, while a few millionaire superstars are no doubt able to approach the game as a business proposition, most players today are still gladiators who face pretty much the same problems their predecessors did, in the glare of a media spotlight that Gent, as a player, never experienced. They are brutalized and exploited by their coaches and owners, by callous fans and by rapacious television executives — and, it must be admitted, by parasitic sports journalists. An old adage comes to mind: if you like to eat sausage, don't look too closely at the process by which it is made. If you are a football fan, it is best not to examine too closely the reality of life in the National Football League. Old habits die hard. I'm afraid I will always be a fan — and a frustrated sportswriter. Peter Gent has warned me on both counts, but it is too late to change the inclinations of a lifetime.

CHAPTER 12

Future Shock

Texas Writing Today and Tomorrow

*Texas, so quickly passing to the forefront in political and
commercial leadership, why not in authorship and criticism?*

— DAVIS FOUTE EAGLETON,
Writers and Writings of Texas (1913)

The pace of change in 1990s Texas is so rapid it induces vertigo in those of
us who are natives of the place. In a way, what I have been writing about —
at least when I have written about the reality rather than the myth; the
myth doesn't change, the reality does — is ancient history, a culture and a
literature that seem products of a distant past. According to an estimate I
saw recently, more than eighty percent of Texans now live in urban areas.
Immigration from other regions — and nations — continues to accelerate.
One can walk for blocks at a stretch down almost any busy street in Dallas
or Houston or Austin and never hear a Texas accent (except one's own).
Demographers predict that at some point fairly early in the next century a
majority of the state's population will be Hispanic.

How do such wrenching and volatile social transformations affect the
state's literature? To reassert a point with which I began these ruminations:
literature inevitably reflects the society and culture from which it issues —
and the society and culture inevitably shape the literature. One outgrowth
of the changes the state is currently undergoing is that we are inexorably
losing — perhaps have already lost — our regional distinctiveness. Do
people residing in, say, the suburbs of Dallas have anything resembling a
genuine sense of place? American culture is now so homogeneous they
might just as well be living in the suburbs of Atlanta or the suburbs of Los
Angeles. In the 1980s commentators coined the phrase "corridor culture"

to designate life in the bland, cookie-cutter suburbs clustered around the interstate highway corridors that connect Dallas–Fort Worth and Austin and San Antonio and Houston. This highway loop encompasses an area where more than half the state's population lives. I don't know if corridor culture is good or bad, but it is certainly a fact of contemporary Texas life.

Once again, I insist on what is no doubt a truism: Texas writers mirror the conditions of their culture. The qualities that in the past made Texas writing distinctive are, if not disappearing, becoming less visible in our literature. It seems to me that writers who think of themselves as *regional* writers will be, of necessity, conservative, even reactionary. In using the word "conservative," I am not suggesting a political stance. Regional writers are not members of any particular political party, nor are they necessarily committed to free market capitalism. Free-market capitalism is not, in fact, "conservative" in any sense of the term. Capitalism is the most radically disruptive of all economic and political philosophies, uprooting individuals and societies at the whim of market forces. It is indeed the agent that fuels the dizzying changes Texas — and the world — are currently experiencing.

True conservatism looks backward to a more stable communitarian ideal. Thus the social and cultural conservatism regional writers (whether consciously or not) espouse usually takes the form of preservation. It is in their vested interest to try to preserve those qualities and characteristics and traditions that make their region unique — and which thus help to make their writing unique. They must attempt to conserve, if only in the imagination, the land in something like its original state, to preserve those unique values and traditions that were nurtured by their culture, their piece of soil.

The literature of our neighbor to the west, New Mexico, provides an instructive paradigm. Recent New Mexico writers, almost without exception, are so reactionary that some of them come full circle and are perceived to be radical revolutionaries. They have been dismissed in some quarters as crazed conservationists or "back to nature" freaks, but they have nonetheless fashioned a vital literature that any region would be proud of. Frank Waters, William Eastlake, Edward Abbey, John Nichols, N. Scott Momaday, Leslie Silko, Rudolfo Anaya, Tony Hillerman — these and other New Mexico writers speak with one voice in advocating such things as the conservation of the natural order; the preserving of the traditions of the state's native populations; the curbing of the insatiable urban appetite to gobble up mountain, desert, and plain; individual and collective efforts to maintain the unique qualities of New Mexico life and landscape. Of course, writers are never powerful enough to halt "progress" and change. Without question, however, these literary folk have had an impact on popular attitudes in present-day New Mexico.

On the other hand, Texas writers seem, for better or worse, ambivalent on these propositions — much less committed to the past and to tradition, more willing to deal with modern life on its own terms. Once again, Larry McMurtry supplies an example. McMurtry's first three novels (published in the 1960s) are set in and around Thalia, an evaporating West Texas town, laid waste by a changing society and by shifting populations and ways of life. From there the author removed himself to a setting more and more Texans in the latter decades of the twentieth century were adapting themselves to: the city. In his introduction to *In a Narrow Grave: Essays on Texas* (1968), McMurtry says that he had thought of calling this collection "The Cowboy in the Suburbs," since that is the story he wished to explore in the essays in the book.

The great theme of Texas life in recent times evolved out of the removal of large numbers of people from village and country to the burgeoning cities and the adjustments, both personal and collective, required by that movement. McMurtry, in such mid-career novels as *Moving On* (1970), *All My Friends Are Going to Be Strangers* (1972), and *Terms of Endearment* (1975) — all set largely in Houston — treats the theme trenchantly and entertainingly. The subject of *Moving On,* for instance, is the disintegration of a modern marriage, demolished in part by the pressures and boredom of contemporary urban existence. Expressing disdain for what he called "Country-and-Western" literature, McMurtry moved on to other urban locales, as well. Later novels are set in Hollywood, Washington, D.C., and Las Vegas. Interestingly, when he finally, triumphantly returned to Texas in his fiction — in *Lonesome Dove* (1985) — it would be through the medium of history and myth, not the actuality of the present.

Clearly the city is a key player in recent Texas literature — and, given the increasingly urban nature of the state, looms even larger in the future. Throughout the twentieth century literary works by Texas writers have featured city settings. For instance, Philip Atlee's novel *The Inheritors* (1940) created a controversy by detailing the scandalous doings of Fort Worth teenagers in the 1930s. The main characters in the novel are dissolute country-club youth, corrupted by their families' oil wealth, who expend their energies in endless rounds of joyless hedonism. Atlee recounts it all with a kind of stilted realism. But despite an occasional work of this sort, it was not until the early 1960s that the Texas city novel emerged as a recognizable subgenre.

Specifically 1963 seems to have been the turning point in the development of Texas city literature. That was, needless to say, a momentous year, the date of the assassination of President John F. Kennedy, the event that gave Dallas, in particular, a history worthy of literary scrutiny. Edwin "Bud" Shrake, in *But Not for Love* (1964), a novel written before the assassination, describes an automobile drive through downtown Dallas: "With a tree there was at least some kind of a sense of history but nobody had thought of that until it was too late and now they had no history except their inventories." After November 22, 1963, Dallas had a history, and few subsequent serious novels about the city have overlooked that date.

Thus *North Dallas Forty*, Peter Gent's scathing critique of laissez-faire capitalism and professional football Dallas-style, contains a brooding historical presence absent from pre-assassination novels: "Back in the early sixties, five minutes past the toll gate, heading for either end, you were out in the West. That was when Braniff's planes were gray. Jack Ruby ran a burlesque house. And the School Book Depository was a place they kept schoolbooks." Georgia McKinley's *Follow the Running Grass* (1969) makes the connection another way: "But at the other end of the space a parade reenacted itself in the mind's eye, the gleaming phantoms of cars moved in the gay light, left Elm Street to turn onto Houston, then make the sharp left turn onto the approaches and enter history."

Shrake's *Strange Peaches* (1972) and Bryan Woolley's *November 22* (1981) are post-assassination novels that place the murder of John Kennedy center stage. Both invoke the frontier mentality as a source of the poisonous atmosphere that prevailed in Dallas in the early 1960s. *Strange Peaches* is set in Dallas in the autumn of 1963. John Lee Wallace, a strung-out ex-cowboy who has become a TV star (his series is titled *Six Guns Across Texas*), has returned to his native Dallas to make a documentary movie about the city, a film that will "tell what the place was really about." One of John Lee's perceptions is that the citizens of Dallas—particularly the rich and powerful—have made the transition from a rural to an urban environment much too rapidly. "Many of them," he says, "had leaped from the farm or the service or the Depression shack into the country club and the opera league."

To such people the simplistic frontier verities still apply. One of the characters, a lobbyist, draws the following analogy in explaining the American political system:

> The rancher wants to protect his cows and his land from the sheep-herders, and so he gets the mayor and sheriff on his side. That's politics. Suppose the rancher needs more land for raising beef cattle, and he asks his congressman to get the army to chase off the Indians. Politics. If the farmers get together and elect their own mayor and sheriff and run off the rancher and sheep-herders, too, that's politics, John Lee.

Given such a view of the world, it is not surprising that the well-to-do of Dallas see Kennedy as their archenemy. He is suave and sophisticated; they are rough-hewn and anxious. He is a liberal intellectual; they are country people still grasping for a higher rung on the economic and social ladder. In sum, Kennedy is viewed as a threat to their wealth and power, a rival to be dealt with in the simplest frontier terms. "Jack's coddling the Russians and wanting test-ban treaties," shouts the lobbyist. "We need a man on horseback to lead this country." Even the good guys, John Lee and his friend Buster (fictionalized versions, apparently, of the author and Gary "Jap" Cartwright), are not immune to the desire for quick and easy frontier justice. Following the murder of the president, they roam the streets of the city looking for "grinning fascist butts" to kick.

Strange Peaches is an exceptionally powerful evocation of urban life in modern Texas. One of the most striking aspects of the book is the vivid contrast between what was, just a few years ago, and what now is. John Lee must try — never very successfully — to reconcile his past self with his present self. The rural ethos of his childhood (two years spent in the country as his father attempted to succeed as a farmer, summer work on West Texas ranches) is juxtaposed starkly with the moral chaos of the modern cities in which he lives. The fundamentalist religion of his early years is a distant, but disturbing, echo in the existentialist nihilism in which he exists.

Of one of his drug trips John Lee says:

> The first lesson acid teaches is that there is no authority for any belief. What is perceived in one condition to be one thing may in another condition be something else altogether. . . . But this didn't bother me. My childhood God had blown off, and I had learned to be without and had built suitable structures from which to make necessary judgments while I waited it out.

In a passage reminiscent of Hemingway's *The Sun Also Rises,* John Lee describes how a column of golden light in a church in Mexico strikes in him "a sort of terror I had not experienced since I was a boy in the Baptist Church — a terror unlike that which comes with acid, for this terror was of my own unworthiness before the unexplainable mystery of God, not a dread of nothing."

The pain of John Lee's guilt and of his existential angst can be dulled only by drugs and by violent action. At the close of the narrative he has discovered in Mexico a wild land where the skills of the frontiersman are still worth having. The modern day outlaw, Erwin Englethorpe, introduces John Lee to the Mexican outback: "it's pure Wild West. Ever'body that's rich enough to have a gun wears it and there ain't no telephones, and a cop or a doctor is liable to be three days away by horseback." Though he is a gun runner and dope smuggler, Englethorpe claims, "I ain't a crook, I'm an adventurer." At novel's end John Lee apparently plans to follow in Englethorpe's adventurous footsteps.

Bryan Woolley's *November 22,* a naturalistic novel of surfaces done in the manner of John Dos Passos, traces the activities of a dozen or so Dallasites during the twenty-four hours of the day Kennedy was shot. Perhaps the novel's chief value lies in its careful recreation of the mood and temper of the city immediately preceding the presidential visit. As Woolley depicts it, the atmosphere is volatile, needing only a spark to ignite. *Wanted for Treason* handbills circulate in the streets. Newspaper advertisements indict the president for dereliction of duty and demand vigilante justice. Extremist political groups spew hate and vituperation at the man in the White House and his eastern liberal cronies (and, within hours after the shooting, try to organize assassination parties for the day of the funeral).

In *November 22,* as in *Strange Peaches,* Dallas is shown to be a frontier city — raw, violent, narcissistic. Many citizens of Dallas who are genuinely disturbed by the assassination worry more about the city's tarnished image that about the dead president. But if Dallas is painted as crass and anxiety-ridden, it is also, in the frontier tradition, a city of opportunity, for rich and poor alike. For the budding tycoon, Rodney Dart, "Dallas was definitely the place to make a million these days." For the illegal alien Luis, the message the city sends is clear: "That everyone could be something, if they worked hard and learned English and were lucky and the Border Patrol didn't take them away."

Those who have made the most of their opportunities have become, of course, the city's civic and corporate leaders. The richest man in town is old J. L. Fisher (a fictionalized H. L. Hunt). Fisher is the most vivid—certainly the most appalling—character in the novel. Others in Dallas's power structure—such as Fisher's right-hand man, a West Texan who calls himself R. Quentin Babcock—have acquired a veneer of polish, or at least a kind of self-imposed blandness. Old J. L. remains a rugged (and ragged) frontiersman to the end. He is said to look "like an ancient desert rat, a cowboy gnome, grotesque behind the big mahogany desk." Fisher's favorite and oft-repeated story concerns an old companion, Buck Pool, now long dead. He and Buck had been prospecting for oil in revolutionary Mexico in 1916, and Buck had shot and killed two Mexican bandits trying to steal their horses. Over the years Fisher's mind has fixed on this episode as a fable of frontier survival: seize opportunities by force, defend them with violence if necessary.

When news of the assassination reaches Fisher, the old man, in his fevered senility, becomes convinced that Buck has risen from the dead to shoot Kennedy because "he's stealing our horses":

> Buck had known something. Buck found out the bandits were coming and circled around and ambushed them clean as a whistle. Kennedy. Connally. All of them. Surprised as hell, never expecting Buck up there with the Winchester, cutting down on them like lightning out of nowhere, bursting their skulls like gourds. . . . Praise God, from whom all blessings flow. The Lord helps those who help themselves. Buck dancing like an Indian, holding the Winchester over his head, hair blowing in the wind, stripping Kennedy and Connally of cartridge belts, guns, knives, leading the horses back to camp, turning to watch the buzzards' circles get smaller and tighter and lower and lower.

In his office atop a modernistic downtown building, Fisher celebrates the killing with canned chili and tumblers of Jim Beam bourbon.

A Dallas novel in which the assassination is rarely mentioned but whose characters live in its shadow is Georgia McKinley's *Follow the Running Grass*. The book weaves, in a dense, high-octane prose, a Faulknerian tale of guilt and of mental and moral derangement. The protagonist, Delmon Goode, a civil-rights lawyer in New York City, returns to Dallas in the mid-1960s to visit his dying mother. Delmon springs from a pioneer Texas family, some of whose members have made enough money to occupy mansions in Dallas's Highland Park: they are, Delmon muses, "a group of hearty, successful people, full of frontier zest and vigor." They are also people "caught in a violent nostalgia for another time; the pinch and grip of it was like a rheumatism; it showed in their faces."

Through the tortured thoughts of Zilla, Delmon's mother, the narrative reaches back over a century of family and regional history, from the family's nineteenth-century arrival in West Texas — "out there, a million miles from nowhere" — to its conquest of the financial citadels of Dallas: a town "come up by violence out of an earth ripped open, come up the way the oil had, rising, spurting higher out of an infertile country." Theo, Delmon's uncle, has traveled from abject poverty during the 1930s Depression to fabulous wealth in the 1960s. And yet that "violent nostalgia" for past times has made Theo a pitiful, perhaps dangerous, victim of old-settler xenophobia: "Trying to take it away," he says of the "Jewish cowboys" invading Dallas, "from us — the old families that built it up."

Coming from such a family, Delmon feels embarrassment and guilt. His career as a civil-rights activist is, clearly, an attempt to find personal absolution, to atone for the sins of his family and region. But Delmon's choice of vocation also issues from a desire to strike out to a new frontier, a motive that has propelled his family from the beginning: "he believed, as his ancestors had before him, that he should move on from whatever ground he held, outward toward some more advanced point . . . leaving behind him a better order than he had found, meanwhile flaying about him mightily to clear the fields of inequality and prejudice, as his people had dug away at the deep-rooted burdock and the jimson weed."

At the close of the novel Delmon is left morally and emotionally disoriented, unable to come to terms with his past or with himself. Still, he finds a symbol of stability in the figure of his pioneer grandfather, the family patriarch. The grandfather had been a buffalo hunter, had, in the family legend, once killed an Indian to save himself and his children. Even as an old man near the end of his life he saw beckoning frontiers to the west, was possessed by the mad delusion that he would soon leave for California to look for gold. At the assassination site Delmon fantasizes the return of his grandfather, a fantasy that effectively links the mythic frontier past with the violent urban present:

Coming into his mind with the full force of the western myth behind him, his grandfather was no longer adjunct to his own mind but had begun his own action — was riding into town for some secret purpose — to oppose evil! Ride out! Ride out! Grandpa had become the western hero — it was Grandpa up on the pony, shining in the sun, the single good man riding into town to some invincible purpose, before whom destiny itself must yield; Grandpa riding alone down the empty middle of the street in the blazing noon of a hot autumn day — riding out, riding out against destiny. For a moment it seemed to Delmon that if Grandpa had been there on that day when the president was shot! That perhaps — even yet . . . .

If Dallas in recent Texas fiction is preeminently the city of reactionary politics, where presidents are slain in the name of historical fantasies blessed by both the left and the right, Houston is the place where murder is merely personal. Thomas Thompson's *Blood and Money* (1976), a nonfiction novel that enjoyed enormous national success, is the prototype of a batch of books that explore the strange subculture of Houston's fast-money set. Laura Furman's *The Shadow Line* (1982), for example, is a novel that probes, with subtle artistry, the connection between money and murder in Houston. Furman writes in a dry, understated, highly polished style, and she possesses an extraordinarily deft touch in describing the texture of life in Houston, the surfaces of things, the sounds and smells, the weather and semitropical plant life. She conveys a sense of the city's shape, its varied districts, the glittering downtown area, the suburbs which inexorably chew away the surrounding countryside: "the cheap motels and surplus warehouses, the neon signs as big as buildings, and the shopping centers that were the town squares for Houstonians who lived in this sprawl."

The newness and rawness of Houston are suggested by seemingly trivial details: people still keep chickens and cows, even goats, within the city limits. As a young city, Houston is frontier territory, a city of opportunity, a place where fortunes may be made overnight. The central character of *The Shadow Line* is Liz Gold, a native New Yorker who has come to Houston in part because it is a boomtown. Liz is wise enough to realize that Houston has made her a different person from the one she was in New York or in Sweden: "Once in a while it came over her that she was in a strange place where she couldn't read the signs for people or the weather. Yet it was for the strangeness she'd come." The disorientation deriving from being "a stranger who recognizes the lack of landmarks" sometimes makes her "dizzy."

Liz is a magazine reporter who is assigned the task of investigating a murder in Galveston that has remained unsolved for a quarter of a century. As Liz digs into the case, a bizarre story involving some of Houston's super rich unfolds. She discovers the power and privilege, including immunity from prosecution, that wealth bestows in a free-form society like Houston's; the frontier city offers freedom and opportunity, but it also breeds injustice and corruption. At story's close, Liz's reformist instincts have been roused, but it is unclear how she will fight injustice or whether her efforts, in the end, will come to anything.

David L. Lindsey has written a series of superior mystery novels, including *A Cold Mind* (1983), set in Houston. These novels feature an unlikely police detective named Stuart Haydon. Haydon is highly educated and independently wealthy. He wears expensive suits and drives a Jaguar. He travels easily between the city's gleaming, upscale downtown and the seamy pockets of life that surround it. Haydon sports a sharp eye for the essences of Houston life:

> Houston has no zoning laws. The supreme authority is money. It is the impetus for manic growth, growth so uncontrolled and uninhibited that it approaches the obscene. The city lies wide open like a promiscuous and greedy woman who gives herself with abandon to anyone who can afford her and wants her. Many can and do.

In Lindsey's fiction Houston is a "city of dreadful night." Here, for instance, is the author's description of a Houston sunset: "A menacing fog engulfed the freeway and scattered the rays of the westward falling sun. It suffocated the city and seemed a major cause for the crawling traffic, weakened by a lack of oxygen." The noxious mists that float over Houston are the Texas equivalent of the fog in Dickens's *Bleak House:* both symbolize the corruption of the social organism. Like Dickens's London or, more to the point, Raymond Chandler's Los Angeles, Lindsey's Houston comes alive through the writer's talented pen.

The plot of *A Cold Mind* is clever, but turns out to be pretty standard fare for fans of the mystery genre. A series of murders of call girls sends Haydon along a path that leads him to — you guessed it — some of the city's richest and most exotic citizens. The conclusion of the novel, though, is unexpected, and it does manage to convey something of the moral atmosphere of present-day Houston. The daughter of one of the murder victims, dismayed by the loops and tangles of the criminal justice system that seem likely to allow the guilty party to go free, blows away the murderer's head with a powerful handgun: "He never would have gotten what he deserved. I heard [he] was going to switch to an insanity plea. You know,

I don't believe insanity cancels out evil actions." This is the Houston way—frontier justice meted out with a vengeance!

Later Lindsey crime novels—*Heat from Another Sun* (1984), *Spiral* (1986), and *Mercy* (1990) among them—entertain while exploring in further detail Houston's singular ambiance. Still later ones have drifted farther afield, to settings in Mexico, Guatemala, and Russia. In Texas in the 1990s, it sometimes seems there is a mystery writer lurking under every rock. A. W. Gray, Bill Crider, Doug Swanson, Mary Willis Walker, Joe Lansdale, Susan Wittig Albert, Kinky Friedman, Jesse Sublett, Thomas Zigal, Neal Barrett, Jr.—this is but a partial list of the talented mystery novelists now pursuing their trade in the state. Moreover, James Crumley and James Lee Burke, native Texans now living in Montana, have built substantial national reputations based on their mystery fiction. None of these writers, however, can match the smooth plotting and elegant prose style displayed in David Lindsey's suspense thrillers.

Of all Texas cities Austin seems the one newcomers take to most readily. Of all Texas cities, moreover, Austin is the one that seems to me to have changed most drastically over the last few decades. Fiction helps the reader track some of those changes. Glimpses of Austin have appeared in Texas fiction for nearly a century. In Ruth Cross's *The Golden Cocoon* (1924), for instance, Austin is little more than an overgrown town. Offering some odd and unintentionally humorous accounts of student life at the University of Texas, Cross's novel tells the story of a young woman from rural Lamar County who uses the city as an arena in which to prove herself. Eventually she marries the governor, runs away to New York where she becomes a famous playwright, and in the end is reconciled with her husband who has become one of President Wilson's closest advisors.

Probably the first full-fledged city novel about Austin—perhaps the first full-fledged city novel in Texas literature—is Billy Lee Brammer's *The Gay Place* (1961). In Brammer's depiction Austin is a pleasant, easygoing town whose raison d'être rests (as even Ruth Cross's novel from the 1920s shows) on two things: education and politics. Especially politics. *The Gay Place* is the book that people who knew Austin well in the 1950s and 1960s recommend to their friends as the best literary projection of the city's unique charm. I am one of those people. When the book was first published, I was a college student (though not at the University of Texas). I immediately bought a copy and read it avidly.

At the time I was interested in state politics and was aware of the small band of liberals making a splash in state government in Austin, knew something about the so-called *Texas Observer* crowd and the *Observer's* brilliant editor, Willie Morris. I thought I could identify several of the characters in the novel. *The Gay Place* is perhaps Texas fiction's most successful roman à clef. Most of its people were drawn directly from real life, from the Austin political scene of the late 1950s. The best-known character in the novel — Governor Arthur "Goddam" Fenstemaker — is a thoroughly compelling literary portrait of Lyndon B. Johnson. Brammer had been an aide to Johnson when the latter was Majority Leader of the U.S. Senate, and his admiration for Johnson appears to have bordered on idolatry.

What attracted me most to *The Gay Place* back in 1961, however, was not the vitality and larger-than-life dimensions of Arthur Fenstemaker. It was, instead, what had attracted me to Hemingway's *The Sun Also Rises* and Fitzgerald's *Tender Is the Night:* the chic, aimless hedonism of the characters, their vaguely bittersweet existential angst and self-pity, their perpetual adolescent navel-gazing. I don't know if he set out to do this, but Brammer became the poet of a generation of Texans that I found attractive. Every generation, I suppose, believes itself uniquely burdened, even doomed. Hemingway proudly displayed Gertrude Stein's description of him and the other 1920s Paris expatriates as the epigraph to *The Sun Also Rises:* "You are all a lost generation." Brammer's portrayal in *The Gay Place* of young (but aging) idealists rapidly becoming dissipated cynics is a memorable literary approximation of a Texas lost generation. Coming back to the book today, I find *The Gay Place* both timely and dated. There are in it descriptions of Austin and the world as it existed almost four decades ago that seem so remote as to be incomprehensible. The city and the political environment of the late 1950s live now only in memory and an occasional rush of nostalgia. On the other hand, the human "flea circus" that Brammer reports on retains its immediacy.

The people — politicians, journalists, assorted hangers-on — still seem to me living, breathing human beings, flawed and fumbling, uncertain and insecure in their daily and professional lives. Their nervous, often absurd caperings are set against the gargantuan backdrop of Arthur Fenstemaker, spouting an endless stream of cynicism and folksy political wisdom. Unlike the lesser mortals around him, Arthur knows who he is, and instinctively he knows the appropriate course of action. He is almost godlike, and he is the glue that holds the three long segments of the narrative together.

In the late 1960s hippies and cosmic cowboys became a prominent part of the Austin milieu. Pat Ellis Taylor's *Afoot in a Field of Men* (1988) is the best literary treatment of hippie life in Texas in the 1960s and 1970s. A series of related stories, the book chronicles the struggles of a character named "Pat," a dropout from the middle-class, suburban rat race, who struggles along in noble poverty, working mostly as a "temporary," in order to pursue her dream of being a writer. Several of the stories are set in Austin, though most are laid in East Dallas. Writing under the name Pat LittleDog, the author published another volume of Pat's adventures, *In Search of the Holy Mother of Jobs* (1991), and almost all of the tales in the latter collection are set in Austin. Taylor/LittleDog's work is wholly unusual and arresting, though it displays a very narrow range of technique and subject matter. Probably, in fact, the writer has pretty much exhausted the possibilities of the subject matter with this pair of slim volumes.

Austin's — and the state's — first real economic boom, created by the surging price of oil, occurred in the 1970s and early 1980s. Texas became part of the Sun Belt phenomenon as people from older, worn-out regions flocked to the South and Southwest in search of new beginnings. Austin became the state's fastest growing major city. According to many of its citizens — Austinites have always been more conservationist-minded than residents of other urban areas in Texas — it quickly became an overdeveloped city. High-rises sprouted overnight like gleaming mushrooms. Industrial and housing projects systematically denuded the surrounding hills of vegetation, leaving them vulnerable to flooding and erosion. Environmentalists fretted and fussed, but development and environmental pillage continued — and continue — apace.

A work of fiction that deals provocatively with this period in Austin's history is Peter LaSalle's *Strange Sunlight* (1984). According to one of the characters in the novel, the emigrés who came to Texas in the 1970s and 1980s were different from those who migrated to other Sun Belt states. The "nuts" who trek to California, he says, go "after confused things like dreams, dreams of movies or religious cults. When the nuts come to Texas they know what they want. Money. This is where the jobs are, this is where the money is."

Austin in the 1980s, as LaSalle sketches it, is no longer the tolerant, easygoing place where college students, legislators, and good old boys mingled freely and, on the whole, good-naturedly. It is, instead, a city where money and material goods supply the validation of one's sense of identity and self-worth. The people who now dominate Austin are Yuppies for the most part, along with a smattering of ex-dope dealers who have been transformed into semi-respectable "developers" and a large contingent of burned-out, vaguely sinister hippies—dregs of the 1960s and 1970s counter-culture.

The central character of *Strange Sunlight* is Jack Willington, a New Englander in his thirties who moves to Austin and lands a job as traveling salesman for a national sporting goods firm. As his commissions grow far beyond his initial expectations, Willington indulges himself in a symbolic purchase: a Mercedes 450SLC. He begins thinking about trading in his south Austin apartment for a condo overlooking Lake Travis. Eventually, through hard work and luck, his success is assured: he is promoted to regional sales manager, an executive-level position within the company.

But all is not well. To reach the executive level, Willington must betray a colleague who suffers an emotional breakdown. He ditches a girlfriend in favor of a *Playboy* playmate of the month; the former girlfriend goes to pieces, finally dying of a drug overdose. Willington's past keeps popping into his consciousness in unexpected ways. When he looks at himself in mirrors, he cannot resist crying. Is Willington to blame for "the sweet mess of things" he finds himself in? Or is the "strange sunlight" of Austin the cause of his disorientation?

A month after being made regional sales manager, Willington goes berserk. He mutilates his Mercedes with a baseball bat. In a fury he kills a man for attempting to sell him pornographic photographs of the dead girlfriend. (The pictures have gone up in monetary value because the girl is dead.) Willington's acts of violence, while irrational, are not without moral significance. They are, of course, his instinctive rejection of a system in which the only standard of value is money—a system in which people, even when dead, are commodities to be bought and sold.

More than a generation ago Erich Fromm warned of the dangers of a consumer society in which "happiness consists in 'having fun,' in the satisfaction of consuming." The modern American, writes Fromm in *The Art of Loving* (1956), is "well fed, well clad, satisfied sexually, yet without self, without any except the most superficial contact with his fellow men." As a result he has become an "alienated automaton," unable to overcome "human separateness" and his essential aloneness.[1] The existential crisis of consumerism of which Fromm speaks, as Peter LaSalle memorably shows, has now spread across Texas much like the boll weevil in an earlier epoch.

Some time in the 1970s music began to assume as much importance in the Austin economy—and self-image—as politics and education. In the 1970s "redneck rock" and country outlaws held sway. Then there was a period when blues and jazz were dominant. Recently more varied forms of avant-garde popular music have flourished in the city's clubs and concert halls. Austin now bills itself as "the live music capital of the world." *Night Time Losing Time* (1989), by Michael Ventura, who as a local columnist for a decade studied the music capital at close range, is a somewhat over-wrought first novel set mostly in 1980 and mainly in Austin, with stops in New Orleans and Lubbock and Quartzsite, Arizona.

The book's protagonist is Jesse Wales (born Giuseppe Andriozzi), a blues pianist whose taste for booze and sex — and very strange women — eventually forces him over the edge. The reader views the Austin music scene through Jesse's knowing eyes. (As a bonus, a lengthy scene in the middle of the book, recounting the filming of a low-budget movie in a dingy club, anticipates 1990s Austin which has become a major hub for filmmaking.) The real subject of *Night Time,* however, is spiritual, not musical. Jesse's quest for his soul leads down some interesting byways, from fundamentalist Christianity to satanism. Ultimately, though, the novel is marred by a straining for effect, a portentousness that too often trails off disappointingly.

Jesse Sublett's *Rock Critic Murders* (1989), a mystery novel laid in Austin in the mid-1980s, is a frothier concoction, but on the whole it is more satisfying because of its very lack of ambition. Sublett is a musician who knows firsthand the sleazy underside of the music business. The narrator of *Rock Critic Murders,* Martin Fender, works as a "skiptracer" by day (a collection agency hires him to hunt people who have walked out on their bills) and a bass player in Austin clubs by night. The plot, which is fairly predictable, hinges on the apparent suicide of a near-legendary guitarist who was an old friend of Martin's, the murders of a couple of small-fry music critics, and a missing kilo of cocaine. The latter item is a red herring, since it turns out that, contrary to expectation, in contemporary Austin concert tickets and real estate are more valuable — and more worth killing for — than drugs.

Sublett writes in the usual hardboiled, wisecracking private-eye mode, but he understands the nuances of recent Austin history. Describing a giant "red and blue and green insect . . . with glass wings and blinking eyes" that for decades had been the symbol of an exterminating company on Lamar Boulevard, he observes: "But it was more than just a mascot. It was an old friend that stayed the same in a sea of change, a reminder of the often quirky personality of a town that was prospering and metamorphosing but that still, in many ways, refused to grow up." The bug, incidentally, plays a role in the complications (and resolution) of the plot.

Though Austin remains a mecca for musicians, the lure that has attracted thousands of musical pilgrims to the city over the past quarter-century is beginning to wear thin. As a rule aspiring musicians are an impecunious lot, and one of the things that drew them to Austin in the first place was its informal and inexpensive lifestyle. But it is hard these days to live cheaply in Austin. The reason for the rise in the cost of living is that, following a period of bust in the late 1980s and early 1990s, Austin is booming again. The economic resurgence is grounded in high-tech electronics, and once more immigrants are streaming into the city, many of them from California. Locals speak of the city's "Californication." The writer who will capture this latest transformation of Austin has not yet made an appearance. The only thing we can be certain of is that he or she *will* appear. Given the imperatives of history and demographics, Texas urban culture — in Austin and in other of the state's major cities — will be a vital subject of future Texas literature.

As the population of Texas becomes ethnically more diverse, it stands to reason that contributions to its literature by writers from the various minority groups will become more numerous. To this point Texans of African American descent have not produced as much literature as their numbers would seem to warrant. But there have been a few black writers worthy of note. One of the earliest was Sutton Griggs, who was born in a small town in East Texas and grew up in Dallas. Griggs published a series of protest novels around the turn of the century, and his *Imperium in Imperio* (1899) remains a surprisingly militant work of fiction. The plot proposes a scheme whereby Texas will be seized and turned into a homeland for blacks on American soil: "Thus will the Negro have an empire of his own." Later novels by Griggs softened the message somewhat, but the generally fiery tone persisted.

J. Mason Brewer, a folklorist who was encouraged and advised (apparently not always wisely) by J. Frank Dobie, published two excellent collections of African American folklore from East Texas: *The Word on the Brazos* (1953) and *Dog Ghosts and Other Texas Negro Folk Tales* (1958). These stories display mostly the humorous side of black life in the region, though there are occasional reminders of the unfairness of that life. At the moment probably the best-known African American writer in Texas is J. California Cooper, who lives in Marshall. Cooper grew up in California and rarely uses

Texas as the setting for her work. She has nonetheless built a national reputation as novelist, short story writer, and playwright. A handful of other black writers from Texas—I am thinking of Lorenzo Thomas of Houston, Harryette Mullen of Fort Worth (though she no longer lives in Texas), and Sunny Nash of Bryan—continue to be active on the Texas literary scene. To repeat, however: contributions to the state's literature by African Americans have been surprisingly sparse.

The story is very different with regard to Texas Mexican writers. Now the most populous minority group in the state, Texas Mexicans will clearly play a large role in Texas's literary future. The first significant work by a Texas Mexican writer appeared in 1958 when Américo Paredes, a professor of folklore at the University of Texas at Austin, published *"With His Pistol in His Hand": A Border Ballad and Its Hero,* an imaginative study of the *corrido* as history and as a literary form. The "Chicano renaissance," a remarkable flowering of the arts among Mexican Americans of the Southwest which lasted from about 1965 to 1975, spawned several important Texas Mexican writers.

One of the best was Tomás Rivera, the son of a family of migrant workers. Rivera toiled in the fields to pay for much of his college education. His *. . . y no se lo trago la tierra/And the Earth Did Not Devour Him* (1970) is a bitter coming-of-age story employing an experimental technique that largely avoids straightforward narration. The novel centers around a boy who questions why God would allow the kind of pain and exploitation his migrant family is subject to. Eventually he curses God, and when the earth fails to part and swallow him, as his mother had told him it would should he ever curse God, his eyes open to cruel reality. He sees that his family's suffering is caused, not by God, but by an unfair economic system, and that the only remedy is to find solidarity with *la raza,* with his people. *And the Earth Did Not Devour Him* is an impressive work. Unfortunately Rivera, who was a busy university administrator, died early (at age forty-nine) and never produced another book.

The most prolific contemporary Texas Mexican writer is Rolando Hinojosa. For a quarter-century, Hinojosa has pursued a project of Faulknerian dimensions: the Klail City Death Trip series, comprising more than a dozen volumes. Each book in the series is autonomous, but it is also a slice from a much larger loaf, part of a lengthy work in progress. The series attempts to recreate the history and culture, in Faulkner's familiar metaphor, of "a postage stamp of soil": Belken County—a thinly disguised version, no doubt, of the author's native Hidalgo Country—in the Lower Rio Grande Valley of South Texas. (Klail City is the county seat.)

Hinojosa believes that the uniqueness of Valley life derives from the fact that it flourishes in a borderland far from the centers of population and power in either the U.S. or Mexico. Valley Anglos and *mexicanos* alike—and on both sides of the river—are shaped by the insularity, the separateness of their shared culture. The writer is most concerned, of course, with depicting *mexicano* life in Belken County, and his fiction memorably projects the sense of community integral to that life: *mexicano* families have lived in Belken County for generations; they share a common language, a common folklore, and common roots in Valley soil.

Hinojosa weaves the folk memory of Belken *mexicanos* into the fabric of his fiction, and that memory extends back to 1749, when José Escandón led a party that established twenty-one settlements on the north bank of the Rio Grande in what is now called the Lower Valley. A number of twentieth-century Valley families trace their ancestry to those original settlers. The Mexican Revolution of 1910–20 is also a historical landmark, as are the turbulent events of 1915–17 surrounding Aniceto Pizaña and the Plan of San Diego. The turmoil of the revolution and associated events had an impact on the lives of all Valley residents and created many Anglo-*mexicano* conflicts that have not been wholly resolved to this day.

All the books in the series, with one exception, are novels. Several of them exist in both Spanish and English versions. The English versions are not exactly translations, but redactions that Hinojosa has fashioned from the Spanish originals. Thus *Estampas del Valle y otras obras* (1972) becomes *The Valley* (1983); *Klail City y sus aldrededores* (1976) becomes *Klail City* (1987); and so forth. Chronologically the series covers approximately half a century, from the 1930s to the early 1980s. While dozens of recurring characters, both *mexicano* and Anglo, appear in it, the protagonists are Rafa (or Rafe) Buenrostro and his cousin, Jehu Malacara.

Hinojosa's fictional technique in most of the works is thoroughly postmodern. Eschewing more traditional modes of narration, he tells his stories by means of various nonlinear (and frequently oral) genres: sketches, letters, interviews, depositions, diaries. The same event is often examined from a variety of points of view, creating a mosaic rather than a linear effect. The only work in the series to employ a straight linear plot line is *Partners in Crime* (1985), subtitled "A Rafe Buenrostro Mystery." Though only partially successful as a mystery story, the novel is one of Hinojosa's most interesting and suggestive works.

Partners in Crime, set in the mid-1970s, focuses on Rafe, Korean War veteran, college graduate, licensed attorney, and lieutenant of detectives in a police unit attached to the Belken Country district attorney's office. In the course of the tale, Rafe and his team are called on to investigate several murders, the most puzzling an execution-style slaying of two Mexican nationals and a Belken County policeman.

Rafe's probings lead him into an underworld tug of war in which well-financed cocaine dealers attempt to supplant nickel-and-dime marijuana smugglers. Unlike most murder mysteries, *Partners in Crime* ends somewhat tentatively; all the loose ends are not tied together. While the ending no doubt disappoints many aficionados of the mystery story, to me it seems an accurate reflection of the real world.

Petty smuggling has been a way of life along the U.S.–Mexico border for a century and a half. Now, as *Partners in Crime* makes clear, with real money to be made in the drug trade, the big-timers over the last couple of decades have moved in. International crime cartels now control Valley smuggling operations, just as American capitalism has come to be dominated by multinational corporations. Thus, as Faulkner's Yoknapatawpha County is ultimately a microcosm of the larger world, so, it turns out, is Hinojosa's Belken County.

The novel in the series set in most recent times is *Becky and Her Friends* (1990), which takes place in the early 1980s. The most recently published, *The Useless Servants* (1993), actually circles back in time to subject matter first explored in an earlier volume of poetry, *Korean Love Songs* (1978). *The Useless Servants* consists mostly of entries in a journal kept by Rafe, a non-commissioned officer in an artillery unit engaged in some of the heaviest fighting of the Korean War. The entries reflect all the disjointedness and shocking immediacy of warfare as described in a day-to-day diary. It is one of Hinojosa's most powerful books, demonstrating the author's continuing growth as an artist.

Aristeo Brito is yet another Texas Mexican writer to emerge from the "Chicano renaissance." Brito's *El diablo en Texas/The Devil in Texas* (1976) is a novel that deserves to be better known than it is. The narrator of the tale, which is divided into three widely spaced chronological segments, returns to his native Presidio to try to understand the place that has been home to his ancestors and to himself. The "devil" of the title appears to be a mythic embodiment of evil in the guise of the Chicano's oppressor. Estela Portillo

Trambley, in addition to her much-praised drama *The Day of the Swallows* (1971), attracted attention with *Rain of Scorpions* (1975), a volume of short fiction set in and around El Paso. Tino Villanueva's poetry collection *Hay otra voz* (1972) is also a literary landmark of the "renaissance."

The freshet of writing by Texas Mexicans that began about three decades ago continues into the present. Texas Mexican writers who have recently published fiction or poetry include Lionel García, Max Martínez, Genaro Gonzalez, Dagoberto Gilb, and Pat Mora. Each of these possesses the technical skills and the artistic resolve to significantly augment the state's literature. Others, as yet unknown, will undoubtedly come to the fore as years unfold.

Thus the future of literature in Texas appears bright. The future of Texas literature, however, is somewhat less certain. The volume of writing and the number of writers in Texas increase yearly, and the maturity and sophistication of at least some of that writing and some of those writers have grown impressively in recent times. Moreover, new forms of writing beckon Texas literary folk. Several established Texas authors — Horton Foote, Robert Benton, and William Wittliff, for example — have carved out successful careers as scriptwriters for motion pictures and television. As the information age continues its explosive growth, perhaps some Texas writers of the future will practice their craft in cyberspace.

Texas changes literally day by day. Some of us fear that the traditional culture, once a solid and (seemingly) permanent part of the Texas landscape, will be swept away in the current of change. Such an eventuality would, in my view, be lamentable. I do not defend every aspect of that culture; obviously it concealed plenty of inequities and injustices. But it possessed an integrity, a gravity, that, to these jaundiced eyes, is sorely lacking in the homogenized pap that masquerades as cultural sustenance in the present day. Still, as my mother used to say, time and tide wait for no man. I will continue to study the state's literary record — snapshots, a kaleidoscope really, of our past — and to await the future with hope and a measure of trepidation.

NOTES

PREFACE

1. Pat Baldwin, "'Texas Monthly' to Mark 20 Years," *Dallas Morning News*, Dec. 20, 1992, pp. 26A–27A.
2. Clifford Geertz, introduction to *The Interpretation of Cultures: Selected Essays* (New York: Basic Books, 1973), pp. 3–30.
3. Richard Slotkin, *The Fatal Environment: The Myth of the Frontier in the Age of Industrialization, 1800–1890* (New York: Atheneum, 1985), p. 16.
4. Bronislaw Malinowski, *Magic, Science, and Religion, and Other Essays* (Garden City, N.Y.: Doubleday, 1954), p. 144.
5. T. R. Fehrenbach, *Lone Star: A History of Texas and the Texans* (New York: Macmillan, 1968), p. xiv.
6. D. W. Meinig, *Imperial Texas: An Interpretive Essay in Cultural Geography* (Austin: University of Texas Press, 1969), p. 7, passim.
7. "The Principality of Texas" (editorial), *Ultra*, Sept., 1981, pp. 3, 41.

1. PROLOGUE

1. John Gunther, *Inside U.S.A.* (New York: Harper, 1947), p. 860.
2. Gregory Katz, "Mexico's Team?," *Dallas Morning News,* Jan. 31, 1993, p. 11B.
3. Meinig, *Imperial Texas,* p. 117.
4. Statistics are from Norman D. Brown, "Texas's Southern Roots," in *The Texas Literary Tradition: Fiction, Folklore, History,* ed. Don Graham, James W. Lee, and William T. Pilkington (Austin: College of Liberal Arts of the University of Texas at Austin and the Texas State Historical Association, 1983), pp. 40–45.
5. See Rhodes's poem "The Hired Man on Horseback," in *The Best Novels and Stories of Eugene Manlove Rhodes,* ed. Frank V. Dearing (Boston: Houghton Mifflin, 1949), pp. 549–51.
6. Bernard DeVoto, "The West: A Plundered Province," *Harper's,* Aug., 1934, pp. 355–64.
7. Gunther, *Inside U.S.A.,* pp. 814–15.

2. ANCESTORS

A portion of this essay first appeared as the epilogue in the reprint of *Cabeza de Vaca's Adventures in the Unknown Interior of America*. Reprinted by permission of

University of New Mexico Press. Another portion first appeared as "Dobie Revisited" in *Texas Books in Review* 6 (1984): 25–28. Reprinted by permission of the publisher.

1. Archibald MacLeish, *Conquistador* (Boston: Houghton Mifflin, 1932), p. 14.
2. One of the few first editions of Cabeza de Vaca's narrative in the United States — a first edition of the 1555 version, published at Vallodolid — is housed in the Southwest Writers Collection at Southwest Texas State University in San Marcos.
3. *La Relación* has been translated into English on several occasions. I use the most readable of the translations, Cyclone Covey's, published as *Cabeza de Vaca's Adventures in the Unknown Interior of America.*
4. I follow here the route mapped by Cleve Hallenbeck in his *Alvar Nuñez Cabeza de Vaca: The Journey and Route of the First European to Cross the Continent of North America* (Glendale, Calif.: Arthur H. Clark, 1940). Some recent historians have challenged Hallenbeck's conclusions, but I find his argument substantially convincing.
5. Quoted in Harry Levin, *The Power of Blackness: Hawthorne, Poe, Melville* (New York: Alfred A. Knopf, 1958), p. 17.
6. Haniel Long, *Interlinear to Cabeza de Vaca: His Relation of the Journey, Florida to the Pacific, 1528–1536* (1939; reprint, New York: Frontier Press, 1969), pp. 24–36.
7. Levin, *Power of Blackness,* p. 5.
8. Alexis de Tocqueville's *Democracy in America,* part 2 (1840) is available in many editions.
9. Richard M. Dorson, "The Voice of the Horned Toad," *Arizona and the West* 4 (Spring, 1962): 74–77.
10. Larry McMurtry, "Southwestern Literature?," in *In a Narrow Grave: Essays on Texas* (Austin, Tex.: Encino Press, 1968), pp. 31–54.
11. Gregory Curtis, "Behind the Lines," *Texas Monthly,* Aug., 1981, pp. 5–6.
12. Henry Nash Smith, "An Enemy of Reactionary Demagogues," in *Three Men in Texas: Bedichek, Webb, Dobie,* ed. Ronnie Dugger (Austin: University of Texas Press, 1967), pp. 101–103.

3. HERDING WORDS

A slightly different version of this essay appeared as "Herding Words," in *Range Wars: Heated Debates, Sober Reflections, and Other Assessments of Texas Writing,* ed. Craig Clifford and Tom Pilkington (Dallas: Southern Methodist University Press, 1989). Reprinted by permission of the publisher.

1. Lawrence Clark Powell, "J. Frank Dobie: *Coronado's Children,*" in *Southwest Classics: The Creative Literature of the Arid Lands* (Los Angeles: Ward Ritchie Press, 1974), pp. 342–55.
2. Quoted in Joe Holley, "John Graves: A Master of Details and Ruminations," *Texas Humanist,* Mar.–Apr., 1984, pp. 40–44.

3. A. C. Greene, "The Fifty Best Texas Books," *Texas Monthly,* Aug., 1981, pp. 158–65.

4. A. C. Greene, *The Fifty Best Books on Texas* (Dallas: Pressworks, 1982), p. 5.

5. Curtis, "Behind the Lines," p. 5.

6. Larry McMurtry, "Ever a Bridegroom: Reflections on the Failure of Texas Literature," *Texas Observer,* Oct. 23, 1981, pp. 1, 8–18.

7. This was Oliver Wendell Holmes's *obiter dictum,* an off-the-cuff judgment that remains definitive.

8. Quotation is from Henry James's notorious catalogue of America's cultural deficiencies in his book *Hawthorne* (1879).

9. H. L. Mencken, "The Sahara of the Bozart" (1917), in *A Mencken Chrestomathy* (New York: Alfred A. Knopf, 1949), pp. 184–95.

10. Donald Barthelme, "Terms of Estrangement," *Texas Monthly,* Jan., 1986, pp. 172–74.

11. Larry McMurtry, "Postscript, 1987," addendum to "Ever a Bridegroom" when the essay was reprinted in *Range Wars,* pp. 40–41. McMurtry also says in the postscript that he had intended to title the piece "Ever a Bridesmaid," but simply typed the wrong word.

12. See Barthelme, "Terms of Estrangement," pp. 172–74.

13. Holley, "John Graves," p. 40.

4. THIS STUBBORN SOIL

This essay first appeared as "This Stubborn Soil: Texas Earth and Texas Culture" in *Southwestern American Literature* 21 (Spring, 1996): 23–28. Reprinted by permission of the publisher.

1. Richard Hugo, "The Triggering Town," in *The Triggering Town: Lectures and Essays on Poetry and Writing* (New York: W. W. Norton, 1979), pp. 11–18.

2. Michel Guillaume St. Jean de Crèvecoeur's *Letters from an American Farmer* (1782) is available in many editions.

3. James K. Folsom, "*Shane* and *Hud:* Two Stories in Search of a Medium," in *Western Movies,* ed. William T. Pilkington and Don Graham (Albuquerque: University of New Mexico Press, 1979), pp. 64–80.

4. D. H. Lawrence, *Studies in Classic American Literature* (1922), a work that has been often reprinted.

5. Edward Abbey, "Hallelujah on the Bum," *The Journey Home: Some Words in Defense of the American West* (New York: E. P. Dutton, 1977), pp. 1–11.

6. McMurtry, *In a Narrow Grave,* p. ix.

7. D. H. Lawrence, "New Mexico," in *Phoenix: The Posthumous Papers,* ed. Edward D. McDonald (New York: Viking, 1936), pp. 141–47.

8. Rudolfo Anaya, "The Writer's Landscape: Epiphany in Landscape," *Latin American Literary Review* 5 (Spring-Summer, 1977): 98–102.

9. Quotations are from Edward Abbey, *Desert Solitaire: A Season in the Wilderness,* pp. 6, 84.

10. From William Butler Yeats, *The Autobiography: Consisting of Reveries Over*

Childhood, the Trembling of the Veil, and Dramatis Personae (1944; reprint, New York: Macmillan, 1953).

11. J. Frank Dobie, *Guide to Life and Literature of the Southwest*, rev. ed. (Dallas: Southern Methodist University Press, 1952), p. 4.

12. Obviously I strongly disagree with Don Graham's argument, in his witty, sometimes hilarious essay "Land Without Myth; or, Texas and the Mystique of Nostalgia," that Texas "has no land myth that empowers and nourishes its devotees." But our disagreement, I believe, is largely semantic, deriving from different definitions of the term "land myth." Graham's piece, for those who desire a more skeptical view of the topic than I provide, appears in *Open Spaces, City Places: Contemporary Writers on the Changing Southwest*, ed. Judy Nolte Temple (Tucson: University of Arizona Press, 1994), pp. 87–94.

13. Quoted in William Goetzmann, "Keep the White Lights Shining," in *Texas Myths*, ed. Robert F. O'Connor (College Station: Texas A&M University Press, 1986), pp. 70–80.

14. T. R. Fehrenbach, "Seven Keys to Understanding Texas," *Atlantic Monthly*, Mar., 1975, pp. 120–27.

15. Elmer Kelton, "Introduction" to the reprint of his *The Time It Never Rained* (Garden City, N.Y.: Doubleday, 1973; reprint, Fort Worth: Texas Christian University Press, 1983), pp. ix–xii.

16. Jon Tuska, ed., *The American West in Fiction* (New York: New American Library, 1982), p. 278.

17. William B. Martin, ed., *Texas Plays*, p. 223.

18. Both quotations from unpublished plays by Vliet are taken from Martin, *Texas Plays*, p. 225.

19. R. G. Vliet, "On a Literature of the Southwest: An Address," *Texas Observer*, Apr. 28, 1978, pp. 18–19.

20. McMurtry, "Ever a Bridegroom," p. 11.

5. TEXAS GOTHIC

A portion of this essay first appeared as "Passions of Racial Hatred Changed Town," *Dallas Times Herald*, Aug. 5, 1984, p. A47. Another portion appeared as "A Twisted Family Feud," *The World and I* 10 (Jan., 1995): 330–34. Reprinted by permission of the publisher.

1. Since 1956 was a presidential election year and Shivers was chairman of a group that called itself Texas Democrats for Eisenhower, President Dwight Eisenhower did not challenge the governor's gambit. A year later, in Arkansas, Governor Orval Faubus was not so fortunate; his defiance of a similar court order was countered with federal military intervention. For a thorough account of the political context of these events, see Robyn Duff Ladino, *Integrating Texas Schools: Eisenhower, Shivers, and the Crisis at Mansfield High* (Austin: University of Texas Press, 1997).

2. See Joan Givner, "Problems of Personal Identity in Texas' 'First Writer,'" in *Katherine Anne Porter and Texas: An Uneasy Relationship*, ed. Clinton Ma-

chann and William Bedford Clark (College Station: Texas A&M University Press, 1990), pp. 41–57. See also Givner's biography, *Katherine Anne Porter: A Life* (New York: Simon and Schuster, 1982).

6. THE WAY WEST

This essay first appeared in *The Texas Literary Tradition*. Reprinted by permission of Don Graham.

1. James W. Lee, "The Old South in Texas Literature," in *The Texas Literary Tradition*, pp. 46–57.
2. It is stunning to consider that some Americans, even some Texans (my students, for example), may have forgotten, or nearly forgotten, that J. R. Ewing, played by Larry Hagman, was the central character of the long-running 1980s TV series *Dallas*. Robert A. Caro's multivolume biography of Lyndon Johnson portrays LBJ as a satanic figure of unrelieved evil, a plausible construction perhaps, but hardly the last word on the subject; see, for example, Caro's *The Years of Lyndon Johnson: The Path to Power* (New York: Alfred A. Knopf, 1982).
3. Jane Kramer, *The Last Cowboy* (New York: Harper and Row, 1978).
4. Frederick Jackson Turner's "The Significance of the Frontier in American History" (1893) is available in numerous editions.
5. McMurtry, *In a Narrow Grave*, pp. 107–108.
6. Larry L. King, "Playing Cowboy," in *Of Outlaws, Con Men, Whores, Politicians, and Other Artists* (New York: Viking Press, 1980), pp. 54–67.
7. Elmer Kelton, "The Western and the Literary Ghetto," in *The Texas Literary Tradition*, pp. 82–94.
8. McMurtry, "Ever a Bridegroom," p. 11.
9. See Henry Nash Smith, *Virgin Land: The American West as Symbol and Myth* (Cambridge, Mass.: Harvard University Press, 1950).
10. Before his death in 1984, Vliet completed a revised version of *Solitudes*. Probably the most important revision was the addition of an epilogue in which the protagonist, Claiborne, is shown some years later as a married man preparing to take part in the Oklahoma land rush. This version was published posthumously under the title *Soledad, or Solitudes*. For purposes of the present discussion, I have used the original 1977 text.
11. Don Graham, review of *Solitudes*, by R. G. Vliet, *Western American Literature* 12 (Feb., 1978): 337.

7. TEXANS AT WAR

A version of this essay appeared in *The Texas Military Experience: From the Revolution through World War II*, ed. Joseph G. Dawson, III (College Station: Texas A&M University Press, 1995).

1. Peter Aichinger, *The American Soldier in Fiction, 1880–1963: A History of Attitudes Toward Warfare and the Military Establishment* (Ames: Iowa State University Press, 1975), p. ix.

2. See John Bainbridge, *The Super Americans* (New York: Holt, Rinehart and Winston, 1961).
3. Aichinger, *American Soldier in Fiction,* p. viii.
4. Eisenhower's famous farewell address to the nation, January 18, 1961, has been reprinted in many collections.
5. An excellent biography of Mackenzie is Michael D. Pierce, *The Most Promising Young Officer: A Life of Ranald Slidell Mackenzie* (Norman: University of Oklahoma Press, 1993).
6. See Stephen B. Oates, *Visions of Glory: Texans on the Southwestern Frontier* (Norman: University of Oklahoma Press, 1970), pp. 25–52.
7. Quoted in Lance Bertelson, "How Texas Won the Second World War," *Southwest Review* 76 (Summer, 1991): 330–31.
8. Don Graham, *Cowboys and Cadillacs: How Hollywood Looks at Texas* (Austin: Texas Monthly Press, 1983), pp. 71–72.

8. A PRAIRIE HOMESTEAD

This essay first appeared in *Texas Studies Annual* 2 (1995): 121–29.
1. James W. Lee, "Arbiters of Texas Literary Taste," in *Range Wars,* pp. 130–34.
2. Harold Bloom, *The Anxiety of Influence: A Theory of Poetry* (New York: Oxford University Press, 1973), pp. 5, 95.
3. See Lon Tinkle, *An American Original: The Life of J. Frank Dobie* (Boston: Little, Brown, 1978), pp. 107–33, for financial details of Dobie's early writing career.
4. Quoted in Al Reinert, introduction to a reprint of Billy Lee Brammer's *The Gay Place* (Austin: Texas Monthly Press, 1978), pp. x–xxvii.
5. McMurtry, *In a Narrow Grave,* pp. 32–34.
6. All subsequent quotations by McMurtry used in this essay (with one exception noted below) are from "Ever a Bridegroom," pp. 1, 8–18.
7. Both quotations are from Givner, "Problems of Personal Identity," pp. 41–57.
8. George Perkins, et al., eds., *The American Literary Tradition,* 7th ed. (New York: McGraw-Hill, 1990), p. 1425.
9. McMurtry, *In a Narrow Grave,* p. 134.
10. See Larry L. King, *The Whorehouse Papers* (New York: Viking Press, 1982), pp. 261–76, for a summation of King's post-*Whorehouse* prosperity.

9. DOING WITHOUT

A version of this essay appeared in *Taking Stock: A Larry McMurtry Casebook,* ed. Clay Reynolds (Dallas: Southern Methodist University Press, 1989). Reprinted by permission of the publisher.
1. Jay Milner, *Confessions of a Maddog* (Denton: University of North Texas Press, 1998).
2. McMurtry, "Ever a Bridegroom," p. 10.
3. McMurtry, "Ever a Bridegroom," p. 17.

4. Larry McMurtry, preface to a paperback reprint of *The Desert Rose* (New York: Touchstone, 1985), p. 5.

5. In late 1997, following the publication of *Comanche Moon,* a prequel to *Lonesome Dove,* McMurtry announced he had "one more novel to write," and after that he planned to focus on composing nonfiction and managing his bookstores in Washington and Archer City. See Kathryn Jones, "'I've Written Enough Fiction,'" *Texas Monthly,* Dec., 1997, pp. 110–13, 147–50.

6. Larry McMurtry, *Film Flam: Essays on Hollywood* (New York: Simon and Schuster, 1987), p. 130.

7. Patrick Bennett, *Talking with Texas Writers: Twelve Interviews* (College Station: Texas A&M University Press, 1980), p. 25.

8. Charles D. Peavy, *Larry McMurtry* (Boston: Twayne, 1977), p. 134.

9. Quoted in Bennett, *Talking with Texas Writers,* p. 26.

10. Reinert, introduction to *The Gay Place,* p. xxv.

11. See Don Graham, "J. Frank Dobie: A Reappraisal," *Southwestern Historical Quarterly* 92 (July, 1988): 1–15.

12. Peavy, *Larry McMurtry,* p. 57.

13. Peavy, *Larry McMurtry,* p. 77.

14. Robert E. Park, "Migration and the Marginal Man," *American Journal of Sociology* 33 (May, 1928): 200–206.

15. Larry McMurtry, "The Texas Moon, and Elsewhere," *Atlantic Monthly,* Mar., 1975, pp. 29–36.

10. MAC THE KNIFE

A portion of this essay first appeared as "Revising the Myth," *The World and I* 4 (Jan., 1989): 343–47. Reprinted by permission of the publisher. Another portion first appeared as "Fate and Free Will on the American Frontier: Cormac McCarthy's Western Fiction," *Western American Literature* 27 (Feb., 1993): 311–22. Reprinted by permission of the publisher.

1. See Hannah Arendt, *Eichmann in Jerusalem: A Report on the Banality of Evil* (New York: Viking, 1963).

2. This idea is developed in Craig Edward Clifford's thought-provoking essay "Horseman, Hang On: The Reality of Myth in Texas Letters," in *In the Deep Heart's Core: Reflections on Life, Letters, and Texas* (College Station: Texas A&M University Press, 1985), pp. 11–22.

3. Lawrence, *Studies in Classic American Literature.*

4. See Richard Slotkin, *Gunfighter Nation: The Myth of the Frontier in Twentieth-Century America* (New York: Atheneum, 1992).

5. Quotations from Richard B. Woodward, "Cormac McCarthy's Venomous Fiction," *New York Times Magazine,* Apr. 18, 1992, pp. 28–31, 36, 40.

6. The other entries in the trilogy, not discussed here, are *The Crossing* (1994) and *Cities of the Plain* (1998).

7. Quoted in Woodward, "Cormac McCarthy's Venomous Fiction," p. 36.

8. Abbey, *Desert Solitaire,* p. 214.

9. Quoted in Woodward, "Cormac McCarthy's Venomous Fiction," p. 31.
10. For a thorough discussion of the sources, see John Emil Sepich, "'What Kind of Indians Was Them?': Some Historical Sources in Cormac McCarthy's *Blood Meridian*," *Southern Quarterly* 30 (Summer, 1992): 93–110.

II. A FAN'S NOTES

A portion of this essay first appeared as "'Rising to Reply . . .,'" *Texas Books in Review* 10 (Fall, 1990): 26.

1. Gary Cartwright supplies an entertaining account of the halcyon days at the *Press* in his *Confessions of a Washed-Up Sportswriter (Including Various Digressions about Sex, Crime, and Other Hobbies)* (Austin: Texas Monthly Press, 1982).
2. H. G. Bissinger, *Friday Night Lights: A Town, a Team, and a Dream* (Reading, Mass.: Addison-Wesley, 1990).
3. J. Brent Clark, *Third Down and Forever: Joe Don Looney and the Rise and Fall of an American Hero* (New York: St. Martin's Press, 1993).
4. The song's lyrics may be found in liner notes for Terry Allen's 1978 album *Lubbock (on Everything)*.
5. Gary Shaw, *Meat on the Hoof* (New York: St. Martin's Press, 1972).
6. Skip Bayless, *God's Coach: The Hymns, Hype, and Hypocrisy of Tom Landry's Cowboys* (New York: Simon and Schuster, 1991); Peter Golenbock, *Cowboys Have Always Been My Heroes: The Definitive Oral History of America's Team* (New York: Warner Books, 1997); John Eisenberg, *Cotton Bowl Days: Growing Up with Dallas and the Cowboys in the 1960s* (New York: Simon and Schuster, 1997); Mike Shropshire, *The Ice Bowl: The Green Bay Packers and Dallas Cowboys' Season of 1967* (New York: Donald I. Fine Books, 1997).
7. Quoted in Gary Cartwright, "Turn Out the Lights," *Texas Monthly,* Aug., 1997, pp. 124–27, 134–37.
8. Golenbock, *Cowboys Have Always Been My Heroes,* pp. 267–70.
9. Cartwright, "Turn Out the Lights," pp. 136–37.
10. Jenkins's novel *Life Its Ownself* (1984) follows Billy Clyde's story through his post–pro football career in broadcasting. Like *Semi-Tough,* the book is a wispy confection — mostly snappy one-liners and raunchy (and, again, often hilarious) farce.
11. See Bill Russell's funny and insightful autobiography *Second Wind: The Memoirs of an Opinionated Man* (New York: Random House, 1979).

12. FUTURE SHOCK

A portion of this essay first appeared as "Contemporary Texas Writers and the Concept of Regionalism," *The Texas Humanist* 2 (Apr., 1980): 2, 10. Reprinted by permission of the publisher. Another portion first appeared as "Slouching towards Houston: The City in Texas Fiction," *The Texas Literary Tradition.* Reprinted by permission of Don Graham. Another portion first appeared as book reviews in the *Dallas Times Herald,* Dec. 30, 1984, and Aug. 25, 1985, and the *Dallas Morning News,* Sept. 5, 1993, and Apr. 30, 1995.

1. Erich Fromm, "Personality Packages," in *The Art of Loving* (New York: Harper, 1956), pp. 5–7.

BIBLIOGRAPHY

The following listing supplies bibliographical data for all primary works discussed or referred to in the foregoing essays.

Abbey, Edward. *The Brave Cowboy: An Old Tale in a New Time.* New York: Dodd, Mead, 1956.

———. *Desert Solitaire: A Season in the Wilderness.* New York: McGraw-Hill, 1968.

———. *The Monkey Wrench Gang.* Philadelphia: Lippincott, 1975.

Anaya, Rudolfo. *Bless Me, Ultima.* Berkeley, Calif.: Quinto Sol Publications, 1972. Reprint, New York: Warner Books, 1994.

Atlee, Philip. *The Inheritors.* New York: Dial Press, 1940.

Baker, Karle Wilson. *Star of the Wilderness.* New York: Coward-McCann, 1942.

Barr, Amelia E. *Remember the Alamo.* New York: Dodd, Mead, 1888.

Brammer, William [Billy Lee]. *The Gay Place: Being Three Related Novels.* Boston: Houghton Mifflin, 1961.

Brewer, J. Mason. *Dog Ghosts and Other Negro Folk Tales.* Austin: University of Texas Press, 1958.

———. *The Word on the Brazos.* Austin: University of Texas Press, 1953.

Brito, Aristeo. *El diablo en Texas/The Devil in Texas.* Tucson: Editorial Peregrinos, 1976.

Bryan, J. Y. *Come to the Bower.* New York: Viking Press, 1963.

Cabeza de Vaca, Alvar Nuñez. *Cabeza de Vaca's Adventures in the Unknown Interior of America.* Trans. Cyclone Covey. New York: Collier Books, 1961. Reprint, Albuquerque: University of New Mexico Press, 1983.

Capps, Benjamin. *Sam Chance.* New York: Duell, Sloan and Pearce, 1965.

———. *The Trail to Ogallala.* New York: Duell, Sloan and Pearce, 1964.

———. *A Woman of the People.* New York: Duell, Sloan and Pearce, 1966.

Cartwright, Gary. *The Hundred-Yard War.* Garden City, N.Y.: Doubleday, 1968.

Crawford, Max. *Lords of the Plain.* New York: Atheneum, 1985.

Cross, Ruth. *The Golden Cocoon.* New York: Harper, 1924.

Dawson, Carol. *Body of Knowledge.* Chapel Hill, N.C.: Algonquin Books, 1994.

———. *The Waking Spell.* Chapel Hill, N.C.: Algonquin Books, 1992.

DeLillo, Don. *End Zone.* Boston: Houghton Mifflin, 1972.

———. *Libra.* New York: Viking Press, 1988.

———. *Running Dog.* New York: Alfred A. Knopf, 1978.

Dobie, J. Frank. *Apache Gold and Yaqui Silver.* Boston: Little, Brown, 1939.

———. *Coronado's Children.* Dallas: Southwest Press, 1930.

———. *The Longhorns.* Boston: Little, Brown, 1941.

———. *The Mustangs.* Boston: Little, Brown, 1952.

———. *Out of the Old Rock.* Boston: Little, Brown, 1972.

Evans, Augusta Jane. *Inez: A Tale of the Alamo.* New York: Harper and Brothers, 1855.

Ferber, Edna. *Giant.* Garden City, N.Y.: Doubleday, 1952.

Flynn, Robert. *North to Yesterday.* New York: Alfred A. Knopf, 1967.

Furman, Laura. *The Shadow Line.* New York: Viking Press, 1982.

Gent, Peter. *The Franchise.* New York: Villard Books, 1983.

———. *North Dallas Forty.* New York: William Morrow, 1973.

Goyen, William. "Arthur Bond." In *Had I a Hundred Mouths: New and Selected Stories, 1947–1983.* New York: Clarkson Potter, 1988.

———. *The House of Breath.* New York: Random House, 1950.

Graves, John. *Goodbye to a River.* New York: Alfred A. Knopf, 1960.

———. "The Last Running." *Atlantic Monthly,* June, 1959, pp. 39–45.

Grey, Zane. *The Lone Star Ranger.* New York: Grosset & Dunlap, 1915. Reprint, Boston: G. K. Hall, 1986.

Griffin, John Howard. *Black Like Me.* Boston: Houghton Mifflin, 1961.

———. *The Devil Rides Outside.* Fort Worth, Tex.: Branch-Smith, 1952.

Griggs, Sutton E. *Imperium in Imperio.* Cincinnati, Ohio: Editor Publishing, 1899. Reprint, New York: Arno Press, 1969.

Hinojosa, Rolando. *Becky and Her Friends.* Houston: Arte Público Press, 1990.

———. *Estampas del Valle y otras obras.* Berkeley, Calif.: Quinto Sol Publications, 1973.

———. *Klail City.* Houston: Arte Público Press, 1987.

———. *Klail City y sus aldrededores.* Havana, Cuba: Casa de las Americas, 1976.

———. *Korean Love Songs.* Berkeley, Calif.: Editorial Justa, 1978.

———. *Partners in Crime.* Houston: Arte Público Press, 1985.

———. *The Useless Servants.* Houston: Arte Público Press, 1993.

———. *The Valley.* Ypsilanti, Mich.: Bilingual Press, 1983.

Jenkins, Dan. *Life Its Ownself: The Semi-Tougher Adventures of Billy Clyde Puckett and Them.* New York: Simon and Schuster, 1984.

———. *Semi-Tough.* New York: Atheneum, 1972.

Jolly, Andrew. *A Time of Soldiers.* New York: E. P. Dutton, 1976.

Kelton, Elmer. *The Day the Cowboys Quit.* Garden City, N.Y.: Doubleday, 1971.

———. *The Good Old Boys.* Garden City, N.Y.: Doubleday, 1978.

———. *The Time It Never Rained.* Garden City, N.Y.: Doubleday, 1973.

———. *The Wolf and the Buffalo.* Garden City, N.Y.: Doubleday, 1980.

Kennedy, Teresa. *Baby Todd and the Rattlesnake Stradivarius.* New York: St. Martin's Press, 1987.

King, Larry L. *The One-Eyed Man.* New York: New American Library, 1966.

LaSalle, Peter. *Strange Sunlight.* Austin: Texas Monthly Press, 1984.

Lea, Tom. *The Wonderful Country.* Boston: Little, Brown, 1952.

Lind, Michael. *The Alamo: An Epic.* Boston: Houghton Mifflin, 1997.

Lindsey, David L. *A Cold Mind.* New York: Harper and Row, 1983.

———. *Heat from Another Sun.* New York: Harper and Row, 1984.

———. *Mercy*. New York: Doubleday, 1990.

———. *Spiral*. New York: Atheneum, 1986.

LittleDog, Pat. *In Search of the Holy Mother of Jobs*. El Paso, Tex.: Cinco Puntos Press, 1991.

McCarthy, Cormac. *All the Pretty Horses*. New York: Knopf, 1992.

———. *Blood Meridian, or The Evening Redness in the West*. New York: Random House, 1985.

———. *Child of God*. New York: Random House, 1974.

———. *Cities of the Plain*. New York: Knopf, 1998.

———. *The Crossing*. New York: A. A. Knopf, 1994.

———. *The Orchard Keeper*. New York: Random House, 1965.

———. *Outer Dark*. New York: Random House, 1968.

———. *Suttree*. New York: Random House, 1979.

McKinley, Georgia. *Follow the Running Grass*. Boston: Houghton Mifflin, 1969.

McMurtry, Larry. *All My Friends Are Going to Be Strangers*. New York: Simon and Schuster, 1972.

———. *Anything for Billy*. New York: Simon and Schuster, 1988.

———. *Buffalo Girls*. New York: Simon and Schuster, 1990.

———. *Comanche Moon*. New York: Simon and Schuster, 1997.

———. *The Desert Rose*. New York: Simon and Schuster, 1983.

———. *Horseman, Pass By*. New York: Harper, 1961.

———. *The Last Picture Show*. New York: Dial Press, 1966.

———. *Leaving Cheyenne*. New York: Harper and Row, 1963.

———. *Lonesome Dove*. New York: Simon and Schuster, 1985.

———. *Moving On*. New York: Simon and Schuster, 1970.

———. *Terms of Endearment*. New York: Simon and Schuster, 1975.

———. *Texasville*. New York: Simon and Schuster, 1987.

Mailer, Norman. *The Naked and the Dead*. New York: Rinehart, 1948.

———. *Why Are We in Vietnam?* New York: G. P. Putnam, 1967.

Michener, James A. *Texas*. New York: Random House, 1985.

Miller, Vassar. *Had I Wheels or Love: Collected Poems*. Dallas: Southern Methodist University Press, 1991.

[Myrthe, A. T.] *Mexico Versus Texas: A Descriptive Novel, Most of the Characters of Which Consist of Living Persons*. Philadelphia: N. Siegfried, 1838.

Owens, William A. *Fever in the Earth*. New York: G. P. Putnam, 1958.

———. *This Stubborn Soil: A Frontier Boyhood*. New York: Charles Scribner's Sons, 1966.

Paredes, Américo. *"With His Pistol in His Hand": A Border Ballad and Its Hero*. Austin: University of Texas Press, 1958.

Perry, George Sessions. *Hold Autumn in Your Hand*. New York: Viking Press, 1941.

———. *The Story of Texas A&M*. New York: McGraw-Hill, 1951.

———. *Texas: A World in Itself*. New York: McGraw-Hill, 1942.

Porter, Katherine Anne. *Collected Essays and Occasional Writings*. New York: Delacorte Press, 1970.

————. *Collected Stories.* New York: Harcourt, Brace and World, 1965.

————. *Pale Horse, Pale Rider.* New York: Harcourt, Brace, 1939.

Rivera, Tomás. *. . . y no se lo trago la tierra/And the Earth Did Not Devour Him.* Trans. Herminio Rios. Berkeley, Calif.: Quinto Sol Publications, 1970.

Shrake, Edwin [Bud]. *But Not for Love.* Garden City, N.Y.: Doubleday, 1964.

————. *Strange Peaches.* New York: Harper's Magazine Press, 1972.

Sublett, Jesse. *Rock Critic Murders.* New York: Viking Press, 1989.

Taylor, Pat Ellis. *Afoot in a Field of Men.* New York: Atlantic Monthly Press, 1988.

Terry, Douglas. *The Last Texas Hero.* Garden City, N.Y.: Doubleday, 1982.

Thomason, John W., Jr. *Fix Bayonets.* New York: Charles Scribner's Sons, 1926.

————. *Lone Star Preacher.* New York: Charles Scribner's Sons, 1941.

Thompson, Thomas. *Blood and Money.* Garden City, N.Y.: Doubleday, 1976.

Tinkle, Lon. *Thirteen Days to Glory.* New York: McGraw-Hill, 1958.

Trambley, Estela Portillo. *Rain of Scorpions.* Berkeley, Calif.: Quinto Sol Publications, 1975.

Ventura, Michael. *Night Time Losing Time.* New York: Simon and Schuster, 1989.

Villanueva, Tino. *Hay otra voz: Poems.* New York: Editorial Mensaje, 1979.

Vliet, R. G. "The Regions of Noon." In *Texas Plays.* Ed. William B. Martin. Dallas: Southern Methodist University Press, 1990.

————. *Rockspring.* New York: Viking Press, 1974.

————. *Scorpio Rising.* New York: Random House, 1985.

————. *Soledad, or Solitudes.* Fort Worth: Texas Christian University Press, 1986.

————. *Solitudes.* New York: Harcourt Brace Jovanovich, 1977.

Webb, Walter Prescott. *Divided We Stand: The Crisis of a Frontierless Democracy.* New York: Farrar and Rinehart, 1937.

————. *The Great Plains.* Boston: Ginn, 1931.

Williams, George. *The Blind Bull.* New York: Abelard, 1952.

Woolley, Bryan. *November 22.* New York: Seaview Books, 1981.

INDEX

Brito, Aristeo, 168
Brook, Stephen, xi
Brooks, Cleanth, 102
Brown, Norman D., 6
Brownsville, Tex., 4
Brown v. Board of Education (court decision), 55
Bryan, J. Y., 83
Bryan, Tex., 166
Bryant, William Cullen, 29
Buffalo Girls (McMurtry), 126
Burke, James Lee, 160
Burleson, Tex., 54
Bush, George W., 98
But Not for Love (Shrake), 153

Cabell, James Branch, 30
Cabeza de Vaca, Alvar Nuñez, 8, 10–18
Cabeza de Vaca's Adventures in the Unknown Interior of America (Covey), 172*n* 3
California (magazine), xi
Camus, Albert, 77
Capps, Benjamin, 31, 34–35, 79
Caro, Robert A., 67, 175*n* 2
Cartwright, Gary, 108, 136, 144–46, 148, 178*n* 1
Castillo Maldonado, Alonso del, 12
Centennial (Texas) celebration, 25
Century (magazine), 102
Chandler, Raymond, 159
Charles V (king of Spain), 11
Chicago, Ill., 49
Child of God (McCarthy), 125
Chisholm Trail, 53
Cities of the Plain (McCarthy), 177*n* 6
Clark, J. Brent, 138
"Clean, Well-Lighted Place, A" (Hemingway), 117
Cleveland Browns, 144–45
Clifford, Craig, xiv, 177*n* 2
Clinton, Tenn., 55
"Cold Mind, A" (Lindsey), 35, 159–60
Coles, Robert, 128
Collected Stories (Porter), 103, 106
Colorado River (Ariz.-Calif.), 130
Columbia University, 140
Comanche Moon (McMurtry), 177*n* 5
Come to the Bower (Bryan), 83

Confessions of a Maddog (Milner), 108
Confessions of a Washed-Up Sportswriter (Cartwright), 178*n* 1
Conquistador (MacLeish), 10
Cooper, J. California, 165–66
Coronado, Francisco Vásquez de, 14, 20
Coronado's Children (Dobie), 20–22
Corsicana, Tex., 60–61
Cotton Bowl Days (Eisenberg), 144
Country Gentleman (magazine), 101
Covey, Cyclone, 172*n* 3
Cowboys Have Always Been My Heroes (Golenbock), 144, 145
Crane, Stephen, 66, 127, 128
Crawford, Max, 89
Crèvecoeur, Michel Guillaume Jean de, 37
Crider, Bill, 160
Crockett, Davy, 83
Cross, Ruth, 160
Crossing, The (McCarthy), 177*n* 6
Crumley, James, 160
culture defined, xi–xii; exportation of Texas culture, 3–5
Curtis, Gregory, 19, 28

Dallas (television series), 67, 175*n* 2
Dallas, Tex., xiii, 12, 25, 35, 36, 58, 60, 96, 101, 108, 140, 142, 143, 147, 150, 151, 153–58, 162, 165
Dallas Cowboys, 5, 138, 143–44, 147
Dallas Morning News, xi, 144
Dallas Texans, 144
Dawson, Carol, 60–61, 62, 65
Day of the Swallows, The (Trambley), 169
Day the Cowboys Quit, The (Kelton), 71
Death Comes for the Archbishop (Cather), 28
Decatur, Tex., 36
DeLillo, Don, 139–41
Denton, Tex., 25
Desert Rose, The (McMurtry), 109–10
Desert Solitaire (Abbey), 39, 126, 127
Devil in Texas, The (Brito), 168
Devil Rides Outside, The (Griffin), 54
DeVoto, Bernard, 7
Dickens, Charles, 110, 159